GENTLE VOICES, BOLD STRIDES

A good story brings joy to the reader; the best stories provide a deeper understanding of the interaction of people with personal and historical events. Fanny Cheung's book, *Gentle Voices, Bold Strides: A Memoir*, does all that and more. It chronicles the life of an extraordinary woman growing up with traditional Chinese values during the rise of feminism. She lived the seismic shift from colonial Hong Kong to Special Administrative Region of China. With this background, Dr. Cheung became a gentle and effective champion for women's rights, mental health, justice, fairness, and kindness. This will surely become one of the best books of the year.

—**Diane F. Halpern**
Former president, American Psychological Association

I have great pleasure working with Fanny at The Chinese University of Hong Kong for over 15 years. Fanny has always impressed me with her clear analytical mind, her calm and gracious manner dealing with challenges and crisis, and her warm and personable character in front of students and colleagues. Serving the university and higher education at large for 40 years, Fanny has made tremendous contributions in not just her own field of psychology, but in education, diversity, and critical thinking. She is a beloved teacher, colleague, and scholar. Reading her memoir brings back a lot of fond memories for me working with Fanny. In my mind, Fanny has always been a sincere friend, a scholarly advocate, instead of a "superwoman."

—**Joseph Sung**
Dean, Lee Kong Chian School of Medicine,
Nanyang Technological University, Singapore

I feel privileged to know Fanny Cheung and to have worked with her over the years. Her gentle but determined art of persuasion has placed her at the centre of improving the status of women in Hong Kong over the last half century. Her memoir reminds me of my own outrage in the 1960s when I received only 75% of the pay of a male doctor. This autobiography is unique; no other publication has documented the history of women's issues — from the personal to the political — in Hong Kong with such detail.

—**Judith Mackay**
Director, Asian Consultancy on Tobacco Control

You may be feeling overwhelmed yet deep inside you still hold this desire to make a difference to the well-being of fellow humans. Turn the pages and you will be fired up.

"We can choose to make the best out of our lives." This book narrates an inspiring journey of how a born-with-silver-spoon girl had by choice metamorphosed into an exemplary champion for empathy, equality, and justice. She played a pivotal role in bringing down the "high wall" of gender stereotyping and inequality in this city and beyond, while leading a rewarding academic career.

"For me, my life had been time well spent." For readers of this remarkable book, your time would be well spent too.

—**Woon Kwong Lam, GBS, JP**
Former Convenor of the Non-Official
Members of the Executive Council of the HKSAR

Through the visionary eyes and passionate commitment of Prof. Fanny Cheung and her collaborators, we come to understand how education and employment opportunities over the past half-century have shaped the evolving role of women in Hong Kong society. These opportunities transformed the demure young girls of the past into the leaders of a modern metropolis.

While tracing her epic fight against tradition and bureaucracy, Fanny is able to entertain the reader with snippets of old-fashioned cultural practices at home or in society. These will certainly resonate with peers like myself. But they will also inform and inspire readers of any age who are interested in learning how resilient women like Fanny could drive change, and challenge authority to make a difference.

—**Shelley Lee, GBS, OBE, JP**
Former Permanent Secretary for Home Affairs of the HKSAR

GENTLE VOICES, BOLD STRIDES

A MEMOIR

FANNY M. CHEUNG

The Chinese University of Hong Kong

Gentle Voices, Bold Strides: A Memoir
　By Fanny M. Cheung

ISBN: 978-988-237-373-0

The Chinese University of Hong Kong Press
The Chinese University of Hong Kong
Sha Tin, N.T., Hong Kong
Fax: +852 2603 7355
Email: cup@cuhk.edu.hk
Website: cup.cuhk.edu.hk

Printed in Hong Kong

CONTENTS

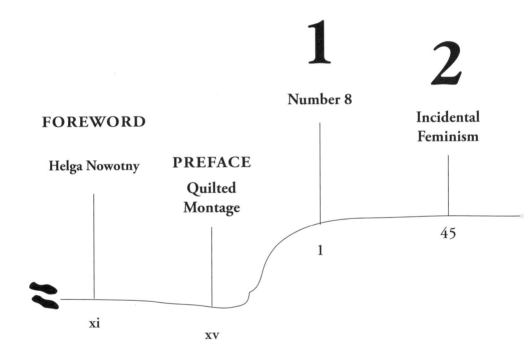

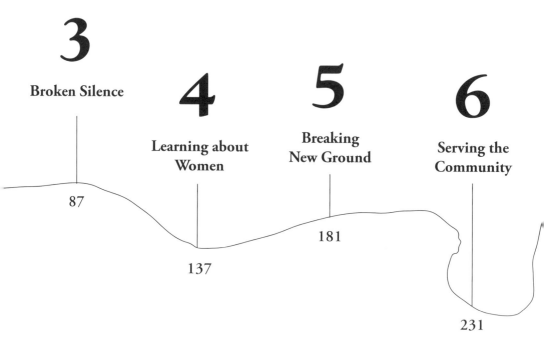

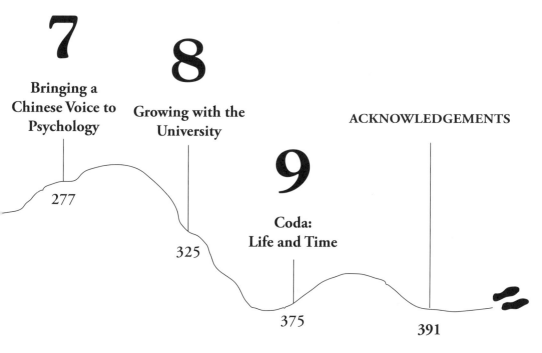

FOREWORD

If I were asked to summarize this memoir, my reply would consist of two words: soft power. Embodied in its author, soft power comes across on every page of this book in her soft-spoken voice with the humility of someone who has excelled in public service, as in her academic career, without ever forgetting that neither is a goal in itself, nor should it serve self-aggrandizement. Soft power speaks with a low voice but knows the direction in which to head. It can summon consensus where many different perspectives are brought together, interests diverge, and prejudice persists. One of the prerequisites for exerting it is the ability to listen before speaking, to include all concerned before an agreement can emerge, while simultaneously never losing sight of what one wants to achieve. It helps to remain focused, even when meeting adversity and not to become distracted by the perks that a stellar career inevitably brings with it.

Professor Fanny Cheung used the COVID-19 lockdowns and the unexpected free time to order personal photographs and family souvenirs, but soon turned her attention to a more systematic journey through her life and career. She takes us through her upbringing in the protected space of a privileged extended family who had settled in Hong Kong in the early days. Her father was an astute businessman who died young, when Fanny was nine years old. With an accomplished anthropological balance of empathy and distance, she describes what life as a child and adolescent was like with the mothers working in the family business and nannies and other domestic staff taking care of the children and daily life. We learn about the complex nomenclature and kinship relations where she was Sister Eleven, meaning she was number eleven out of her father's thirteen children. We get insights into dining rituals, Buddhist prayers and Confucian values, immersed in the quiet and slow pace inside a home that shielded the children from knowledge of the lives outside.

Already at an early age her feminist instincts were awakened through a series of incidents that made her stand up against perceived injustices that disadvantaged or discriminated against girls. As a pragmatist, she brushes aside theoretical discussions about feminism and conveys that the foundations of her life-long advocacy for women's rights and her pioneering work for bringing awareness about gender into Chinese society were laid early in life. She observes astutely that the respect and authority commanded by her grandmother was not real power, but rather the symbol for transmitting filial piety across the generations.

We then follow young Fanny as a foreign student to the USA and her doctoral studies in psychology at the University of Minnesota, from where she returned to Hong Kong after graduation. Unlike the younger generation of today, the location of her workplace remained the same for forty years, directing her drive and professional knowledge to changing society. After a series of stints in community service, she came to know of life outside her protected upbringing as a young girl. She encountered many instances of violence against women, the poor handling by the police if they were reported, and the imposed silence or indifference by the women's families and wider community. This led her to find her voice and break the silence, becoming a campaigner for the "war on rape" and addressing one of the gravest social injustices at the core.

Her scientific background made her realize that the most adequate instrument to bring awareness of the experience of women to society and policymakers was to gather evidence and render women's situation visible. Professor Fanny Cheung pioneered women and gender studies in Hong Kong and was influential in expanding them to other parts of Asia. Her strong advocacy of gender equality and equity took her directly to where action was needed, from combatting sexual harassment to gender blindness in statistics. When she became the first Vice-President for Research at The Chinese University of Hong Kong (CUHK), she brought gender consciousness to the administration and her colleagues, promoted women leadership and improved the working environment for women in academia.

She fought successfully for the disaggregation of statistical data, engaging in the development of indices for gender inequality and analyzing the situation of women in the labor market. Yet, numbers alone are not sufficient to capture the experience of women. Together with an American colleague, she launched an international research project based on interviews with women in leadership positions in different cultural settings. The study revealed the many similarities of being a woman—regardless of the cultural gender settings in which they worked—and resulted in a major publication against cultural stereotypes.

The peak of her engagement for women's rights came when she was appointed chair of the Equal Opportunities Commission. This implied stepping down as Dean of the Social Sciences Faculty of CUHK, hiring a management team and becoming fully involved in breaking new ground, from anti-discrimination laws to redesigning pedagogic methods and trying to meet the expectations from women's groups. It took her out of the academic comfort zone into a highly politicized environment. There, the air becomes thinner the higher the function. Dealing with the media proved to be especially challenging, as she had to deal with media distortions and hostile reactions. The legacy she left by tilling the soil and sowing the seed proved long-lasting and impressive.

Among Professor Fanny Cheung's many academic achievements, bringing a Chinese voice to psychology stands out. She questioned the assumed universality of the MMPI, a standardized and widely used personality test. Thanks to her efforts and those by Chinese colleagues, a standardized and validated translation of the MMPI into Chinese was accomplished for the first time, followed by significant changes to accommodate indigenous Chinese Personality Assessment Inventories. In a global world in which cultural differences persist, the dogma of a standardized universal structure of personality gave way for culture and multicultural perspectives to enter the psychological mainstream.

The book ends with a moving tribute to her husband Japhet, reminding the reader how important emotional support is not only for the individual, but for public achievements of women. It is based on mutual respect and the firm belief in gender equality, which still need to be firmly anchored in society. Her recent experience of retirement marks a new phase in her life, but as this memoir shows, there are novel ways of continuing to be active.

Soft power can be wielded by men and by women alike, and even by a country. When Professor Fanny Cheung started her impressive career, no role model existed for her. She created one that will encourage younger women in different phases of their lives and wherever they are to continue along the path opened by her: to become self-assured leaders in serving their communities.

Thank you, Fanny.

Helga Nowotny
Professor Emerita of Science and Technology Studies, ETH Zurich

PREFACE

QUILTED MONTAGE

COVID-19 Lockdown

The outbreak of a novel coronavirus pandemic across the world in early 2020 was a major global disruption that wreaked havoc in every aspect of human life. Governments, local communities, health and school systems, businesses, families and individuals were unprepared for the risks and chaos that ensued. Difficult decisions had to be made on how to safeguard people's lives and protect their livelihoods, where to allocate scarce resources, and how to mitigate the economic, social, health and mental health impact at the collective and individual levels.

To reduce the spread of the virus that caused what is now called the Coronavirus Disease 2019 (COVID-19) before pharmaceutical interventions became available, about half of the world's population was under some form of lockdown. By early 2020, an unprecedented scale of over 3.9 billion people in more than ninety countries or territories had been asked or ordered to stay at home by their governments.

People across the world reacted differently to these restrictions. In many Western countries, there was resistance to the imposition of restrictions on their personal freedom. Protests in opposition to lockdowns were held in the United Kingdom, the United States, Australia, Germany, the Netherlands, Canada and New Zealand. Overall, most people complied with them, whether out of self-interest to protect oneself or out of legal or moral duty to support the authorities. Nevertheless, these lockdowns subsequently impacted food security, supply chains, the global economy, education, tourism, sports and leisure, domestic violence, and mental health. They also introduced new modes in our ways of living, such as online shopping, working from home, Zoom teaching, or staycations instead of overseas travelling.

Having just retired by that time was a saving grace, in that I did not have to manage a working life. Even though the COVID-19 pandemic disrupted the multiple travel plans that my husband had painstakingly prepared (and then cancelled) for my retirement from full-time appointment, stealing three years from our post-retirement itinerary, it afforded me the time to slow down and reflect on different aspects of my life.

During the lockdown periods in 2020 and 2021, when I could not go anywhere other than to take walks around my home estate compound, I spent time at home going through my stacks of photo albums, starting with the first album of black-and-white photos given to me by Sister Three when I was ten. I digitalized all the photos I wanted to keep and compiled them into a folder with over 12,000 items in classified subfiles. These photos reminded me of my family as well as different stages of my life—as a student, a professional, and an advocate. I felt fortunate to have lived a meaningful life, being able to contribute to the advancement of gender equality and bringing a Chinese voice to academic psychology, as well as witnessing with pride major historical epochs in my lifetime, including the reunification of Hong Kong with our motherland, and the rise of China on the world stage.

During these three years of border control when we could not travel overseas, I received several international psychology awards and invitations to present keynote addresses at virtual conferences, for which I had to prepare video recordings. These presentations gave me the opportunity to summarize key aspects of my career development and share my experiences with the younger generation. The reverberating feedback I received from the online talks was that I should write up these experiences as inspirational legacies. I agreed that when I was promoting public education on mental health or gender equality, using lived experiences of real people touched people's hearts and was effective in communicating empathic messages.

I was humbled by these accolades, but in the mentality of a typical Chinese woman, I was always hesitant about tooting my own horn. Few people knew about my family background, much less about my relationship to a statue standing in the building bearing my grandfather's name in the university I served for forty years. I was known for what I had done and not where I came from. Many successful professionals in Hong Kong recall their childhood in poverty, as that was the era when their families escaped from war-torn China and started new lives in Hong Kong. They grew up in wooden squatters and the rudimentary public housing estates while their parents worked hard to make a living, and made it through their educational achievements. I was among the privileged minority who had access to overseas education. In those days, girls in families with limited resources had to quit school to work in factories in order to support their brothers' education. The minority of Chinese women educated overseas usually came from more affluent families.

All along, I had kept my personal life private and shielded from my professional persona. In this modern age of information and communications technology, I still refused to open a Facebook, Instagram, or Twitter (X) account. I preferred to be known for my work untainted by the lens of my background. However, my friends and colleagues persuaded me to share my life story, not only to record various aspects of my work, but more importantly, as a testimony to the historical contexts of the social progress of our times. Without knowing where we came from, the next generation often took what we now enjoyed for granted and only complained about not having all that they wanted.

Why Write My Life Story?

Having written objective academic papers throughout my professional life, I found it a new challenge to venture into writing narratives about myself. I didn't think I was a good storyteller. Yet, when I recounted tidbits from different episodes in my life, others told me those stories were interesting. Quilting these fleeting tidbits into a coherent montage was another matter. Quilting is a traditional folk practice in different parts of the world done by sewing blocks of at least three layers of cut fabric together with different patterns, which can tell a story or convey a message. I did not intend to analyze my psychological development in the way that I wrote psychological reports of my patients. Nor did I delve into the archives to produce a scholarly historical record, even though the backdrop of the historical periods that contextualize my story can illustrate the interconnected societal vicissitudes over the past decades. I just wanted to recount through my lens the events and engagements that underlined my passion and compassion and that had enriched my life paths. Resembling a participant observer in anthropology and sociology, I recorded those episodes in my life history to inform the sociocultural landscape in which I played a role. Like the multiple layers of padding of a quilt that creates a three-dimensional surface, the historical and social contexts illustrated the nuanced complexities underlying my stories.

This retrospection has deepened my understanding of my historical and cultural heritage, as well as illuminated more seasoned insights on the geopolitical landscape around us. Instead of a chronological autobiography, I have painted a kaleidoscope of my life, as I reminisce about episodes interspersed with flashbacks and diversions around the themes, together with related historical facts. From the patchworks in this saga, one may find the interplay of traditionalism and modernity: patriarchal family systems, old-fashioned customs, Buddhist and folk rituals, Confucian values, and collectivism on the one hand; Anglican and Catholic schooling, overseas studies, global outreach, feminism, and autonomy on the other hand. These patchworks reflect the cultural dynamics and social progress in Hong Kong in the context of global development. There are glimpses of my life in Hong Kong from its colonial rule to post-reunification transitions, interspersed with my sojourn in the United States during the 1960's tumultuous era of protests, followed by the meteoric rise of China on the world stage in the background. Snapshots of my life engagements provide traces of the advancement of gender equality, social activism, and higher education, as well as contentions in academic globalization, hegemony, and multiculturalism in the past fifty years. They also illustrate how one can shape one's work to serve the wider community and create meaning in life, which starts from nothing.

To me, this blissful voice from my life serves less as an indulgence in nostalgia but, more importantly, as a reminder of where we came from, how we got there, and how far we have gone. We can learn to appreciate that what we enjoy now is not a matter to be taken for granted and aspire to what still needs to be done.

NUMBER 8

Number 8 in the 1950s.

1

In Hong Kong, the number eight is remembered as the car license plate that was auctioned off at five million HKD (worth about thirteen million HKD in 2023) to an industrialist tycoon in 1988, the highest record for a license plate up to that time. In the Cantonese dialect, the number 8 (八 *baat*) and prosperity (發 *faat*) are homophones and is regarded as a lucky number. To our family and our close associates, the number eight has a totally different meaning. It is the code or common name we use to refer to the Cheung family. Number 8 was more than the address of our family mansion—Number 8 Macdonnell Road—a road that was named after a former British colonial governor like many streets in Hong Kong. It was a household in the form of a microcosmic corporation. It was a stage of characters and lives. It represented an institution of feudalistic norms and rituals. It embodies our collective and individual identities. It recalls nostalgic memories of pride and joy, as well as threat and avoidance.

The Family Clan

Our family—consisting of my grandmother, my father, his three younger brothers, their wives and offspring—lived in the same house, a big mansion of five stories with an

Grandfather Cheung Chuk Shan's portrait in the living room of Number 8.

in-house elevator. Altogether, my grandmother had twenty-eight grandchildren stretched over three decades. By the 1950s, extended households like ours were disappearing except for a few old families.

The external architectural design of our house and the major pieces of furniture were in Western Art Deco style, but many traditional Chinese fixtures were embedded inside. Traditionalism was prominent behind the modern façade of the building. So was the family system, which preserved feudalistic values and traditional norms. The first object that greeted everyone when we entered our home was the large painted oil portrait of my grandfather, Cheung Chun Kam 張椿錦, alias Chuk Shan 祝珊, which was prominently displayed above the marble fireplace in the living room. Few of us in my generation had met our grandfather, as he died in his early fifties in 1936 in Guangzhou, before most of his grandchildren were born. My father and his brothers revered him as patriarch of the family, and the family's philanthropic foundation, Cheung Chuk Shan Estate, was named after him.

After my grandfather's death, my grandmother and my father, as the oldest son, took up the small rattan ware company he started called Cheung Kam Kee 張錦記. The first character was the family surname, and the second character was part of my grandfather's birth name. The last character 記 *Kee*, which means "remember," was commonly used in old-style Chinese shop names. It could be used as a reminder and in a way, a trademark, for customers to remember the shop or the products they sell. Everyone in the family worked for the business. Through hard work and frugality, the family expanded its business and accumulated savings that were invested into properties in Guangdong. After Guangzhou was occupied by Japanese invaders in 1938 at the beginning of the Sino-Japanese war, my grandmother and my father escaped to Hong Kong in a wooden boat filled with water chestnuts to cover their hidden silver coin savings. Two of my uncles were dispatched to look after the family businesses in Macau and Guangzhou Bay, a foreign concession leased to the French Republic at that time. The family members remaining behind in China were all brought to Hong Kong one after another after the war. The last to arrive was my father's first wife, who had previously refused to leave Guangzhou because she enjoyed the comfort and status of being in charge of the shop there. It was only after being pressured by my father's second brother, who was fearful of communist rule, that she finally left with her two youngest children in 1950.

My father, Cheung Yuk Kai 張玉階, started a trading company in Hong Kong using the same family store name at Number 10 Wing Kut Street in Central. Although he only had three years of traditional education in the home village, my father was an astute businessman. He expanded the business to Western pharmaceutics, which were very profitable during and after the war, and especially during the Korean War. He further invested in land and real estate development in the 1950s. The first major project was a newly reclaimed piece of land in Causeway Bay consisting of warehouses and shipyards, which was turned into a residential and jam-packed shopping precinct now known as Paterson Street.

As the oldest son and head of the family, my father upheld the idealistic tradition of keeping the extended family as an undivided unit with shared assets. Everyone living under the family household would be taken care of. He guided his younger brothers to join the family business and entrusted his youngest brother and his eldest son to be the joint executors of his will upon his death. We children were not told anything about the family business or decisions; those were adult affairs.

The Cheung brothers in 1950. From the right, Fanny's father and Uncle
Four in front, Uncle Three and Uncle Two at the back.

Uncle Two, Cheung Yuk Ki 張玉麒, was the most educated and
intelligent. He was the only one among my father's generation who received
university education in China. He worked for the Guangzhou government
for a few years upon graduation. After joining the family in Hong Kong, he
was a capable partner with my father in business strategies. Tragically, he died
young at age thirty-five in 1953 from drowning when he tried to rescue his
wife's sister at Shek O beach during stormy weather. His twenty-five-year-old
widow became a devout Buddhist and vegetarian. My father promised that
the family would take care of her forever. Apparently, Uncle Two's smart genes
were inherited by his sons. His oldest son, my first cousin, Albert, was a child
prodigy who skipped grades throughout primary and secondary school, got into
college at age fifteen and received his master's degree in physics from Stanford
University at age eighteen. He inspired me to leave for the United States
before finishing secondary school so that I could skip a couple of years in my
education (eventually, I got my PhD degree slightly earlier than his doctorate at
Berkeley). Albert was the idol in the family when we were young—the Einstein
of Number 8.

Uncle Three, Cheung Yuk Luen 張玉麟, was more well-known in Hong Kong society because of his public roles in charity, for which he later got the honor of MBE (Member of the Order of the British Empire) from Queen Elizabeth II, the reward system handed out by the colonial government for contributions to the colony. He was more laid-back and enjoyed Cantonese opera and socializing. After my father's death, he took up a leadership role in the Tung Wah Group of Hospitals and the Five Districts Business Welfare Association, which represented businesses from the counties in Guangdong from where our family originated. He acted as the external affairs minister of Number 8. He seldom stayed around in the house. My most vivid memory of him was the fancy wedding ceremony of his second marriage in the luxury Baroque-style Peninsula Hotel. With blended traditionality and modernity, the bridegroom and bride marched down the banquet hall in Western tuxedo and wedding gown to bow to my father—who, as head of the family, wore the traditional Chinese jacket馬褂 *magua* over his robe 長衫 *cheongsam*—and to the senior sisters-in-laws dressed in heavily embroidered formal wedding attire 裙褂 *qungua*. We young children all dressed up as flower girls and pageboys. Such a scene was the epitome of the blending of traditionalism and modernity among Chinese high society in colonial Hong Kong.

Uncle Four, Cheung Yuk Leung 張玉良, attended secondary school in Hong Kong and was the only son who knew English. He was disciplined to the point of rigidity. He disliked socialization and maintained a clockwork routine. He came home to greet our grandmother after work every day during our dinner time, but he did not eat with us in the dining room. He retired to his own room to eat his dinner alone, which consisted of the same simple dish of steamed fish and vegetables, plus a papaya for fruit. He was very health conscious and seldom ate out. The one time when he had to, he brought his own food with him. Our cook was alarmed by the awkward order to add the papaya to his rice and fish so that everything could fit into the thermos, which he brought to his dinner. My father entrusted him to run the family business after his death. As a shrewd businessman, he expanded and restructured the family companies into a conglomerate of subsidiaries upon further subsidiaries, an intrigue which emerged later in the lawsuit my Aunt Two brought against him in 1990 when Number 8 was disbanded and demolished.

Uncle Three's wedding at the Peninsula Hotel, 1958.

The Cheung sisters-in-law in 1959. From the right, Aunt Two, Fanny's mother, Aunt Three at her wedding, Big Mother, and Aunt Four.

Working Women

Following the tradition of my grandmother, who worked with my grandfather to start the small cottage business in China, the adult women in Number 8 all worked in the family business. While the adult men worked on the business development and external liaison, the women worked in the back office.

My Big Mother (大媽 *dama*, a term that refers to the principal wife of men with multiple wives), the first wife of my father, was illiterate. She was sent to look after the warehouse in Kennedy Town. The laborers working there were from my father's home village, so Big Mother could communicate with them in their dialect. She stayed in a bedroom on the roof of the warehouse during the week and came home on the weekends. When we visited her, the kind laborers would put us on a trolley and give us a joyride through the grounds of the three-story warehouse in and out of the huge goods elevator.

My mother, Aunt Two, and Aunt Four were literate and worked behind grilled windows in the back office of the retail shop, Cheung Kam Kee. The shop attendants would clip the invoice and the banknotes in a little gadget on a cable, pull the string, and shuttle the papers to the back office. My mother and my aunts recorded the sales, kept the bookkeeping and inventory, and returned the receipts and change via the cabled shuttle. Apparently, money matters could only be entrusted to family members. When I visited them in the shop, I always gazed at these flying shuttles with fascination.

For a few years when Aunt Four was recuperating from multiple childbirths and a few miscarriages (she had eight children), my big Sister Three was taken out of junior high school to take up her place. My big brother was already working with my father and uncles in the family business. Sister Two was the favorite of my grandmother who sheltered her from distractions from her studies. She was the first family member who studied overseas and got her medical degree in Ireland. Sister Three was initially reluctant and continued to attend school. Uncle Four went to her school principal who then told her to serve the family first. She took her unfair treatment in stride and continued to complete her studies in night school on her own. Finally, she was able to further her university education in Australia after five years' delay.

Aunt Three was my uncle's second wife and joined our family a few months before my father died. I suspected that Uncle Three's first wife could not stand the constraints of the feudal family system of Number 8, and she left a few years after their marriage. We learned that she later went to study law in the UK. Aunt Three stood apart from her sisters-in-laws as she came from a renowned family in Hong Kong and graduated from an English-speaking secondary school. She did not go on to university. As a socialite who enjoyed a leisurely lifestyle, she fit easily into my uncle's public relations role.

Work or no work, childcare and housework were taken up by the team of household staff. The mother's role was obscure. When we were older, my mother tried to assume that role in the form of feeding us the nutritious slowly cooked soups apart from our communal meals. She ordered the special ingredients on the side and directed my nanny to make sure that we would be served those nutritious soups every afternoon before our communal dinner. She would be dismayed if we did not finish the bowl of soup, as if we were rejecting her.

Much more so than the Jewish mothers' chicken soup, slowly brewed soups have acquired a special symbolic meaning of love and care in Cantonese culture in southern China. Concocted with rich seasonal ingredients and brewed for hours, these soups are supposed to be nourishing. Cantonese mothers swear by them and serve soup with dinner every day. A few years ago, when I asked my students at the university, they told me that the tradition was still ongoing. When they went home on the weekends, their mothers would serve them soup to replenish the malnutrition they suffered living in the dormitories. Mothers-in-laws would teach their daughters-in-laws soup recipes to ensure that their sons continued to be well fed so that they would come home.

In Hong Kong, having soup soon adopted a circuitous symbolic meaning. At one time, businessmen asked each other whether they had "had their soup yet" as a code term for visiting their mistresses. It was alleged that instead of serving a regular full meal, mistresses put all their loving care in serving their men nutritious soup so that the men would not become too full by the time they returned home to have dinner with their wives. There was even a restaurant started in 1988 with the name "Number Two's Beautiful/Marvelous Soup" 阿二

靓湯 specializing in good soups with a branch at the Hong Kong International Airport. These restaurants have closed in recent years.

Names and Numbers

Chinese people list their surname or family name first, followed by their given name. In English, the order is reversed, with surnames listed as last names, and given names as first names. When we go overseas, we conform to the Western style of listing our names, putting our surnames after our given names to avoid creating confusion. Some early Chinese immigrants in the United States had their surnames changed to their given names by the immigration officers because they told their names in the Chinese order during their interviews.

Most given names in southern China have double characters, with one of the characters kept constant among siblings. In the old days, the characters for the male names were prescribed in the family genealogy archives. In our family, all the sons of the second generation, other than two, had 堂 *Tong* as the second character in their given names. It was easy for others to recognize that they came from the same family. For the girls, my father's daughters all had 妙 *Miu* as the first character in their given names. Chinese characters are complex, covering multiple meanings, depending on their etymology and pairing with another word. The character "Miu" could mean being marvelous, wonderful and subtle. After the death of Uncle Two's infant daughter, all my other uncles' daughters adopted the character 慧 *Wai*, which means wise and bright. These were characters related to Buddhist concepts. Many people told me that my Chinese name "Miu Ching" 妙清 (the meaning of the second character includes clear, clean, and pure) portrayed the image of a Buddhist nun.

Somehow on my birth certificate and that of one of my sisters, the cursive fonts in the handwriting of the registrar officer placed the dot over the "i" in Miu behind instead of above the letter. Subsequent government documents typed by other government officers made our English names into "Mui," the spelling with which I have been stuck in my official identity. We never bothered to apply for an official change in the spelling of our names, as we used our Chinese names in Chinese writing, and in English, we were given English names by which we would be called.

In my primary school, the expatriate teachers found it hard to remember the Chinese names of forty students in a class. During Primary 3, we were told to go home and get ourselves an English name. Otherwise, she would assign names like "Mary" or "Jane" to us at her pleasure. My parents did not know any English. My older Sister Six, who was in Form 2 at the time, was reading a romance story in which the heroine was called "Fanny." She was enchanted by the story and asked me to report to my teacher this English name. We started addressing our classmates with their English names. This was part of the colonial heritage.

At home, our seniors would call us by our Chinese names. We could not address our seniors by their names in reverse as it was against propriety. Other than my own parents, the uncles, aunts, big brothers, and big sisters were addressed by their numbers, such as Uncle and Aunt Two, or Big Brother for the Number One brother, then Number Two big sister and so on. In our family, the numbering of boys and girls follow the same order.

My mother is my father's second wife or concubine. That posed a problem with the numbering as his first and principal wife was already called Big (Number One) Aunt by my cousins. My mother's secondary status could not take on the same number. My cousins were asked to call her just "Aunt" without the "Big." My father's children were supposed to call my mother "Ah Niang" 阿娘 to differentiate her from "Ah Ma" 阿媽 or "Big Mother" 大媽, which was reserved for my father's first wife. In secondary school, my mother's group of children decided to discard this old-fashioned address and started to privately call our mother "Mama," which was still different from Ah Ma. (It was our little revolution, treading onto the grey areas, but we never dared to ever call our own Mother Ah Ma, the usual reference to one's mother, but reserved it for my father's first wife at Number 8. Rules, guidelines, and traditions were strictly adhered to in Number 8. Everyone must stay low and under the radar to stay out of trouble.

I am number eleven out of my father's thirteen children, including my half-brothers and half-sisters. I was called Sister Eleven by my younger brothers and cousins, and Number Eleven young miss by our servants. My Big Mother's seven children were numbered one, two, three, four, five, eight and ten, whereas my mother's own children were numbered six, seven, nine, eleven, twelve and thirteen. We did not make any distinction which were half-brothers or half-sisters. All of us third generation in Number 8 lived under the same roof, ate the same meals, and obeyed the same strict rules.

We addressed our cousins with the same numbering system based on their patrilineality. As the Chinese terms for brothers and sisters are the same for paternal cousins, there could be repeated numbers which we tried to distinguish by adding "big" and "small" before the same number.

The House

In 1950, the year I was born, my father bought a two-story building on Macdonnell Road to be the family home. The original house was severely damaged by a fire in 1952 and then rebuilt into a five-story building above a street-level entrance gate and a garage. Beginning in the early 1960s, an Indian doorman wearing a Sikh turban would open the gate for us and direct guests to either walk up the stairs or take the indoor elevator upstairs to the main hall. Contrary to the hierarchical structure of our household, everyone, including the domestic servants, could use the indoor elevator. When we were young, skipping up and down the staircase was faster than waiting for the elevator. This saved the elevator from becoming a toy for us.

Our cars were parked on one side of the garage. The other side of the garage was turned into the living quarters to house the big family of my father's cousin. There the cousin and his wife operated a cottage food stall selling aromatic Hong Kong style coffee, tea and toast to the nearby drivers or patrolling policemen who came in to take their break. In those days, it was natural and common that families took care of less fortunate relatives.

Four floors in the building were designated as residential areas. My grandmother's bedroom was on the ground floor, next to the ancestral hall with the ancestral tablets and shrines of various deities where she prayed every day.

The Buddhist Hall on the fifth floor of Number 8.

My father and uncles would burn incense and kowtow to the ancestral tablets when they came home from work every day. We would do the same during Chinese New Year, and on the birth anniversaries of our deceased ancestors. On those occasions, we would help to fold the origami gold and silver paper ingots piled onto layered paper bowls. An adult would light the pile, make a deep bow and quickly shuffle the offerings into the side furnace to ensure that our ancestors were well provisioned in their afterlife.

In the ancestral hall, there was a plaque with the I-Ching wise saying: "A family that accumulates goodness will have superabundant happiness" (積善之家，必有餘慶 *Jishan zhi jia, bi you yuqing*). There was also a framed script of *Master Zhu's Maxims on Managing the Home* (朱子治家格言 *Zhuzi zhijia geyan*) hanging on the side wall. I don't remember reading the script when we were young. It was supposed to teach the values of being disciplined, hard-working, frugal, and leading a simple life. As far as I can remember, nobody taught these scripts to us. Yet subtly but surely, these values permeated throughout our lives in Number 8, particularly to the wives and children.

When the first black-and-white television set was bought in the late 1950s, it was placed in the antechamber between the living room and the ancestral hall. The children were allowed to sit around a long couch to watch Rediffusion

In the ancestral hall on the ground floor of Number 8, 1979.

TV, the first television station in Hong Kong, for about half an hour before and after dinner. By the time the wireless television broadcasting company TVB commenced broadcasting in color in Hong Kong in 1967, I had already left for my studies in the United States.

All the parents, except Aunt Two (widow of my father's second brother) lived on the third floor in their large ensuites, which the trepid children were warned not to disturb. I think the adult men ate their dinners in their own rooms as I don't recall eating with them in the Victorian-style communal dining room at the back of the ground floor. However, the mothers would eat with the children in the communal dining room when they came back from work. We were only allowed a place at the large dining table since primary school when we were old enough to feed ourselves with chopsticks. Before then, we would be served soft food in our own rooms by our personal amahs (domestic servants) or nannies. Around the large dining table, we all had our own marked ivory chopsticks. The food plates were placed in a turntable in the middle. My grandmother and Aunt Two were Buddhist vegetarians and ate separately at another long dining table on the other side of the room.

Before starting to eat, we had to address our seniors to invite them to start eating. The mothers would first address my grandmother and then one another.

Then the children would start together to address each generation one by one in order of seniority. The youngest ones, who had to go through the rounds of addressing everyone older than them, ended up being the last, after the others had started to eat. Before leaving the table at the end of the meal, we went through a similar round, saying to our seniors who were still sitting at the table "take your time eating." These were daily ceremonial procedures which we all had to go through solemnly. Any digressions from the children during these procedures would receive stern looks from the seniors, upon which the mother of the offending child would feel disgraced.

The children were grouped according to their parents into big bedrooms on the second floor. There was a large communal bath area with rows of children-sized face basins and toilet cubicles of different sizes. The toddlers sat on a row of potties. I stayed in a room with my two younger brothers and our personal amah on the second floor until Primary 5 after my father passed away, when I moved upstairs to my mother's room. The children's rooms expanded into the fourth floor later when the population of children grew. There were still enough rooms, as the older children had left home by the time the youngest cohort was born.

Air conditioning was a rarity in those days until my father first set up window air conditioners in the adults' rooms in the late 1950s. With windows and doors opened in the high-ceiling rooms, there was always a nice breeze coming into the house. Electric fans added to the air circulation. During hot summer nights, our amahs rolled out straw mats on top of our mattresses to keep us dry during our sleep. They would wave black goose feather fans at us to cool us and themselves. It was believed that having electric fans blowing directly at us during sleep was bad for our health. In those days, life without air-conditioning was not an issue. Nowadays, with more high-rise buildings sprouting up on the road and more cars polluting the environment, air conditioning has become a life necessity, generating more noise and heat around us.

My age cohort consisted of six girls with whom we played group games in the ground floor front terrace and back garden, where there was a goldfish pond with a miniature rockery. When the tap was turned on, the mini waterfall flowed from the top to the pond. In the summer, a couple of blooming water lilies floated on their leaf pads. When she was pleased, my grandmother would allow us to take a few pieces of breadcrumbs from her plastic bag to feed the goldfish. During the summer, we had more leisure time, and we could run around and have fun in the garden when the adults were out at work. If we became too loud, my grandmother's maid would come out to hush us not to disturb my grandmother's afternoon nap. Playing hide and seek in the garden was not a fair game. We could always go upstairs from the back staircase to different floors. The strategy was to remain stationary and wait till those in hiding got bored and reappeared on their own.

My grandmother was a devout Buddhist. There was big hall on the fifth floor which housed a formal Buddhist shrine with three large, gilded Buddha statues and a row of kneeling pads where my grandmother led the bi-monthly prayers on the first and fifteenth day of the lunar month. On these occasions, the adult women put on the formal Buddhist brown robes. Aunt Two would lead the Buddhist chants in mixed Chinese and Sanskrit and others would accompany her with the percussion instruments to keep the tempo: the "Mokugyo" (a wooden drum in the shape of two fish facing each other), the bell singing bowl, and copper prayer bells. We would follow the chanting without knowing the meaning, waiting for the sound of the singing bowl that signified the final verse. Then we took turns to place the smoldering incense sticks into the incense burner. On those days, we all ate vegetarian dishes for lunch and dinner. These were our bi-monthly formal rituals, which seemed overly serious to us children.

To compensate, chicken, fish and meat dishes would be added on the next day (the second and sixteenth day of the month), which was called 做禡 zuo ya, as food to offer to the land god for blessing. The chicken thighs were always designated by my grandmother to her favorite grandsons (never to the granddaughters). My grandmother would also bestow her prized harvest of Sapodilla fruit from the tree in the back garden to her favorite grandchildren every year. Occasionally, I was lucky enough to get half of a fruit, only after the boys. I suppose I was in her favor as I was always the only one around in the afternoon playing the piano in the living room while she was reading the Buddhist chant book in the ancestral hall. I was also probably the most studious of this cohort of her granddaughters. She would often ask me to come over to pronounce a word she did not know. The Sanskrit translation was also foreign to me, but I tried my best to give her the pronunciation which satisfied her.

Special foods other than the regular meals were served during Chinese festivals. Before Chinese New Year, the team of domestic helpers assisted the cook to steam stacks of turnip cakes and fry bean paste dumplings. These would be served to guests coming to pay the New Year call to my grandmother, but we always managed to snatch a few pieces of the goodies from the kitchen. In the evening of the Mid-Autumn Festival, heaps of fruit of the season—pomelos, star fruits, and persimmons—and boxes of moon cakes would be placed with auspicious foods including steamed baby taro roots, which supposedly could drive away the devil, and water chestnuts, which rhymes with being intelligent and clever, and sweet round dumplings, which symbolized reunion, on a big table on the roof terrace. After the adult women made offerings to the moon, we could enjoy the festive food while playing with the lighted lanterns in the shape of rabbits or star fruits.

The most obscure festival was the Qiqiao Festival, which took place on the seventh night of the seventh lunar month. This festival originated in the Han dynasty from the legend of the love story between a heavenly weaver fairy and a poor cowherd on earth. After the fairy was forcibly taken back to heaven, the persistence of the cowherd eventually moved the Emperor of Heaven to allow the couple to meet on the bridge built by magpies over the Milky Way once a year. On the night of the festival, young girls were asked to worship the celestials to gain dexterity in needlework as talent for being a good wife, and to make wishes to marry a good and loving husband. Not too many people in Hong Kong celebrated this festival, but my family still did when we were young. The offerings did not include much food except fruits, but there were plenty of toiletries like soap, talcum powder and the "Two Girls" (雙妹 *soeng mui*) Brand of Florida Water, a popular cologne manufactured in Hong Kong. After our mothers prayed to the heavens on our behalf, these offerings were distributed to their daughters, as well as to the eagerly awaiting amahs.

That was the Number 8 in which I grew up: Old fashioned, solemn, restricted, and frugal (not knowing how the average citizens of Hong Kong were living back then). Yet everything and anything we children needed was taken care of, seemingly by the amahs.

On the Street Where We Lived

Number 8 Macdonnell Road was located in the Mid-Levels, halfway between Victoria Peak and the waterfront. In 1904, the British colonial government banned nearly all Chinese residents from the Peak under its official pretext to protect the health of Hong Kong's European residents, keeping them away from the city's older districts near the waterfront which were squalid, overcrowded and rife with disease. Before World War II, the Mid-Levels area below Victoria Peak and as high up as Macdonnell Road was home to people from privileged ethnic backgrounds, including Portuguese, Eurasians, and wealthy Japanese. This racial segregation policy was only repealed in 1946 by the colonial government after the surrender of the Japanese occupying forces in World War II. The rise of the Chinese merchant class led to the opening up of land leases of these formerly restricted zones to be auctioned. Several social institutions were located on Macdonnell Road, including the headquarters of YWCA, St. John's Ambulance, The First Church of Christ, Scientist, and St. Paul's Co-educational College, my alma mater. The peak tram going up from the Garden Road terminus to Victoria Peak had a stop on this road.

Until secondary school when we could independently go out, we stayed inside this Number 8 fortress. Other than the occasional outing to the Botanical Garden which was a three-minute walk from our house, and the bird's eye view of the peak tram track as we stopped by the bridge on our three-minute walk to our school, our glimpses of the outside world came from the balconies where we watched the ongoing life on Macdonnell Road. With envy, we peeked at our schoolmates passing our house in groups to have lunch at the canteen at the YWCA, while we took our monotonous daily lunch among ourselves in the dining room. Like the Western saying that the grass is greener on the other side, the Chinese would say the food next door always tastes more delicious. We seldom had the chance to go out to meals as a group of children, except for the Christmas set lunch at Ruby Restaurant in the Man Yee Building in Central. Ruby Restaurant is part of the collective childhood memory of my generation, who remember it for its classical music record concerts after Sunday lunches. We always probed our classmates about the menu at the YWCA and what the delectable dishes were. The only time I got to try the famous Almond Jello was

The original Number 8 Macdonnell Road, 1951.

Number 8 Macdonnell Road in the 1970s.

when I accompanied Sister Five to her piano lesson at the YWCA. Her piano teacher sometimes treated us to the delicious dessert after class.

Other than students from our school, the pedestrians were mostly dog owners walking their dogs in the afternoon. Occasionally, we heard passing vendors call out their wares. Our favorite was the one selling "airplane olives," so named because each twisted packet of three pickled licorice olives would be flung up to our balcony with precision after we surreptitiously threw our coins down to him with full strength. In those days, all the buildings in Macdonnell Road were low rise, so it was possible for the airplane olives to be flung upstairs. Other than this aerial contact, we could only watch the others pass by. When we heard the recycling collector bang his pots and pans, calling out to buy old metalware, one of the servants would sneak downstairs to the front gate to hand over the hardware from the garbage to get some small change. The newspaperman also came to collect used newspapers. Before we were aware of environmental protection, this simple recycling economy helped to preserve the environment. Modern life creates more waste that is sent to the landfill.

By the time the China Motor Bus route 12A started to operate on Macdonnell Road in 1961, these pedestrian vendors had disappeared. Only a few stationary vendors remained, offering flowers, key cutting, plumbing, and car washing services. After new hawker regulations were introduced in the 1970s, some of them became licensed as fixed pitched stalls. Their trades are inherited by their children and grandchildren up to this day. Bus 12A gave the residents new convenience. Our cook was no longer driven to the market by the chauffeur. Students could take the bus to school instead of walking up the hill if they did not have a family car. We did not have to walk through the Botanical Garden in the hot summer to go to Central. The first generation of single-decker Bus 12As did not have air conditioning, but it was airy enough. One of the bus drivers was super friendly and always patiently waited for passengers running after the bus. He became so popular that he issued his work schedule to the regular passengers.

These were the lives of Hong Kong from the (restricted) perspective of us residents in Number 8. Life was seemingly quiet, slow, peaceful, frugal yet plentiful. We had little knowledge of the lives of ordinary folks, workers, and hawkers who were struggling to make a living in the 1950s. I often wondered what these people were doing away from Macdonnell Road, but at my young age inside a protected cocoon (which I never realized until I had accumulated more experience with life of real people outside), my imagination did not carry me too far. How I longed to experience life outside of Number 8!

Notwithstanding its fortified façade, there was an unbeknown easy access to the garden of our house. I only discovered the loophole in Primary 6 when a boy who sat behind me in my class called me up by phone. He lived in the new building compound at the top of Garden Road, one level above our house. Every afternoon, he and his friends played football on the lawn above our garden. That day, he accidentally kicked the red plastic football over the fence, and it dropped into our back garden. I told him to wait for me at the front gate and I would return the ball to him. He replied that there was no need as he knew how to get in, and I could wait for him in the garden. I was alarmed to find him hopping with ease over the low stone fence between our front terrace and the courtyard of Number 10.

Number 10 Macdonnell Road was a mysterious building. It consisted of a long and narrow neoclassical style two-story building on one side and a simple block for utilities and the servants' area on the other side of the courtyard. Nobody seemed to be living there. In the morning, cars with a military license plate would drop off several civilian expatriates in business suits and frocks who walked up past the courtyard into the shuttered building. The windows were always shut even during the summer. The Chinese chauffeurs would wait in the servants' area during the day. In the late afternoon, the officers were picked up by the same cars. The building became empty.

The chauffeurs had befriended the florist selling flowers from a wooden stall under the huge Bauhinia tree across the street from our two houses. The florist was allowed to fetch water twice a day from the servants' area for his buckets of flowers, even after the office was closed, as the front gate was not locked.

The unlocked gate gave access to my dashing classmate, who had observed the topography of our buildings and knew exactly how to get in without going through our doorman. The row of potted plants on top of the waist-high stone fence was no barrier. In the late afternoon, nobody was out in the garden. He stayed to chat with me and afterwards, left the same way he came in. Over the next few months, the accidents happened more often, presumably a pretext for him to come look me up. We just sat on the steps in the garden and chatted. In school, we did not talk to each other but just played with our own single-sex groups of friends. This short-lived childhood romance of the red plastic ball lasted until the end of the term.

Despite the curiosity we harbored, we never found out what secret activities were involved in Number 10. The adults never talked about our neighbors. When we were young, we did not know what military intelligence or spies were until the 1962 release of the first 007 James Bond movie, Dr. No. Under colonial Hong Kong, ordinary citizens would not have heard anything about the existence of the Special Branch of the Royal Hong Kong Police Force, established by the British colonial government of Hong Kong in 1934 originally as an anti-communist squad under MI5 (the UK's Security Service) with assistance from MI6 (the UK's Secret Intelligence Service), until after it was disbanded in 1995 prior to the return of the sovereignty of Hong Kong to China in 1997. By the time I returned to Hong Kong in 1975, Number 10 was vacated and later sold to a Chinese family. My cousin got to know the daughter who invited us to visit her, and we had a glimpse of what was inside the neocolonial style building. The rooms had high ceilings and there were wooden shutters behind the glass windows. There was no hint of its former life. A few years later, the family redeveloped the building into a high rise. With the mushrooming of these redevelopments, the landscape of our serene Macdonnell Road has been transformed forever.

Scenes from Childhood with My Father

My father died of cancer in 1959 at the age of forty-six when I was only nine years old. He had suffered multiple episodes of treatment and relapses for eight years. I did not know what cancer he had until I joined The Chinese University of Hong Kong (CUHK). The then-Dean of the Medical School,

Prof. Gerald Choa, told me that he was one of my father's doctors, and it was nasopharyngeal cancer. In the last few years of his life, my father's tumor was bulging from his neck. It grew bigger by the year to the size of a tennis ball. I got very upset and angry whenever I saw children on the street pointing their fingers at his big tumor with curiosity. That helpless feeling probably inculcated in me the determination to counter social stigma and support the disabled and disadvantaged when I grew up.

My memory of my father was during the last stage of his life, when he was semi-retired from his business but still active in his philanthropy and engagements in the Chinese business community, including the Tung Wah Group of Hospitals and the Chinese General Chamber of Commerce. I was not old enough to witness his business success or the way he ruled over the family. I only recognized the names of his friends who were the first generation of successful Chinese businessmen in Hong Kong, whose second generation later became business tycoons. I wish I had had the chance to learn from him his entrepreneurial acuity and social skills had he lived longer. I can only remember him as a loving father and a respected elder, an image that was somewhat veiled and distant, and yet so close to my heart all these years.

Ferries and Piers

Once a month, my father would take my mother and her youngest children to visit his friend's villa in the New Territories and enjoy seafood dinners there. We started early in the morning. To cross Victoria Harbour to Kowloon before the first Cross-Harbour Tunnel in Hong Kong was opened in 1972, the car had to take the Yau Ma Tei vehicular ferry which ran every twenty minutes from Central to Yau Ma Tei. I cannot remember how many of us piled into the car. In those days, enforcement of passenger limit was not stringent. We children were always cuddled on the floor level of the passenger back seats. If a traffic policeman was spotted nearby, we were warned to duck our heads down. On the ferry, we could stretch our legs and walk around until the whistle blew to announce the approach of the pier on the other side.

On busy Sundays, the cars had to line up on the pier. Sweepers would rush to the car and try to clean the windshield with their chicken feather dusters.

Our driver always waved them off, as the car was clean. I felt sorry witnessing this scene when poor people were just trying to make a living. Sometimes, my father would give them some small change to send them off.

With no highways back then, the country road to the New Territories took hours. We generally stopped halfway at the Carlton Hotel on Tai Po Road for refreshments. We could enjoy a panoramic view of Kowloon from the hotel restaurant. By the time we arrived at our destination, it would be just in time for lunch. My parents would then go with their friends to the fishermen's wharf to buy seafood, leaving us to play with the other children. When we returned after the sumptuous dinner, we children would all fall asleep in the car while we waited for the vehicular ferry on the Kowloon side.

The vehicular ferry pier was near the Wing Lok Street Pier, commonly known as the Triangle Pier, where goods between Hong Kong, mainland China and Southeast Asia were loaded and unloaded. There were many pier laborers called coolies hired to carry the goods from the pier to the shops and warehouses in Sheung Wan. Once, our car was stalled near the pier when there were many pedestrians and coolies crossing the street. I can still recall a vivid image of the bloodshot eyes and strain on the face of a coolie carrying a very heavy load three times his size on his back. He tried to stop to take a rest, but his hirer rushed him on like a donkey. Tears swelled in my eyes. My father comforted me and said I was a silly girl. In retrospect, that was my first memory of empathy for human suffering. Why did so many folks have to live such a painful life? These questions were too big for my little brain. I just felt sad for those people.

Every year after the Chinese New Year, my father and mother would take us to Macau to visit Popo, my maternal grandmother, and celebrate her birthday in a fancy Chinese restaurant. In the 1950s, before the jet turbo and hydrofoil Macau ferries were introduced, we took the SS Fatshan steam ferry, which took four hours from the Sheung Wan Ferry Pier to reach Macau. We were always excited to watch the halocline in the sea, the distinct boundary where yellow freshwater and dark blue saltwater met near the estuary of the Pearl River as we approached Macau. If the sea was rough, we were given salted ginger to hold in our mouths to ease our seasickness.

Popo lived in a small three-story house with my Brother Nine and an amah. Brother Nine had a mental handicap and could not speak. Allegedly, he was a bright and smart baby when he was born. However, during the time Number Eight was being rebuilt, some of the young children crowded in the living quarters upstairs from the family store in Wing Kut Street. He caught meningitis during his infancy, resulting in his intellectual disabilities. It was before I was born. Evidently, the presence of an exceptional child in Number Eight would disrupt the peace. My father decided to ship him to Macau under my Popo's care. In those days when training facilities for children with intellectual disabilities were nonexistent, rich families usually hid their children from sight. Poor families had to carry the burden without any support.

I did not know anything about mental disabilities when I was young, not until I became a psychologist. I only remembered being afraid of Brother Nine because he would lurch towards us in excitement when he saw us. I didn't know how my parents felt about him, but he was out of mind except for the yearly visit. Nobody talked about him in Number Eight. No one taught us how to relate to him. I only remembered the fun side of staying in the Macau house, where we could lower a basket from the second floor to buy bread and biscuits from the street vendor. After I returned from my studies in America, my mother told me that the loyal amah who took care of Brother Nine all her life had a heart attack and died, leaving Brother Nine sitting by her corpse helplessly when my Popo had gone back to China for a brief visit. As Popo was getting too old to manage Brother Nine, he was sent to an institution for people with mental disabilities run by the Catholic Church in Macau. I did not know what physical ailments he had apart from epilepsy, which ran a risk of premature death three times higher than the general population. He died a few years later. Those were the sad lives of Brother Nine, my Popo, and the loyal amah. While their physical needs were taken care of, there was really no life.

In Hong Kong in the 1950s, people viewed mental disabilities and psychiatric illnesses as mysteries, shrouded in superstition and social stigma. Through the efforts of non-governmental organizations and the early pioneers, educational, training, and residential services for people with physical and mental disabilities were introduced in the 1960s. The first special school for children with intellectual disabilities was set up in 1965. It was only in the

1970s when the concept of equal participation, mutual respect, and integration for individuals with and without mental disabilities began to be promoted in Hong Kong. A series of government White Papers on Rehabilitation during the 1980s and the 1990s finally established a comprehensive policy and service model for the prevention and rehabilitation of different forms of disabilities, with an increasing emphasis on public education and social integration. Unfortunately, up to now, capacities for these facilities still could not satisfy the demand, and social rejection, especially of people with mental disabilities, is still prevalent in the community.

My Brother Nine was born too early to benefit from these social changes. In retrospect, I could understand the decision made by my parents at that time. They kept us in the dark when we were young. Who am I to voice my regret or disapproval of my parents' decision as a daughter when there was nothing that I could do then? Nevertheless, my resolve to care for people with mental disabilities in Hong Kong had compelled me to engage in the New Life Psychiatric Rehabilitation Association for over 45 years as a volunteer, a committee member, the chairperson of the executive committee, and now its president.

Actresses and Movie Stars

Next door to the family pharmaceutical store in Wing Kut Street was Lok Yu Tea House, which has since become the iconic traditional Chinese restaurant famous for its tea and dim sum. My father took his daily morning tea there. When I visited him at the office, I would be taken to join him at his usual table in the tea house. The waiter would bring me a basket of barbeque buns (叉燒包 *charsiubao*), the typical dim sum for children. I always refused, as one bun would fill me up immediately. I preferred the little custard tarts instead. The female cleaner would then come over with her broom and chat with my father, saying how much I looked like a certain famous movie star, whom I did not really know or care for. I would flinch when she tried to pinch me on my cheek. She was the embodiment of the wicked witch of the East!

In the summer when I was six years old, I joined my father in a small stone cottage rented in Shek O Village near the beach for vacation. He apparently had sponsored the Cantonese opera performances offered to the deities around Yue

Lan Festival, or the Hungry Ghost Festival, in the lunar month of July. I told my father I was dazzled by the beautiful opera costumes. He asked someone to take me backstage and deposit me on top of a stack of chests in the dressing room of an actress. I didn't know her name or how famous she was. I was just fascinated watching how she painted her face, tied her hair back, pasted the black sideburns and hair strips on her face and forehead, wore her head gear with jewelry pins and pendants, and then put on the layers of silk garments and adorned slippers. At the end, she looked like a completely different person. Air-conditioning was uncommon and was not installed in the wooden shed built for the performance. There was just a small electric fan in the dressing room. It was impressive how the actress still managed to keep her cool under the heavy makeup and costume. The dressing room was more interesting to me than the front stage as I was too young to understand the story and what was being sung with the loud cymbals and gongs.

I later got to see more actresses when my father took us to the Bay Garden Restaurant which was opened at the waterfront on Paterson Street, before the typhoon shelter was further reclaimed in Causeway Bay. On weekends every few months, movie stars were invited to pose for photographers in the restaurant's garden. I recognized that they were famous icons from Loke Wan Tho's 陸運濤 Cathay Film Studio such as Ge Lan 葛蘭, Lucilla You Min 尤敏, and Julie Yeh Feng 葉楓. I had never been enthusiastic about celebrities or pop idols. I was oblivious to the fanfare. The restaurant also had a jazz band for dancing that played in the evening, which put me to sleep. In retrospect, I reckon that my father made use of these facilities to promote the family's newly-developed real estate in Paterson Street.

Paterson Street

The typhoon shelter outside Paterson Street was a more conventional favorite hangout for my father. In the 1950s, many Tanka 蜑家 boat people lived on sampans in the shelter. My father took us on sampan rides in the evening when the floating hawkers rowed around to offer their seafood and congee dishes. Other sampans offered fruit and Chinese desserts. Singers of Cantonese opera accompanied by traditional Chinese instruments provided entertainment in return for a fee. The typhoon shelter was lit up to become a night market. In those days, food hygiene did not enter our minds. The dishes were washed on the sampans and dirty water were thrown overboard. The famous dishes from the typhoon shelter of fried chili crabs and boiled sea snails with seafood sauce have become incorporated into the popular menus of modern seafood restaurants on land. Until the typhoon shelter was reclaimed to make way for the Cross-Harbour Tunnel and later the Eastern Corridor, when the Tanka sampan population was relocated, the typhoon shelter was a tourist attraction. My mother used to take us there for a treat occasionally after my father's death.

Another enterprise my father started at Paterson Street was bringing the Japanese department store, Daimaru, to Hong Kong. Daimaru was one of the major department stores located in many cities across Japan. He negotiated with the Japanese corporation on a partnership that revolutionized Hong Kong's retail shopping landscape. The store was more modern than the local department stores (Wing On and Sincere, both owned by friends of our family) at that time. The wide variety of merchandise was attractively displayed on well-spaced counters. The food court on the ground floor sold novel Japanese food. Customer service was the hallmark, and the local staff were well trained in Japanese etiquette and gift wrapping. At the entrance to Paterson Street, Daimaru became the landmark of Causeway Bay, which developed into the busy shopping hub it is today. I remember the home movies my father showed about his trips to Japan together with the Chinese businessman, Mr. Liu, who was the broker of the deal and later became the Hong Kong store's general manager. Unfortunately, my father did not live to see its opening in 1960, which was one year after his death. My uncle sent my mother to work with the Japanese supervisors in Daimaru for five years. Daimaru later closed its doors in 1998, succumbing to the rising rent in the district and the cut-throat competition from other Japanese stores.

Death and a Funeral

Conscious of his mortality, my father often went off with friends who were Feng shui masters and aficionados to look for land plots in the New Territories with excellent geomancy as future burial sites for family members. These remote sites made visiting the graves a challenging outing. My grandfather's bones were transposed from Guangdong to a traditional tomb in the middle of nowhere in Junk Bay (now Tseung Kwan O), where my grandmother was later buried with him. We had to ride our family yacht from Blake Pier in Central to Junk Bay, whence we were transported to the beach by the local fishermen's sampans. We walked for another twenty minutes through the shrubs before reaching the tomb, followed by our helpers carrying the offerings. With the development of the New Town in Tseung Kwan O after our family clan moved out of Number 8, no one organized the tomb visits. I have no idea what happened to the tomb, as it is no longer legal to have private burial sites in Hong Kong.

By 1959, my father's cancer had worsened, and he was in and out of the Hong Kong Sanitorium. On November 6, I was taken out of my Primary 5 classroom by my amah, who came to fetch me and my younger brother in Primary 1. All my siblings went to the hospital and later that evening, my father was moved back home because my grandmother wanted him to die in Number 8. He was placed on a bed in the large living room facing the terrace. Everyone knelt around him all night, while the adult women chanted Buddhist prayers. One of his attending doctors was there throughout the night. Before dawn the next morning, the doctor took his pulse and announced that he was dead. There was loud wailing all around. I must admit that at age nine, I did not truly comprehend what was happening and the meaning of death. I just followed the instructions I was told in a daze. I remember having some strong strange feelings, but I don't know what they were, back then or now.

The funeral was an elaborately choreographed affair. At that time, the largest funeral hall was in the International Funeral Parlor located in Wanchai, where Asian House is presently located. My mothers and all my father's children wore white mourning clothes covered by a thin surcoat of sackcloth. The women wore a white hood and a white knitted flower hairpin. My uncles and cousins also wore white gowns while the women wore blue knitted hairpins. We knelt on the side of the altar mounted with my father's big portrait. The funeral director arranged the visitors who had come to pay their respects to line up in front of the altar, and then bowed three times before turning to bow to us, whereupon we bowed back on our knees.

The funeral vigil lasted a few days. The funeral hall was lined with floral wreaths and condolence blankets against the wall. At the reception, relatives and staff helpers recorded entries and thanked the visitors with a packet of white and red envelopes containing a dollar bill, a piece of candy and a small white towel. There were shifts of Buddhist monks and nuns providing non-stop prayers and chants. Now and then, we would follow the monks to circle around the hall during the chants, holding a joss stick with both hands to be deposited in the incense burner on the altar at the end.

In addition to the bags of gold and silver paper ingots that our relatives helped fold as they sat to one side during the wake, paper models of our house, our cars, a troop of servants as well as some of my father's favorite belongings, such as his cameras, were arranged. These were burned as offerings to ensure that he would not miss his worldly luxury in his afterlife.

On the day of the funeral, my oldest brother held my father's portrait to lead the coffin to the funeral van. The funeral procession, with a loud marching band and a troupe of Buddhist monks and nuns, paraded through the streets that my father had travelled in his last days, probably to ensure that his spirit would rejoin his body and not be left behind. From Wanchai, we first marched to Paterson Street in Causeway Bay, followed by Happy Valley where my father was hospitalized in the Hong Kong Sanitorium, then back to Central, stopping in front of Wing Kut Street for a special rite of offerings to his businesses. We then proceeded to the Final Farewell Pavilion near the main Chinese cemetery in Pokfulam for another prayer ritual before ending at the Tung Wah Coffin Home on the hill above Sandy Bay. My father's coffin was stored temporarily there before his tomb site in Fanling in the northern New Territories was ready. At that time, the coffin home served the important function of providing a temporary repository for dead bodies waiting for transportation back to their hometowns in mainland China for a proper burial. I cannot remember how much walking we children had to do, but each of us was escorted by an adult helper. We probably were transported by car part of the way. In those days, it was still possible to apply to hold funeral parades through the streets. I only remember hearing the loud gossip from pedestrians on the sidewalk, who were wondering how many wives my father had with such a large entourage.

In the forty-nine days (seven days times seven weeks) after my father's death, we wore mourning clothes, unless we were wearing our school uniforms when we went to school. Buddhist nuns came to perform prayers held in the ancestral hall in our house every evening. The rites were more elaborate on the first, third, and seventh weeks after the day of his death. More gold and silver ingots and new paper models were burned. Although we were all very used to ceremonial rituals in our mansion, these daily rituals had a very different atmosphere. The "normal" solemnity of Number 8 turned starkly grim. Whether for show or for real, it seemed as if all the adults were breathing heavier air, carrying a heavier heart, and mournful of the loss.

Other than a display of respect befitting one's status and wealth, I suppose these elaborate funeral rites could serve the function of releasing grief through mourning. My mother vehemently believed in the importance of these Buddhist rites to ensure that after her death, her soul would pass into the Western Land of Bliss. She had already made arrangements with a Buddhist temple for prayers to be held at her eventual passing. As an agnostic, I loathe formalistic religious rituals. I would rather have a simple cremation and have my ashes scattered. After one or two generations, it is uncertain who may attend to our graves, which will eventually be abandoned to a state of disarray. So why waste precious land? There could be many other means to remember our legacies.

My father's own tomb site was bought from the New Territories villagers in the name of a fruit farm. It was in a hillside behind the Gurkha military camp in Fanling in the northern New Territories. Before the village houses were developed nearby, there was no vehicle access to the hillside except through the private road of the military camp. Twice a year when we visited his tomb, we had to explain our purpose to the soldiers guarding the gate. Somehow, they always let our cars pass through. We paid the nearby villagers to help cut down the overgrown grass and shrubs so we could find our way among all the tall trees, up the heavily vegetated steep hill to reach the tomb. As my mother aged—and by now, my generation was also getting old—we no longer had the physical strength to climb up the steep bumpy hillside to sweep the grave. The tomb site was mostly left unattended. An earlier attempt to exhume my father's bones for reburial in a cemetery fell through when we could not get enough enthusiasm from my half-brothers and half-sisters in America to consent to the project, and my mother did not dare to go forward alone for fear that she would be blamed for the action that might damage the fengshui of anyone in the family.

The Household Staff

Ms. Yeung

Our housekeeper-cum-governess, Ms. Yeung, was the key figure in our household. Ms. Yeung was a spinster who had attended a conventional Chinese girls' school in Hong Kong known for being old fashioned and strict, at the time when few women had finished secondary education. Wearing a simple cotton cheongsam with her permed hair brushed back, she always looked stern. She lived in our house and managed the team of up to eighteen domestic servants, including the cook, the communal cleaners, laundry worker, garden cleaner, and our personal amahs/nannies. The two male chauffeurs stayed downstairs in the garage and seldom showed up inside the house. A part-time male gardener came twice a day to water the plants on all the balconies and tended the young potted plants on the rooftop before they were ready for rotation.

As our tutor, Ms. Yeung imparted traditional Chinese values and proper manners in us, starting with our first lesson in the *Three Character Classic* (三字經 *Sanzijing*). She conducted the initiation rite for our writing by holding our hands to dip the Chinese brush in the ink pad, and then tracing the lines of simple characters in the grids of Chinese nine-square writing paper. She next taught us to recite the first two paragraphs of the *Three Character Classic*, which stated the basic belief in the inherent goodness of mankind and the importance of education. At our young age, we just repeated the words without understanding what we were reciting.

In the morning, Ms. Yeung checked the pantry, ordered provisions, and kept the grocery accounts. In the afternoons, after we had biscuits and milk for afternoon tea, she supervised the homework of those of us in the lower forms of primary school. In the living room on the fourth floor, we had assigned seats around a long Mahony table with a row of trimmed drawers on the sides. We were supposed to keep quiet and concentrate on our homework while she walked behind us. If she was out of sight, we would start chatting and playing around. As soon as we heard the click clack of her slippers, we quickly resumed our position at the table. Homework class was dismissed at six o'clock, when we would take our baths before going down to the communal dining room for dinner.

As our mothers went off to work in the family business during the day, Ms. Yeung was the only adult who ate lunch with us. We were all afraid of her as she would tell us off and report our misbehaviors to our mothers. She instilled in us the traditional discipline of sitting still at the lunch table, "no talking when eating and when in bed" (食不言，寢不語 *shibuyan, qinbuyu*), and proper table manners like not touching the "Lazy Suzy" turntable when someone else was picking up the food. If she were around nowadays, she would forbid playing with mobile phones at the dinner table, which would be a good thing. She ensured that we handled chopsticks properly, always holding up the bowl with the left hand while using the right hand to hold the chopsticks. Fortunately, none of us were left-handed. Once, when Ms. Yeung stepped aside during lunch, I played mischief by inciting the other children to all switch our chopsticks to our left hands. It took her half a minute to discover the anomaly around the table and we were given a scolding. Luckily, she never found out that I was the culprit. Otherwise, my mother would have received the humiliating report.

As Ms. Yeung was our tutor, we addressed her as "Master" Yeung, which in Chinese mean "teacher" irrespective of gender. As we were young, we addressed all the amahs with *jie* 姐, which means big sister, added after their given name.

Oi Jie, My Nanny

Oi Jie 愛姐 joined our family when I was born. She was in her late twenties when she came back from a short stint with an overseas Chinese family in

Annam (now Vietnam). She stayed with us until her seventies, when she finally retired due to poor health. She looked after me, and then my two younger brothers until we left home. After my mother moved out of Number 8, Oi Jie continued to serve my mother and supervised my mother's Filipino domestic helpers. We considered her part of our family. My mother helped her to invest her savings in stocks, bought her a small flat when she retired, hired an Indonesian domestic helper to nurse her as her health deteriorated, and managed her final years in an old-folk's home and then her funeral rites when she died.

Coming from the tradition of *majie* 媽姐 (domestic servants or amahs from Guangdong) who remained single throughout their lives, Oi Jie was proud of her professional identity. Her signature *majie* uniform of white cotton tops with Chinese buttons and black silk trousers were always kept pristine. She wore her thick black hair in a long pigtail which was only shampooed about once a month. Before important festivals, she would go to the traditional hair combing woman (like our modern hairdresser) in one of the stalls on the steep stone slabs of Pottinger Street in Central, where her hair was fine combed with *baohua shui* 刨花水 (a gluey substance of wood shavings soaked in water) to make it soft and shiny before being braided tightly and tied with a red string at the end. She had been so intimately attached to her pigtail that I was surprised to find it cut off many years later in her fifties. She said it was too much trouble keeping up with long hair and it was too hot during summer months. I think it might also be because her hair was thinning out. I felt disappointed that she did not save the cut pigtail as her treasured souvenir. The act seemed like a determined break from her youthful glory.

Oi Jie's loyalty and dedication to the "little masters" under her ward was unquestioned. She ensured that we did not lose out on our fair share of central provisions. She protected my younger brothers if they got into squabbles with their peers. She became well known in the neighborhood, as she always screamed out to my younger brothers not to run so fast or cross the road without her while she chased behind them with her wagging pigtail, carrying their schoolbags in the three-minute walk to school. At home, she followed me around with a bowl of slow brewed soup to make sure that I would finish it before going out.

With Nanny Oi Jie as a toddler at the Botanical Gardens, 1954.

Although she was always gentle with us, Oi Jie was territorial over her position. She kept an eagle eye over any junior servant who was hired to help her out. I remember when I was a nine-year-old, one new child-servant barely over thirteen was asked to shampoo my hair for me. She was not a "little sister" (妹仔 *mui jai*), who were girls from poor families sold at a young age to work as domestic servants in traditional China, under the condition that they be freed through marriage when older. In 1922, the colonial government passed a law in Hong Kong to abolish the practice. However, girls over thirteen could still be employed in non-industrial establishments. The new child-servant was inexperienced and once used water that was too hot to wash my hair. When I complained, the poor girl got badly scolded by Oi Jie and disappeared a week later. I really felt sorry for causing her demise. In later days when my mother lived alone and hired another Filipino domestic helper to assist her with housework, Oi Jie guarded her kitchen stronghold ferociously and often pushed the Filipina out of her territory.

When I was a teenager, I once asked Oi Jie why she did not want to get married. She said she did not want to, which was a non-answer. I reminded her about a man who came to visit her at Number 8 when I was in Primary 1, and how she walked with him to the Botanical Garden across from Macdonnell Road, bringing me along with her. I saw him trying to grab her hand and she shook him off. She later confessed that it was a cousin of her former employer. It must have been more than that for she had given him a few loans that he never repaid, which might have explained the end of the relationship.

For her other family members back in her home village in Guangdong, Oi Jie saved up my parents' worn clothes and sent them in packages with small sacks of rice and cans of cooking oil. In the 1950s, China was poor, food was scarce, and oil was precious. Every other year, she got a break to go back to her home village. She would pack as much as she could into two big bags, which she carried on a shoulder pole while piling the surplus clothing on herself. One time, she was questioned by the Chinese customs official about why she was wearing four thick trousers in the summer and was given a fine.

Oi Jie's favorite relative was her brother's daughter, whom she sponsored to come to Hong Kong to study. After junior high, the niece went to work in a factory and then got married. She was good to Oi Jie and would take her out to dinner now and then. Unfortunately, she died of cancer a few years later, and Oi Jie was heartbroken. I was pleased to find that later in life, one of her nephews had moved to Hong Kong. He and his wife often visited her in her retirement and took care of her until she died. I appreciate that they still upheld the traditional Chinese virtue of showing gratitude to Oi Jie for her benevolence earlier in life.

Pecking Order

Under different patronage and given their diverse personalities, the domestic servants formed an implicit pecking order. Standing apart was the nanny of Aunt Three's first son, Sei Jie (四姐), which means Sister Four. Allegedly, she was the fourth concubine of a former minor official in China but lost everything during the wars. She impressed the others with an air of arrogance that she had seen big times. Distancing herself from dirty work, she often gave instructions to the junior servants on the proper way of doing things. She had the privilege (or audacity) of rolling her own cigarettes and had a puff occasionally on the balcony, even though nobody in our family smoked. The other servants stayed out of her way. Even Ms. Yeung refrained from crossing her path, as Sei Jie reported directly to my aunt. She did not stay around too long as her obesity started to give her health problems.

Chun Jie (珍姐) was the smart one around whom the others revolved. Despite having little education, she could read and write. She helped the other illiterate servants to read their letters from home. She often served as the negotiator and peacemaker to resolve their conflicts. Although her primary duty was taking care of Aunt Two's children, she was frequently conscripted to the role of envoy for the family, as she was well versed in Chinese customs and niceties. Before weddings, she delivered the wedding gifts of my uncle and oldest brother's brides in stacks of red round boxes on a pole for their betrothal ceremonies. She was sent to visit and pay amends to the neighbor's porter at the hospital when he was hit by a Coca-Cola bottle that had been thrown out of the toilet's window by my little brother, in his fumbled attempt to destroy the evidence of the forbidden sugary drink. After Number 8, Chun Jie followed the older of my aunt's twin daughters after her marriage to take care of the next generation of children.

The most diffident and bullied one was Shun Jie 順姐. She was sent to the family as a dowry of Aunt Two who was married to Uncle Two in China at age eighteen. Initially a personal attendant of my aunt, she later took part in caring for her children. Shun Jie was kind-hearted and non-competitive, which befitted her name, which means to go along smoothly. She always got left out and ended up with the leanest portion for dinner. I don't know why she did not have a fixed bed but had to roll out a canvas bed with wood poles every night to sleep in the corridor outside my aunt's room. Maybe Chun Jie already shared the bedroom with the children, and for whatever reason, she did not get allocated a bedspace in the servants' quarters. Her health was generally weak, and her face always looked pale. In addition to taking brewed herbal medicine all the time, she frequently slabbed ginger slices on her forehead when she slept. The trademark was a blood spot on the bridge of her nose, sustained from constantly pinching between her eyebrows, which she claimed could relieve her headaches. She felt inferior to the others, who teased her for being a weakling. Shun Jie's boldest feat was sneaking the biggest piece of roast pork thigh bone strewn with meat chunks from the kitchen during feasts and bringing it to my twin cousins for their snack. She reasoned that with their widowed mother being a vegetarian who only took them to visit the Buddhist temple with her on weekends, the twins were often deprived of good food. Her dedication was reciprocated by my other twin cousin, who took her under her wing when she married into a prominent family. Shun Jie stayed there until she passed away in old age and my cousin arranged to have her buried in her husband's private family cemetery as a family member.

Undercurrents in Harmony

As a fair and respected patriarch, my father kept the family in harmony, which consolidated the collective. I do not recall any scenes of open conflict or fights among the adults or children. The common good of the family always came before the interests of individuals. By following norms and rituals prudently, the adults averted discord. The young children played innocently together, like we were all siblings. That was my father's old-fashioned idealism, as was the belief of many traditional Chinese extended families in the early days.

To avoid provoking jealousy, the daughters-in-law kept a low profile and refrained from flaunting themselves or their children. What they feared most, however, was their own children's transgressions bringing shame to their nuclear branch. They disciplined their children in private and reminded them that their misconduct was an unfilial act.

Brother Seven, my mother's second child, was the thorn in my mother's standing. I remember a fiery scene shortly after my father's death, when she flared up in a wailing fit after receiving a complaint about my brother. I cannot recall what the complaint was about, but it must have been serious. She commanded him to kneel and admit his wrongdoings before my father's photo on top of the small shrine she kept in her room. The rest of us had to kneel with him as a deterrent and reminder that misbehavior by any one of us could sink the whole boat. A few years later, Brother Seven and Brother Eight, my half-brother, were sent off to Sydney and Dublin respectively to attend boarding school under the guardianship of my two older half-sisters, who were attending college there. I presume that was a form of exile due to their truancy and poor results in school.

My mother's sunken boat warning was not groundless. Sister Ten, my half-sister who is one year older than I am, reminded me of an incident in which she and I were summoned to receive a lesson from my grandmother. That was in 1962 when my father's oldest son moved out of Number 8 with his wife and two young sons. We later learned through the grapevine that he had piled up a huge gambling debt and was expelled from the family. Sister Ten and I were my father's only children still at home and old enough to be summoned. Out of the blue, Grandmother threatened that if we did not behave ourselves, we would not have rice to eat (which also meant dinner). Sister Ten was deeply aggrieved that she had been reprimanded for no fault of her own. She was traumatized by the injustice and burst into tears. She rushed back to her room to pack her bag with the intention of running away from home as a passive protest but was led back inside the house when an amah saw her sniffing at the front porch. On the other hand, oblivious to whatever misbehavior my grandmother had in mind, and convinced that I was innocent of any wrongdoing, I retorted nonchalantly that without rice, I could eat bread instead. Sister Ten still remembers with admiration my bold resistance to injustice without succumbing to my emotions. Staying aloof helped me to ride above the swirls of the undercurrents at Number 8.

After the death of my father the patriarch, the dynamics among the sisters-in-laws shifted. The widows lost their protector and receded to the background. When the widows stopped working in the family business, they lost the right to use the family car. Aunt Three took the limelight, armored by her natal family background and her husband's societal role. Heedless of the due respect expected to her seniors, she assumed a lofty standing with special privileges, in the name of her contributions to the family companies. While still retaining the appearance of courtesy, Aunt Four watchfully aligned herself with the axis of power. Yet, harmony was maintained so long as the matriarch, my grandmother, was still around.

Legacy of Number 8

After completing my studies in the United States in 1975, I returned to Number 8. Nine years had passed. Cheung Kam Kee had closed by then. Other than Uncle Four, the rest of the family members no longer worked in the family business, which had expanded into a publicly listed conglomerate focusing on real estate. Until 1971, the two, thirty-one-floor commercial buildings constructed in 1967 in Central—Realty Building and International Building—were the tallest at that time. Realty Development Corporation owned the two commercial buildings plus other pricey properties in the Mid-Levels. Via a share swap, Realty Development Corporation became part of the holdings of Wheelock Marden & Company, a large real estate corporation with old British capital headquartered in Hong Kong. In 1977, Uncle Four held 10 percent of the issued share capital of this listed company.

At Number 8, the housekeeper, Ms. Yeung, had already retired, and there were fewer inhabitants. Among the twenty-eight grandchildren, only the youngest children of Uncle Three and Uncle Four, who were still in secondary school, were staying there, as well as me and one of my twin cousins. The others had either gone overseas for studies, settled there, or had got married and moved out. The house had not changed, and the microcosm of its social structure and dynamics still permeated across the board. Even after the house was demolished and the family split apart in 1979, Number 8 kept its ethos in its inhabitants' outlooks.

After my grandmother's funeral in 1978, my mother started to get anxious. She sensed the end was coming and she would not have a home. Number 8 was the only home she knew in her adult life. My Big Mother had already migrated to San Francisco, where most of her children had settled. My mother and Aunt Two were widows who had no say in the family decision. After an announcement was posted in the name of the family company holding the property that Number 8 would be demolished in 1979, my mother reluctantly accepted a compensatory "gift," which she used to buy another flat on

Macdonnell Road. She insisted she would not consider staying anywhere else in Hong Kong, as this was the only street where she had lived.

Shortly after the announcement of the demolition of Number 8, Uncle Three was discovered dead in his sleep from a heart attack when his servant went to wake him up in the morning. Apparently, deep in his heart, he did not want to leave Number 8 even though he and Uncle Four had already arranged to move to the Peak with their families.

To everyone's surprise, Aunt Two—who had been peaceful and reticent throughout her life in Number 8—refused to move out of the house. With remarkable resilience, she stood firm and would not budge even after the utilities were shut off. Eventually she filed an injunction and won a settlement in which she was allowed to stay without rent in a flat in the redeveloped high rise for the rest of her life. Later, it was discovered that her assigned flat was deliberately cut into half the size of the standard flats and the other half was turned into a duplex of the flat below.

With the support of her son-in-law, who was a distinguished lawyer, Aunt Two filed another lawsuit in 1981 against the family asking for equal distribution of the family assets, recalling promises from her late husband and my late father that the family would always take care of its members and remain undivided. It was a complex lawsuit involving the Qing customary laws and an intricate matrix of family company holdings. It was unclear when the collective family unit was transformed into individual ownership with shareholdings that did not include the rest of the family. It was beyond my knowledge and interest. It would take a team of business legal experts to uncover the web of transactions of the collective unit's assets. At that time, it was rumored that Uncle Four had retained all the top law firms in Hong Kong. After a stressful trial, my aunt lost the first tactical round and decided to give up the lawsuit, returning to her Buddhist devotion. We never got to learn the truth about the legal battle.

Despite what happened to them, my mother and Aunt Two persisted in their allegiance to the family name and rituals even when they lived away from Number 8. They always referred to the family rules and customs, and how things would have been done in Number 8. They were still sensitive to how others in the family would view them and worried about their children bringing shame for any misdeeds. In her new home, my mother kept all the photos and tablets of the deceased senior Cheung family members on the shrine table and prayed for them every day. Until she developed Alzheimer's disease, she remembered the dates of their birthdays and death anniversaries, making special offerings on those days. She could not relinquish her identity as a Cheung family daughter-in-law.

For our generation, who grew up as pupae in the protected cocoon, our metamorphosis was as fascinating as butterflies. Having been a participant observer in Number 8 might have stimulated my interest in the study of psychology and cultivated my emotional intelligence. From navigating the labyrinths of familial hierarchies throughout childhood, I have learned to be sensitive to organizational structure and interpersonal dynamics. I have gained the skill to relate to assorted characters irrespective of whether they were likeable. Yet, I queried how the concept of genetic and environmental interaction in human development could be simplistically applied to my family, as all twenty-eight grandchildren developed diverse personalities and led varying life paths. The family environment was not consistent across time cohorts, positions, and circumstances. Some have succumbed to, some survived, and some transcended the ethos of growing up in Number 8. Number 8 was more akin to a cooperative than a family, as it was commonly perceived. Until I was married and witnessed how my husband related to his nuclear family members, I did not realize what intimate family relationships were like.

We don't have a choice about being born into this world or into which family, but we can choose to make the best out of our lives. As for myself, pursuing a steady professional career throughout my adult life and not having to worry about food on the table afforded me the luxury of being indifferent to material wealth and worldly ambition. Perhaps, helping my grandmother to pronounce the vocabulary in her Buddhist prayer books over the years had also made an imprint on my Zen-like attitude to a life without desires. My psychological reactions to the vicissitudes of Number 8 have fostered my disdain for greed, my conviction in fairness, and my compassion for the disadvantaged. Cognizant of the discrepancies in the two worlds—between my privileged family and the society at large—I became convinced that those of us who were more fortunate should contribute to the cause of the less fortunate. I did not subscribe to the life of leisure enjoyed by some of my family members, even those in my generation now, whose daily lives only consist of shopping, travelling, fancy dinners, clubbing, playing Mahjong, or other entertainments. Many of them never had to bother with the chore of having to earn a salary, cruising through life as a good life was meant to be. While they were entitled to their hedonistic pleasures, I considered it more gratifying to find my voice and pursue a deeper meaning in my own life.

INCIDENTAL
FEMINISM

The floral clock of University House,
UC Berkeley University, 1969.

2

Feminists are stereotyped typically as being militant activists and often anti-men. In the movement for women's emancipation, Western feminists have advocated for and gained equal rights and equal access to public life for women. However, throughout the different waves of Western feminism, there have been different factions of feminists with different ideologies and strategies. Instead of working together towards outcomes, the factions unfortunately often attacked one another for "political incorrectness." Any time "politics" is brought into the discussion of issues, we find more conflicts and power struggles. In the 1960s, radical feminists have taken to the streets to burn bras and condemn "male chauvinist pigs." Third world and Global South women scholars have critiqued American and European feminism as culture-bound and only relevant to developed industrialized societies. Some contemporary protests for women's rights in the Western world have evolved beyond anti-men to anti-transgender rights. A chaotic "Let Women Speak" event in Australia in March 2023 made headlines when it was joined by anti-transgender demonstrators and the far-right National Socialist Movement. Local politicians accused the protesters of being Nazi allies and spreaders of hate. These extreme images of women's rights advocates exaggerated in the media have tainted the label of feminism.

Many Chinese women leaders have shunned the label of a feminist. Some of the more traditional women even reject feminism altogether. Some told me that I didn't look like a feminist as I spoke softly and maintained a feminine demeanor over my diminutive body frame. Nevertheless, I have been regarded as an advocate for women's rights and a pioneer in gender studies in Chinese society. For me, labels are inconsequential. Anyone who believes that a woman has the right to live her own life without the need to fulfill preconceptions of what a woman should be, or who promotes women's advancement and gender equality, can be regarded as a "feminist." As such, I consider myself a feminist although I was not versed in the orthodox ideologies of various forms of Western feminism. As a pragmatist, what counted to me were the issues, actions, and outcomes. The orthodoxy of numerous "isms" through the decades, culminating in the current conservative right-wing backlash and anti-woke hysteria in America, reveals why I preferred the principle of the middle way and the value of harmony in our Chinese culture.

How did I become a feminist? It was not due to my nine years studying in the U.S., where many people thought I was trained in feminism. I have never taken any courses in women's studies or feminist theories. When I was an undergraduate at Berkeley, feminists marched on the streets in militant rallies. I detested the antagonistic rhetoric as well as the boisterous tactics. Confrontation was not congruous with my cultural heritage and traditional upbringing. Growing up in an extended family with strict Confucian norms and social hierarchies, Chinese traditional gender roles were not and could not be questioned. Harmony was paramount and conflicts would not surface. Power structures were enigmatic.

A Patriarchal Family Headed by a Matriarch

My father, as the oldest son, was head of my extended family until he died in 1959 when I was nine. My three uncles and all the children living under the same roof followed his mandate. After my father's death, Uncle Four, who took over the reins of the family business, assumed the ultimate authority, because

Fanny's grandmother and her in the back garden of Number 8, 1976.

Uncle Two had died even earlier in 1953 and Uncle Three was less interested in business or management. As authority figures, these adult men did not actually interact with us children. Reference to their edicts would be sufficient without their physical presence.

On the other hand, my grandmother was the matriarch to whom everyone, including my father and my uncles, paid filial respect. Her sheer position portrayed paramount authority. Every Chinese New Year, everyone lined up in order of gender (males first) and seniority and then knelt before her to present her with tea, kowtowed, and wished her longevity and good health. We were then each rewarded with a red packet from her.

Occasionally, my grandmother would make critical comments on misbehaving grandchildren. Her daughters-in-law were more mindful than the grandchildren themselves when their children were involved. In retrospect, I think my grandmother was more the figure head put forth to symbolize the essential values of filial piety and obeisance rather than the real center of power.

In our patriarchal family, boys were favored over girls. However, in Confucian tradition, education was revered. All of us children were encouraged and supported to study as much as we wanted and as far as we could go. Good scholastic performance was rewarded. At the end of each school year, my father would host a ceremony in the ancestral hall and pin a gold or silver medal

Fanny's father giving out scholastic awards in the ancestral hall, 1956.

on those of us who came within the top three places in class. I was one of the lucky ones. Under this scholastic shield, I gained my self-esteem at Number 8 and did not discern any disadvantage being a girl. It was only after my feminist sensitization thirty years later that I rediscovered the gender nuances in my household. Back then, the explicit hierarchy of sons over daughters-in-laws was accepted as a matter of fact. On the other hand, the power connections of the daughters-in-law via their husbands bestowed differential status. Widows had no power base and thus no say. For the grandchildren, normative gender roles were prescribed in the name of good behavior. Scholastic success was recognized as paramount good behavior that overrode childhood concerns about unequal distribution of favors to boys over girls.

Wife and Concubine

My father's first wife was arranged by my grandmother through a matchmaker in Guangzhou. My grandmother once told me that she went with the matchmaker to look at the potential bride in her father's butcher shop. My grandmother was satisfied that the candidate was plump and had big round buttocks, which meant she would be good for breeding children. Big Mother lived up to her prognostic and mission. She bore a total of seven children for my father during his travels between Hong Kong and the mainland until she came over and joined the family with the youngest two of my half-brothers and half-sisters, Brother Eight and Sister Ten, after the civil war in China.

My mother, being the concubine, married my father when she was only sixteen, twelve years junior to my father. Even without the prognostic, she bore my father six children, with her first child, Sister Six, born when she was age seventeen. In my teenage years, I asked my mother why she would agree to become a concubine, which to me was inconceivable.

Even though polygamy and concubinage was still legal in Hong Kong at that time until the marriage law was reformed in 1970, it was old fashioned. Few people realized that this practice prevailed for so long in Westernized modern Hong Kong. Many years later, after I started research into gender issues in Hong Kong, I learned that all other Chinese societies had abolished polygamy and outlawed concubinage after the fall of the Qing dynasty in 1911. It was only in colonial Hong Kong that the Qing customary laws were maintained, when Britain proclaimed sovereignty over Hong Kong Island in 1841. To pacify the local inhabitants when he took over Hong Kong, British Admiral Charles Elliott, the first administrator of Hong Kong, declared that Chinese laws and customs would be preserved. This reference to the Qing customary laws has impacted gender equality in different aspects of Hong Kong life up to this day, including the 1972 New Territories Small House Policy, which gave each male—not female—descendant of the indigenous villagers registered in 1898 the grant to build one village house. This Small House policy was not prescribed by the Qing customary laws. When the late David Akers-Jones was the then-Secretary for the New Territories, he exploited this cultural custom as a cost-saving compensatory measure to get the indigenous villagers' support for new town developments in the New Territories. The Small House Policy was specifically exempted in the Sex Discrimination Ordinance that was passed in 1995.

The 1971 Marriage Reform Ordinance passed by the Legislative Council, which finally abolished polygamy and concubinage in Hong Kong, was credited

Big Mother (middle) and some of the children, 1957.
Front row from the right: Sister Ten, Brothers Twelve, Seven, Thirteen, Eight,
and Fanny. Back row from the right: Big Brother and Sister Six.

Fanny's mother (middle) and her five children (from the right in front):
Brothers Thirteen and Twelve; at the back (from right to left):
Fanny, Brother Seven and Sister Six, 1959.

to Mrs. Ellen Li Ts'o Sau-kuan (李曹秀群), the first female councillor, who proposed the bill. Married women were subsequently allowed to hold property and petition for divorce since 1972 with the passage of the Married Persons Status Ordinance and the Matrimonial Causes Ordinance, respectively. When I met Mrs. Li in her late nineties in 2004, she confessed that it was in fact a male councillor, Oswald Cheung, who initiated the idea, but he passed the role to her as it would be more persuasive coming from a female councillor. I thought she was being too modest.

Under this historical context and the prevailing social norm, my mother did not question the marriage proposal to become a concubine in 1944. My mother was my maternal grandmother's only child, and the family was poor as her father died young. After one year of secondary school in Guangdong, she left for Macau with her mother to escape from the Japanese invasion in Guangdong province. Toward the end of World War II, she came to Hong Kong to seek refuge from her distant cousin and look for a job. Her cousin happened to be a friend of my father. At that time, her cousin was also pursuing a concubine, which was fashionable among Chinese men, and got my father interested. My mother figured that during the Japanese occupation of Hong Kong, it would be safer to get married than being a young single woman. She recalled that my father was persistent and would trail behind her even when she was invited to tea by another suitor. She just needed a haven. She did not mind being a concubine or secondary wife, which would put her in a lower position in the social hierarchy, as she was my father's favorite.

Self-Reliant Women

My mother was bright and eager to learn. Even though she did not finish secondary school, she took private English and Japanese lessons from tutors who came to our home on weekends after my father's death. She was dispatched by Uncle Four to work at the Daimaru Department Store, which my father started in Hong Kong as a joint venture with the Japanese conglomerate. She built up good working relationships with the Japanese managers and their wives with her rudimentary Japanese language skills. After my uncle took her off the position five years later, she started her own fashion wholesale business in

Fanny's mother (left) at Daimaru Store with her and
the Japanese manager's wife (right), 1959.

defiance, based on the merchandising knowledge and skills she had learned at
Daimaru. In the back of her mind, there was probably the fear that as a widow,
she would be at the mercy of my uncles and might lose the financial support for
herself and her children any time. At first, she naively tried to hide her business
from the knowledge of other family members, claiming she was just helping in
her cousin's office, in the fear that she would be officially prohibited from doing
so. In such a small business world, it was impossible to conceal her commercial
activities. Apparently, Uncle Four turned a blind eye and it remained a hushed
secret in Number 8.

After the dissolution of Number 8, my mother pursued her business in
full-fledged mode. Before high fashion and luxury brand names were common
in Hong Kong, she imported European women's and men's fashion, as well
as Japanese children's wear to the local large department stores. Every year,
she flew to Europe to select samples which were then shown to the buyers of
the department stores. She had built personal friendships with the buyers and
prodded them to support her by placing maximal orders for her merchandise.
While she was generous in treating her business associates and friends, she was
frugal with herself. With a lean budget on her travels, she skimped on food and

wasted little time. Yet, now and then, she would take us to a popular Chinese restaurant to enjoy expensive delicacies such as small bowls of shark fin, to ensure that her children would not be deprived of good food after their father was gone. Singlehandedly, she ran this business for fifty years with her blood, sweat and tears, accumulating her independent wealth, enough to provide a good living for all her children as well as support the education costs of the next generation and other relatives until she retired in her eighties.

With our mothers engaged in working outside of the home all day at Number 8 and coming home only to eat dinner and sleep, we did not have good role models in mothering, unlike what we saw in our schoolmates' mothers, who often gathered at the school gate to pick up their children and talk to the teachers. We children were practically brought up by our personal nannies at home, supervised by our governess-cum-housekeeper, Ms. Yeung. Of course, they could not fill the gap of the role of mothers. All in all, we grew up surrounded by women who made a living to support themselves, and we learned about the importance of self-reliance. Some of the older domestic helpers from the generation of *majie* remained single and stayed with our family for decades. *Majie* were from Guangdong province and worked as amahs in Hong Kong and Singapore between 1930 and 1970. However, I didn't think any of our domestic helpers swore to reject marriage, unlike the special group of *zishu nü* 自梳女, meaning "women who combed up their own hair into a bundle" with a special comb in a right-of-passage ceremony with a vow not to get married. That was a tradition common in Shunde county of Guangdong in the nineteenth to twentieth century, where young women swore to be spinsters and formed a sisterhood. They rejected marriage, which was equated with a loss of freedom. Many of these women came to Hong Kong to work as *majie* with a distinctive professional identity to support themselves independently.

Our older group of domestic servants worked in our family for most of their lives to support their own families. Isolated from the outside world, they missed their marriage opportunity. Nonetheless, they were conscious of saving money for their old age. At Number 8, they formed a collective mutual fund association (標會 *biaohui*) into which each one would deposit her small savings and would have the option to withdraw a sum with interest when money was needed. The collective fund association was an ancient folk system allegedly dating back to over 2,000 years ago, and took the form of private small-amount credit loan that had the function of earning interest and raising funds for merchants. At Number 8, one of the smarter helpers, Chun Jie, took charge of the account and chaired meetings with the members every month. That was before personal banking accounts were common. As economy in Hong Kong began to flourish, some of our younger servants left one by one to work in the factories or to get married.

By the 1970s, the generation of *majie* in Hong Kong was disappearing, replaced by the importation of foreign domestic helpers, initially from the Philippines, and later from Thailand and Indonesia. By 2024, the total number of Filipino domestic helpers exceeded 200,000 for the population of 7.4 million in Hong Kong. Like the *majie* who sacrificed themselves to take care of us, this generation of Filipino women made similar sacrifices, leaving their families and children behind to take care of our families and children so that women in Hong Kong could go out to work. The foreign domestic helpers saved up to send money home for their families to buy land and build houses. Targeted by loan sharks in financial companies, many ignorant foreign domestic helpers were lured into high interest loans and became indebted for years. Some returned home to find their husbands had gone off with their mistresses and their children alienated and rebellious. Others who were unmarried but had contributed to support their siblings all through their work life were abandoned and left to struggle on their own upon their retirement. Such was the sad story of women's domestic work in those days. These women sacrificed themselves without complaint to take care of their employers' families and to provide a better living for their own families, so that their female employers could enjoy the opportunity to work outside of home. The labor force participation of women in Hong Kong had vastly increased from 42 percent in 1971 to 57 percent in 2023, with 76 percent of women with post-secondary educations employed outside of the home. However, this transfer of "women's work" from one group of more affluent women to another group of deprived women was not the goal of women's liberation.

Germinating Seeds of Gender Equality

Looking back, I think there may have been early traces from my childhood and youth that foretold my lifelong engagement with gender equality. Memories of my school days unearthed the seeds of my development as a self-reliant young woman starting to question women's submissive and stereotypic roles.

Battle of the Sexes

Back when I was in Primary 6A at St. Paul's Co-educational College Primary School, I learned from the daughter of Uncle Four, my same-aged cousin, over lunch one day that girls in her 6B class were being bullied by the boys. During recess, the boys chased and poked them with the school hymn books. St. Paul's was and still is today an elite co-educational school esteemed for its academic excellence, moral values, and school discipline. Fighting, even among boys, was unheard of.

"Why didn't you fight back?" I asked my cousin.

"We can't; we are girls."

My cousin was timid. So were the 6B girls. Maybe they were also afraid of breaking school rules. To me, this was not right; this was not alright. I rallied our daring 6A girls to advance to 6B during recess. waving our own hymn books to chase away the boys. Our triumphant Amazon warriors were emboldened by our early victories. Some girls started to upscale our weaponry to elastic bands with paper bullets. At this point, I withdrew from the battlefield. My mission of protecting the meek girls and upholding justice was accomplished. I was not interested in warfare for its own sake. More importantly, the new weapon was contraband and subject to school discipline if caught.

As the new battle continued, I heard that our Form Mistress, Teacher Leung, was starting to interview selected members of our class. Teacher Leung Pui-king 梁佩琼 was a serious and stern teacher. She wore a simple cotton traditional Chinese cheongsam and flat walking shoes. She spoke with a firm low voice. She inspired awe whenever she entered the classroom every morning with her solemn looks, whereupon we would stand up and bow to her to say good morning.

St. Paul's Co-Educational College Primary 6 class photo with class teacher
Ms. Leung Pui-king, 1961, Fanny is second from the right in the second row.

With the initiation of Teacher Leung's investigation, I got scared as I was certain that we would be punished for the fights. Weeks passed, and I had not yet been called, while my comrades-in-arms had been summoned one by one. I dared not ask them what happened, feeling guilty that I was the one who instigated the battle. I checked indirectly with the boy sitting behind me, who seemed to know what was happening. Teacher Leung wanted to find out what the fight was about and who started it. I was getting nervous. As a model student who had been getting A grades for good conduct throughout primary school, I would lose my title of "excellent student" this year. The term was coming to an end but still, I had not been summoned.

The report cards were distributed on the last day of class. Sheepishly, I peeked at my conduct column first. My A grade was still there! Underneath, Teacher Leung wrote the comment "a brave act standing up for justice" (見義勇為 *Jianyi yongwei*) in the remark's column! This was totally beyond my expectations. Unfortunately, the top girl who had continued the battle with the contraband weapons and became the de facto leader after my departure lost her excellent student title.

We should never forget how good teachers can affect the life course of their students. I was too young to have the courage to approach Teacher Leung at that time to thank her for her fair-minded judgement. I was just relieved for having escaped punishment. However, my admiration for her wise verdict had prevailed to this date. I regret having missed the chance to tell her how she inspired my confidence to fight for justice in my later life. This happy ending taught me the value of taking up action to right wrongs, particularly when the weak are oppressed by the strong. I suspect Teacher Leung's remark in my report card in my formative years subconsciously encouraged me to get involved in helping the marginalized in our society, on top of the academic work in psychology and gender studies that I pursued throughout my adult life.

St. Paul's Co-Educational College Girls

At St. Paul's Co-ed, the name by which our school was known, girls stood their ground among boys. Particularly, in most classes, the top students were all girls from Primary One until senior secondary school, when more boys were streamed in science subjects and girls into arts subjects. Then the brighter boys began to shine. The superiority of girls' school performance throughout primary and junior secondary school prevails to this day. This may be attributed to girls' cognitive aptitude in languages as well as their better concentration in class, which make a positive impression on schoolteachers. The Hong Kong Education Department's attempt to balance secondary school placements by sex in the 1980s led to the subsequent investigation and lawsuit by the Equal Opportunities Commission (EOC) under the Sex Discrimination Ordinance, a controversy which will be described in greater detail in Chapter 5.

The students' top positions in primary school were maintained consistently until Form 1 in secondary school at St. Paul's. The same girls maintained the top three positions year after year. However, with new students who were admitted in Form 1 based on their excellent public examination results, and a greater variety of subjects being offered in secondary school, the top ranks became more fluid. Facing threats to the status quo, the top girls became keenly competitive, although they pretended to be indifferent. They would probe into how much preparation the others had made for the examinations. I had never been number one all along and I did not really care. I had always been the top third in primary school, and that was good enough for my confidence.

I reasoned that being number one meant I could not go any higher and could only be overtaken. I had more sympathy for my classmates who did less well and suffered from the disfavor and prejudice of the demanding teachers in our school. Many of them lost their self-esteem in school and felt inferior throughout their lives, even though graduating from this elite school could already be a prestigious status symbol by itself.

Reaching number one in class was not my intention. I was never a competitive person—whether in school, at work, or in social activism throughout my life. During the final examination period in Form 3, I suddenly realized that my grades in the earlier examination papers were surpassing the top girl, who was getting a bit uneasy with me. I did not mean to hurt or challenge her. In the last examination paper, which was English composition, I deliberately loosened up and wrote rather casually on the given topic off the beaten track. Lo and behold, to my surprise, I got an even better grade, apparently for the creative and novel style in my composition.

I accepted the fortuitous crown with humility. Being top of my class gave me a new leadership position to negotiate with the teachers on class assignments on behalf of the rest of the class. One afternoon, when the folk-dance instructor did not show up for our extracurricular lesson after fifteen minutes, I led our classmates (all girls) to unilaterally dismiss the less-than-popular class and go home. The folk-dance class had been arranged by our physical education teacher for girls only and we all had to stay behind after class to learn these seemingly meaningless Western folk dances for no purpose, wearing our incongruous sports shorts. Of course, the PE teacher was furious when she found out, but she could not fault me because the instructor was late in the first place.

In contrast to the scholastic renown of St. Paul's Co-ed, its strict school rules were antiquated. The girls' Chinese-style blue cheongsam uniform had to be loose on both sides and at least four inches below the knees, while the slits around the knees should be no more than four inches. This fitting ensured that girls could not take long strides. However, the restraints did not stop our athletic classmates from lifting their cheongsam by the waist and skipping up and down the stairs to race to the ping pong tables during recess.

Our secondary school principal, Miss Bobbie Kotewall, an unmarried Eurasian woman, always wore a Chinese cheongsam, although hers was more stylish. It was common for teachers to wear traditional cheongsams, which presented a more mature and formal image. Every morning, Miss Kotewall presided over morning assembly on stage, portraying an icon of dignity and authority. She instilled moral values through her daily briefings and sermon. Although she appeared formidable on stage and she would not tolerate misbehavior, she was actually a very kind woman who cared about all her students. When we met her between classes, she would greet us by name and ask us how we were faring. Her memory of the names of all the students as well as those of their siblings in the school was impressive. One time, when she learned about some of our senior boys getting into a street fight with boys from our neighboring school, St. Joseph Boys', she did not scold the culprits. To our surprise, at the morning assembly, she told our senior boys to invite the St. Joseph boys to come to our school to fight it out. We all looked up to her with profound reverence as our beacon and role model. With Miss Kotewall as our inspirational idol, many St. Paul's alumna made outstanding accomplishments in life.

During our time in school, only academic excellence counted; gender was not a conscious identity in our co-educational school. Still, boys usually played with boys and girls with girls during recess. The rare pairing between a boy and a girl during or after school hours would be subject to teasing by other classmates. At that time, we did not question why the woodwork class was only taken by boys and the domestic science class only by girls in Form 1 and Form 2. It was just the prescribed curriculum without any choice. I did wonder about it back then why there was this segregation, but never articulated it in terms of restrictive gender stereotypes. These concepts were too abstract for my young mind. (This gender-based curriculum persisted in secondary schools in Hong Kong until after the Equal Opportunities Commission was established in 1996, which I was fortunate to steer through its infancy.) It seemed "natural" that when we had to choose between the Arts and the Science streams in upper forms, there were mostly girls in the Arts stream and much less girls in the Science stream. Except for girls who were excelling in their science subjects, most girls were subtly steered to the Arts stream. In my Arts class of forty students, there were only five subdued boys who were dominated by thirty-five assertive girls.

I left St. Paul's after Form 4, when I questioned why I should go through another school year just to rehearse what we had learned already in the Form 4 curriculum, purportedly to ensure we got good results in the School Leaving Examination and brought more honor to the school. I did not want to be bound by the prescribed school path. As I gazed at the night sky in our terrace in Number 8, I grew curious about life beyond our stone fortress, beyond Macdonnell Road, beyond Hong Kong, beyond this world, and even beyond the stars. There was nobody around to answer my curiosity. I yearned for a life on my own yonder from the sterility of my protective cocoon and the bondage of the feudalistic undercurrents in Number 8. I was keen to explore new learning arenas. I started to apply to high schools in California where some of my older sisters were studying. In my application for Grade 12, the last year in American high schools, I indicated that I was going into the last year of secondary school, which was Form 5 in Hong Kong, equivalent to Grade 11 in the American system, thereby skipping a year like what my cousin Albert, the Number 8 prodigy, was admired for.

Gender Shock in Teenage America

As a foreign student in the U.S., I had to enroll in a private boarding school. Sister Six was attending a Catholic women's college in San Francisco, where the nuns introduced me to the Convent of the Sacred Heart in Menlo Park. It was a last-minute arrangement, and I got admitted at the end of August in 1966. To prepare for the colder weather in America, my mother quickly bought me four overcoats, which I carried in my arms boarding the plane to San Francisco as my suitcase was too full. A former St. Paul's classmate who was returning from his summer vacation to his high school on the East coast of America was on the same flight from Hong Kong. He and his three friends gallantly carried

At the Sacred Heart Convent senior prom in 1967.
Fanny is second from the left, front row.

my four coats when we disembarked in San Francisco airport. Sister Six, who picked me up at the airport, was surprised I was so game, having picked up four male suitors on the plane. Even though I was ready to carry my own load, two suitcases and four coats in my arms did look a bit overwhelming. I did not reject being the recipient of courtesy or just four pairs of helping hands. My sister, ever the romantic, had a one-track mind. To me, the nature of boy-girl relationships was not limited to the stereotype of courtship. Cross-sex and same-sex friendships could both be platonic and valuable.

I encountered my first gendered culture shock in Menlo Park at the age of fifteen. For the first time in my life, I was in an all-girls boarding school. I was amused watching the stress and strains of American teenage girls under the old-fashioned Catholic rituals and bourgeoisie social propriety. In this upscale pristine campus surrounded by red brick walls, we had to curtsy in response to the castanet clicks of the nuns as they approached, fully clad in old habits.

We were awakened every morning when one of the nuns came into our rooms, sprinkling holy water into the palms of our hands stretched out from our beds, whereupon we would make the sign of the cross. No cigarette or bubble gum was allowed on campus. Only senior girls had the permission to go out without guardians on the weekend.

Weekends in Menlo

Several girls in my senior class had cars and at times I was invited to join their weekend outings. They wanted to initiate me into their American culture. Making a stop during their pleasure rides around town, they would light up their cigarettes at ease and offered me one. I was not sure that the girls liked cigarettes necessarily, but being off campus, it gave them freedom to smoke. They insisted that I joined them, as everyone was having one. In my own family, smoking and gambling were strictly forbidden vices that would bring havoc to the gods in heaven. The health hazard about smoking was already well known, but I was not in the position to lecture them. Above all, the smell and taste of cigarettes did not appeal to me at all. I did not want to waste their cigarette. Despite my refusal, they kept pushing a cigarette on me. I figured that they did not want me to be different. As a compromise to my nonconformity, I offered to hold a lit cigarette as a reserve for anyone who would like a second one. They were happy to settle at that, seeing all of us holding our lit cigarettes in hand.

Friday nights in the dorms were phenomenal. Girls would congregate around the only telephone booth in the corridor (those were the days before mobile phones). At the ring of the phone, they would lurch forward to see if it was a call for them. I was amused to watch them, waiting passively, yearning for calls to go on a date. The girls who got a call proudly marched back to their rooms. After the weekend, they keenly shared stories of their trophies. Having dates boosted their self-esteem. To me, it was pathetic that one's esteem was dependent on the telephone booth and boys. Maybe this was not much different from the yearning for "likes" or "followers" on girls' social media nowadays.

As for myself, I'd rather spend the weekends in the lovely ground of the campus, practicing my piano and studying my books. There was a small stable in the campus ground and one of my classmates took me to feed the horse that she was learning to ride. I wrote to my mother and told her that I wanted to learn riding too. The reply was a terse and definitive "NO." Girls should not ride horses. She did not explain, but I later figured out that Chinese mothers discouraged active sports that might tear their daughters' hymen before marriage. Looking back, we girls were discouraged from sports, as good girls were supposed to stay home and study hard. With mostly sitting and little physical activity throughout my youth, I suffered from osteoporosis as I aged and fractured the neck of the femur below my hip when I had a fall. I only picked up regular physical exercise from my athletic husband after we got married, but it was too late to build up my bone density.

With restricted mobility, fractures in a women's old age can often prove to be fatal. Medical research has estimated that the one-year mortality after sustaining a hip fracture is about 30 percent. Through the intensive treatment of my dedicated physiotherapist for two years, my commitment to daily stretching exercises upon waking up (in the same ritual as sticking out my hand every morning to receive holy water from the nun in Menlo) and daily exercise at the gym to build up my muscle strength, I managed to restore my mobility. I now consider it my mission to remind young girls and their mothers that bone density does not grow much beyond our late twenties; they should take up weightbearing exercises and refrain from unhealthy dieting early in life.

One weekend in Menlo Park, a junior high girl approached me to take her out, as I was the only senior girl on campus. The American senior girls had either gone home for the weekend or were out on a date. The foreign students, the majority of whom were from Latin America, had left on their weekly shopping spree in the nearby Stanford shopping mall. The young girl asked me why I didn't go out. I told her I came there to study.

"How are you going to get married if you don't go on dates?" she asked.

I realized it would take too much effort to explain to her young mind about marriage not having to be a woman's destiny, or to convince her that staying single happily could also be a worthy option. To stop her from more ludicrous questions, I explained that I did not have to worry about it: we Chinese had arranged marriages, a practice which had actually been outdated by two generations at that time. I hid my chuckles when she seemed to take it seriously, a look of cultural enlightenment on her young face.

In sympathy for this chubby and socially awkward girl, whom I learned came from a broken family and was not popular among her peers, I agreed to take her out for a short walk down the road outside campus. As soon as we passed by a store, she quickly sneaked in and came out with a pack of cigarettes. She pleaded with me to hold the pack she paid for, as she was too young to buy cigarettes.

"You are so young; cigarettes are not good for your health," I warned her.

"No problem. I smoke all the time and I like it," she insisted.

She lit a cigarette, took her first puff, and started a coughing fit. I took her to a Baskin-Robbins nearby and bought her an ice cream instead. I could see the gratification in her face as she licked her chocolate ice cream cone. She finally admitted she enjoyed the ice cream much better.

Why did these girls have to smoke? Was it to show their rebelliousness? Or was it to prove their maturity and independence? In the late 1960s, Virginia Slims capitalized on the popular feminist movement to promote their cigarettes to women with the slogan "You've come a long way, baby," equating smoking Virginia Slims with being independent, stylish, confident and liberated. Was that liberation or was that subjugation to capitalism?

Senior Proms

Getting close to Christmas, the senior class' December Ball would take place in the posh St. Francis Hotel in downtown San Francisco. There were two proms for the senior class, one before the Christmas break and one closer to graduation. The girls would all put on heavy make-up and wear long evening gowns, escorted by their beaus in tuxedos. Selection of their escorts was the most important topic in their social forum.

I had no previous experience with dancing parties. I left St. Paul's after Form 4, before the last year of high school when the school-leaving party would be held. Anyone in the class could opt to join, and usually small groups of friends would go together. There would be music and dance, but also other performances. In any case, that party would not be as fancy as this debutante-style ballroom event.

My history-cum-music teacher, Miss Tremelle, wanted to make sure I was prepared for my Christmas ball. She took me under her wing when I surprised her with my perfect score in the history quiz one month after I arrived at the school. My research paper on President Harry Truman was also shortlisted for an interschool oral competition (I had no idea who Truman was before writing the paper and was relieved that I was not selected for the interschool competition). She had not previously expected serious studying from the foreign students. Most of the Latin American students came to the U.S. only for finishing school to learn social graces in preparation for marriage when they returned home.

Mindful that I would not know any boys shortly after my arrival, Miss Tremelle kindly approached her former Chinese classmate, who was then a doctoral student at Stanford, to take me to the ball. When my cousin Albert, the Number 8 prodigy, also a Stanford alumnus, learned about it, he rejected the choice. That guy would be too "old" for me. He decided to take over as big brother and escorted me to both balls. He made sure all the social proprieties were followed, including bringing me a prom corsage and buying me drinks during the cocktail reception. The pomp and vanity were senseless to me, but I surely appreciate my cousin's brotherly protection, nonetheless.

The top girls at the Sacred Heart Convent all aspired to go to nearby Stanford University. I had no experience doing college applications and there was no guidance from my family. I only learned about the Scholastic Aptitude Test (SAT) before having to take it in December, three months after my arrival in the U.S. Unlike students nowadays, who are sent to years of tutorial classes for the SAT, I studied the test practice book I borrowed from the library as I applied for the December test session. In the end, none of us got into Stanford, but I was accepted by the University of California at Berkeley, which was a world apart from the proper and feminized catholic convent. My exposure to the American teenage identity at Menlo opened my eyes to the futility of sexism. The counterculture at Berkeley was another eye-opener.

Awakening in UC Berkeley

Civil Rights Movements

In the 1960s, the Free Speech Movement began in Berkeley, giving rise to a period of student activism during which students fought for political freedoms. Every day when I walked across campus from Sather Gate to Tolman Hall, with the Psychology Department building on the north side, I passed by impromptu speakers standing on top of boxes in front of the student union building. With dogs running around and African drums playing in the background, I could not hear what the speeches were about. There were frequent rallies in front of the administration building in Sproul Plaza. During my time at Berkeley, students demanded funds to set up the Third World College for ethnic studies, battled against the university's attempt to reclaim the People's Park to build a carpark and student hostels, and later, faculty joined students in the anti-war moratorium. These protests often disrupted lectures when students rallied for class boycotts and clashed with police and the national guard who were sent in to curb the disturbance. Living in the dormitory right next to Telegraph Avenue, the epicenter of violence, I learned a lot about tear gas and its antidotes, as well as Molotov cocktails. For three terms, my psychology classes were suspended close to exam time when some sympathetic professors did not want to cross the picket lines of the protesters. We ended up writing papers instead of going to those classes and there were no final exams. I was disappointed that I was deprived of my classes, as studying was my purpose for being there. As foreign students, we had to pay a hefty tuition fee.

During the height of the disturbances, the then Governor Ronald Reagan (who later became the 40th President of the United States) sent in troops on horseback to quash the crowds of protestors. Even for those of us who were not in the protests, we were not spared. One day during our swimming class, we had to be rushed out of the swimming pool when the instructor told us that the helicopters were flying in to spray mace to clear the campus. Mace was a chemical that irritated the eyes and caused dizziness and immobilization. I thought chemical weapons were only used on enemies but not your own people. After the Kent State University shootings by the Ohio National Guard, killing four college students in May 1970, there was further outrage on campuses across the country. Many departments at Berkeley, including mine, joined the moratorium and shut down for the rest of the term again.

Although I did not endorse the violent tactics of the protesters, I was impressed with the nationalistic patriotism that American students manifested in their anti-war movement. Coming from colonial Hong Kong, we had not developed a sense of national identity or any interest in politics. We were officially identified as British subjects. In our history curriculum, we did not learn about contemporary China beyond the end of the Qing dynasty. The colonial mandate of the University of Hong Kong, the only university in Hong Kong for over fifty years before the Chinese University was established in 1963, was to train rule-abiding civil servants who would not question the system. It was an awakening for me to witness young people and intellectuals in America standing up to express their belief that it was wrong for their country to engage in an aggressive foreign war conjured by the military industrial complex, politics, misinformation and lies.

The Chinese Student Association

Berkeley was a large school, and the Psychology Department was one of its biggest. The typical undergraduate class size was 300 to 500. I hardly knew any professors other than my advisor, the teaching assistants in our tutorials, and a handful of fellow student in psychology in the same class. There were few Chinese or Chinese-American students enrolled as Psychology majors. Most of the Chinese students studied science or engineering, especially the boys.

At the UC Berkeley Chinese Student Association Charity Ball reception, 1970.

However, there were many Chinese students on campus, including American-born Chinese and foreign students from Hong Kong and Taiwan (mainland China had not yet established diplomatic relations with the United States). There was a separate club for Chinese-American students. The Hong Kong students in the Chinese Students Association (CSA) formed my primary social network.

At UC Berkeley, there were two clusters of Hong Kong students at the CSA: the party-goers and the service volunteers. Every term, there were mixers where boys met girls. Girls from nearby women colleges would also be invited to join. The girls would be seated on the side waiting to be invited to dance by boys, fretting with anxiety the risk of becoming a wallflower. At that time, I did not know how to articulate my reactions toward all this. With my juvenile cynicism, I stayed aloof. These mixers could be fun for others, but the indignity of such a marketplace was distasteful to me.

At least, we had a choice. Naturally, I leaned into the service community in the CSA. Every week, we went into San Francisco Chinatown to give English language tutorials to new immigrants. I became active with several CSA committees and helped to prepare newsletters to cover events back home, Chinese migrants in the Bay Area, and on CSA activities. The senior Hong Kong graduate students guided us on learning more about contemporary China.

This was the early period of the Cultural Revolution in China. There was a sense of idealism about equality in China where women could hold up half the sky. In my political science class, my Chinese-American professor praised the Cultural Revolution as a form of true democracy and total equality. This was so different and refreshing from what was portrayed in mainstream media about the evil Communist China that it energized many of the young minds on campus, me included. A couple of enlightened Hong Kong students quit school to return to China to work in the rural fields with the laborers and farmers. Sad to say, a year later, they became disillusioned and had difficulty picking up their studies again after leaving China. I wondered what my political science professor would say about the meaning of democracy a few years later. I remained skeptical whenever "democracy" was touted as an absolute universal value without showing how it improved people's lives. The picture of centuries of havoc wreaked by Parisian mobs in the name of liberty, equality and fraternity during the French revolutions always came to mind.

Every year, the CSA would elect a new president. In my senior year, the potential candidate was a dandy party socialite who only attended the mixers but had not served in any of the committees. The other veterans had already served their time on the Executive Committee. Having participated actively in several committees, I believed that I could at least make more substantial contributions than the dandy could. To block his potential candidacy, I came forward with my intention to run for president. The outgoing president was supportive. The vice-president, a serious-looking graduate student and a second-generation immigrant with conservative views, solemnly advised me that it would be better for me to run as vice-president. I asked him why. He said it would be better for a woman to be vice-president; there had never been a female CSA president before. Why couldn't I be the first? I was puzzled by his illogical rationale, which galvanized my resolve to run and win. I went ahead with my candidacy, disregarding his "brotherly" advice. The dandy, probably sensing my battle-readiness, decided not to run, and I was elected as the first female CSA president at Berkeley.

An annual glamorous event for the CSA was the Charity Ball held in December. The purpose was to raise funds to be donated to a selected charity back home. Students in the Bay Area would join and nominate candidates from their colleges to compete for the Charity Ball queen. One of the criteria was the amount of raffle tickets that the candidates' camp sold and the funds that they raised. That would make the competition less of a beauty contest and a more worthwhile cause to me.

As president, I had to host the ball. Before I set off early to help with the preparation, I found my then-boyfriend sitting pensively in the living room of my apartment. For the first time, he confided in me the pressure he felt from his peers about having a girlfriend who was in the limelight and in a "superior" position. I had never thought about our relationship in terms of power structure. Why should a man be seen as the underdog if his mate excels in achievement, be it academic or financial? Conventionally, men were supposed to be more accomplished than women, who were only judged by their looks. Even though my boyfriend did not see our relationship that way, it took him some effort to overcome the peer pressure. I appreciated his honesty and resolve, but I had since become more aware of the conventional gender power structure under which men were supposed to be superior and dominant and women to be inferior and submissive.

Two decades later, one of my students examined this question in her undergraduate thesis. In a survey, she asked college students what differences in attributes were most unacceptable in their mates. Her results confirmed the conventional norms. While boys found it difficult to have a mate who held a higher degree or earned more money than themselves, the least acceptable was to have a mate who was taller in height. The reverse pattern was found among the girls, although to a lesser degree.

If we are to promote women's status and advancement, we need to address these normative biases at the same time. Can't men feel prouder of their mate's accomplishments? Why do they need to put themselves down as if in competition with their mates? Subsequently, in my study of top women leaders published in a 2008 book[1], this issue was also explored. Among successful women leaders who stayed in a happy marriage, their husbands tended to be confident of themselves and regarded their wives' accomplishments as their family's pride. They became their wives' best champions. Some of my young students who read this book asked me where such husbands could be found. I did not have a ready answer, but I told them that I could attest to these findings based on my first-hand experience in my marriage of thirty-eight years with my husband. Otherwise, I'd have rather stayed single.

Doctoral Studies in Minnesota

With the credit unit system at Berkeley, I did not realize how quickly I had accumulated enough units to graduate at age nineteen. At that time, I only knew I would go on studying as far as I could. University education opened the doors to continuous learning and offered the pursuit of ideas and fundamental truths that set me free. While learning was a good story that should never end, there were milestones along the way. To continue my studies, I had to be admitted into a graduate program before I graduated. Psychology being a large department with hundreds of majors, my advisor only remembered me as "a good student" every term when I visited him to sign my study plan. Without any career guidance or vocational preparation, I hastily applied to several graduate programs. Fortunately, I got accepted by several schools into their PhD programs, and I chose the University of Minnesota(UM), which was associated with the famous Minnesota Multiphasic Personality Inventory (MMPI) mentioned in all introductory courses of psychology. (Without the guidance of mentors, that was how young naïve souls made their big decisions, decisions which could significantly affect their eventual career and life development.)

---

1 Diane F. Halpern and Fanny M. Cheung, *Women at the Top: Powerful Leaders Tell Us How to Combine Work and Family* (Chichester, UK: Wiley-Blackwell, 2008).

Before moving to Minnesota, I went home to visit my family. Other than my cousin Albert, the child prodigy and Stanford alumnus who was studying for his physics PhD at Berkeley, there was nobody else in my extended family who was going into a doctoral program. For my mother, whose secondary education was curtailed by the Japanese occupation in World War II, my academic pursuits were a sufficient source of pride. She did not understand what the difference was between a bachelor's, master's or doctoral degree. She was just proud to have her daughter (instead of one of her sons) help her gain some credit and status in Number 8. On the other hand, one of her sophisticated and worldly-wise mahjong friends was more direct with me: "How are you ever going to get married with a PhD degree?" she asked.

At age nineteen, getting married had not yet entered my mind. I did not mind staying single, which should be a choice and not a failure for women. To me, it was more important that I would be able to pursue my studies and support myself in the future with my education. Self-reliance would free me to fully pursue my life interests apart from being the clinging vine of Number 8. After the tumultuous wars in China when many families lost their fortunes and wives lost their husbands, mothers in our generation often told their daughters that only education and knowledge, not any external belongings, could give them security in the future. Even now, women's economic independence is still an essential condition for gender equality.

At the turn of the twenty-first century, there was a grim joke in mainland China about three types of people: men, women, and female PhDs. Female PhDs were singled out as anomalies who would not be seen as women. As more women got into higher education, female graduate students worried about becoming ineligible in marriage and becoming "leftover women" when they got a PhD. Even though gender equality has been advanced in indicators like literacy and higher education enrolment up to the master's level in mainland China since the twenty-first century, and more women were getting their PhDs (38 percent of PhD graduates in 2016 were women, according to the Ministry of Education), this social "stigma" still posed an implicit barrier.

Strange Women in Centennial Hall

During my first year at the University of Minneapolis, I stayed in Centennial Hall, a co-educational graduate dormitory. I soon met a group of Hong Kong undergraduate boys in the common cafeteria shared among the quadrangle of dorms. We often ate together as a group and chatted in Cantonese. As a graduate student in psychology, I became the boys' big sister and advisor. After about half a year, an inquisitive freshman became bold enough to knock on my door and spoke his mind.

"I have been wondering….You know, you don't look that strange to me."

"Why am I supposed to look strange?" I was baffled.

"But you are getting a PhD degree!"

"Do I look strange?"

"No."

"Then why should a woman going for a PhD look strange?"

"Okay…that's all I wanted to ask." He left abruptly. He was either convinced by my logical quip or was embarrassed by his illogical utterance.

Nowadays, there are more female PhDs even though they are still in the minority. Back in the early 1970s, it was rare among Chinese students from Hong Kong to study for a postgraduate degree. Those few of us who did were oddities.

There were only three Chinese women in Centennial Hall; the other undergraduate female dormitory was several long blocks away from this quadrangle. Linda was a tough-minded third-year postgraduate medical school student who always wore rolled-up shirtsleeves and chunky-style trousers. She looked like a tomboy in the eyes of the Chinese young men. She liked intellectual discussion on social affairs and educated us on scientific medical knowledge. Our conversations over dinner spilled over to late night. With a keen interest in good Chinese food, which was hard to find in Minnesota, she would get exhilarated when we reminisced on food from Hong Kong. In the absence of a pantry in the dorm, she would improvise a "feast" with what could be concocted in my small electric rice cooker in my room.

There was another mature Hong Kong woman in a postgraduate architecture program who insisted on feeding us and would regularly barge into our rooms any time she cooked us anything. Architecture students worked late into the night in their studios. In the still of the night, I could hear her calling my name from the staircase even before she reached my door, oblivious to the other residents who might be sleeping already. She insisted that steamed egg custard was nutritious and good for our skin in this cold dry weather. I must admit that I enjoyed this popular Chinese dessert, but having it every week was overkill. Incongruous with her motherly bearing, Amy wore long hair and fashionable miniskirts. From behind, she looked like a young beauty. She acted our age, but given the wrinkles around her eyes, everyone was trying to guess how old she was. That remained a mystery still discussed many years later.

So, we, the three Chinese women in Centennial Hall, must have been considered oddities in the eyes of the young Hong Kong undergraduate boys.

Rescue of a Battered Wife

The university's International Students' Advisors Office, under the director Dr. Paul Pedersen, was active in engaging international students in cross-cultural communication. As a foreign student in psychology, I helped to play the role of the "cultural gap" to highlight the problems in cross-cultural counselling in his training workshops. Soon, I became a volunteer in his office, offering help to Chinese students who were spotted as having problems with their grades.

In my second year, when I was starting my first practicum at the university hospital, Dr. Pedersen asked me to help in a counselling case for a couple from Taiwan. The local Chinese church approached his office as there was no Chinese-speaking counsellor in Minneapolis. I got permission from my practicum supervisor to see them in my hospital office. The middle-aged couple ran a small souvenir shop selling knick-knacks from Taiwan. The husband did most of the loud talking throughout the sessions. He said that his wife had difficulty adjusting to life in America, as she did not speak English. He complained about her overall incompetence. When I got to speak to the wife separately a few weeks later, she had gained enough confidence to break her silence. She rolled up her sleeves and showed me the scars from

With Prof. Paul Pedersen from the University of Minnesota
on his visit to Hong Kong, 1991.

his beatings and the burn from a hot iron. She said he would get angry with her if she did not or could not do what he wanted. She now only wore long sleeves and long pants. She told me not to let her husband know about what she told me, as she would get further beatings. I was alarmed by the injuries but was frustrated by the dilemma of having to keep the discovery a secret. Domestic violence was not included in my psychology courses at that time. Psychology of women and gender issues were not and are still not part of the core curriculum in psychology. I felt inadequate in how to address the problem. Later in my teaching career, I always included topics on violence against women in training my clinical psychology students. However, the few textbooks on the psychology of women were primarily based on Western women. That prompted me to eventually edit a handbook[2] in 2020 with an international perspective to illustrate the intersectionality of culture, race, class, and religion in understanding the psychology of women.

Controlling my indignation during the counselling sessions, I tried to gently raise the topic of marital relationships with the abusive husband, but I

---

2   Fanny M. Cheung and Diane F. Halpern eds., *The Cambridge Handbook of the International Psychology of Women* (Cambridge, UK: Cambridge University Press, 2020).

was not getting anywhere. He only talked about his wife's problems every time. Given my inexperience, there was not much progress I could further make. The husband could not gain what he wanted from the sessions and the couple did not come back.

One weekend a few months later, I got a call from the wife. She had been beaten up again. She had just run away from home but had nowhere to go. At that time, I was living off campus with three other Chinese girls in a small townhouse in Dinkytown north of the Minneapolis campus. I considered putting her up in our basement. But then, the husband knew me and could trace her to my place, and we would not be safe. We did not know what the husband might do if he showed up at our door. We had no knowledge of shelters for battered women in the community and had to scramble to find our own resources.

Linda, the medical student, had moved to a townhouse further away from campus. She came forth to offer her place for the wife to stay. During the next two weeks, the wife hid in Linda's townhouse. Every time she ventured out, she would open the back door shakingly, peeking around left and right, before she would sneak out of the house. Linda was a staunch advocate of social justice and was fearless. Her courage and our group support calmed the wife's nervousness.

Two weeks later, the wife said that she had connected with her daughter and her church. She moved out of Linda's place. Later, we learned that with the help of the church, she was living with her daughter away from her husband. That episode was my first exposure to violence against women. Our makeshift solution was not evidence-based or grounded in psychological literature. It was not until several years later after I returned to Hong Kong that I became involved in the movement and started research on violence against women.

Fallen Women in an Off-Broadway Play

In the spring of 1973, the International Students Advisors Office contacted me again. The off-Broadway play, *The Basic Training of Pavlo Hummel*, was coming to Minneapolis. The director of the play wanted to recruit a few Asian women for the local production. I had not seen the play before and had never acted

The University of Minnesota anti-Vietnam War student
strike on Washington Ave., 1971.

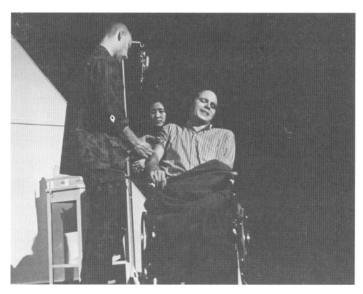

Acting in an off-Broadway play,
The Basic Training of Pavlo Hummel, in Minneapolis, 1973.

on stage. Out of curiosity, I thought this could be an interesting learning experience about American theater and went to the audition. This play by American playwright and novelist David Rabe was the first in his anti-Vietnam War trilogy. In the first scene, the key character, Pavlo Hummel, an American GI, was killed with everyone else when he mindlessly grabbed at a live hand grenade tossed into the Saigon brothel he was visiting. Apparently, the Asian women to be cast were the mama-san and a prostitute in the brothel. These stereotypic sex roles of Asian women prevailed in popular shows like the West End blockbuster *Miss Saigon*, in which women resorted to sex work to survive in their worn-torn countries. Tragically, Kim in *Miss Saigon* killed herself so that her son with the American GI who deserted her could be taken to a better life in America, analogous to the tragic ending of Cho-Cho-San in Puccini's *Madame Butterfly*. These pathetic stereotypes of Asian women would not fit me. The director concurred. At that time, there were few Vietnamese students in Minnesota. The roles were eventually filled by a Japanese-American and a Chinese-American student respectively. To Americans, all Asians looked alike anyway.

Even though I did not fit the script, it occurred to the director that I could present a refreshing contrast in the role of an innocent refugee village girl seated in the foreground, holding onto her basket of clothes in front of the brothel. He created this character for me. It provided a symbol of the brutal war in which innocent lives, as well as societies, were meaninglessly destroyed. I did not have to say a word before I was killed with everyone in the grenade attack in the first five minutes of the play. So much for my brief acting career. Being in the cast, however, gave me the opportunity to observe the alcohol, sex and profanities behind the scenes in American theater, a vast contrast to my virtuous upbringing at Number 8. It also brought home the sexual exploitation of women, especially in times of war and armed conflict. It prompted me to ponder: Are sex workers victims or survivors of wars and poverty? Are sex workers enslaved by pimps or traffickers? If not, are sex workers entitled to choose how they make a living? What right do we have to moralize about prostitution? The feminist discourse on prostitution remains diverse and the disagreement between the pro-prostitution and anti-prostitution feminist

Fanny's first car, a Pontiac Tempest, 1972.

stances was particularly contentious. I still don't have a simple answer to these questions.

The Woman Driver Heroine

A common stereotype of women drivers were that they are poor drivers who were hesitant and had difficulty making quick decisions. While neuroscience research has shown a link between gender differences in spatial perception skills and brain structure differences in the parietal lobe, it could not be established whether it is caused by biology or experience or their interaction. In everyday life, men were more likely to take up the driver's seat. Among the Chinese foreign students, girls seldom had cars but would ask some of the boys who owned cars to drive them to run errands, move house and furniture, heavy grocery shopping and so on. Boys who had cars were popular.

I learned driving in my last year of college, as I believed that it was a basic survival skill that would give me independence. I took group lessons from a driving school and then practiced with one of my young cousins who just passed the test herself. The test in Berkeley was easier than that in San Francisco, which was hilly and busy with traffic. Nevertheless, given my limited practical training, I was nervous and was extra careful during the test. At the end of the driving test, I looked timidly at the examiner. The burly examiner said the reason he would pass me this time was that if he failed me then, I would be driving even more slowly and blocking the traffic. He lectured me to practice driving for two more months before going out on a busy road, upon which I gratefully agreed. Even though I knew in my heart that I was driving much like the "typical woman driver" then, I was happy to get my driver's license in my first trial, breaking this gender divide.

In my second year of graduate school, I had to go to my part-time job in the twin city of St. Paul, which was quite a way from our townhouse in Minneapolis. I did not expect to get that job but applied for it out of curiosity. It was the position of a counsellor for women returning to take courses at the University of Minnesota Extension after a break in their studies. I had little exposure to the issues of returning students, but apparently the three African-American interviewers were impressed with my cultural sensitivity during the interview and offered me the job. It took me an hour to take the public bus to get over to St. Paul. Public buses ran infrequently. I did not feel safe waiting for the bus when it got dark.

I gathered the advice of a few car owners and bought a used car like everyone among my friends. It was a Pontiac Tempest, a mid-size two-door car which was sturdy enough for the Minnesota winter. Linda was a car aficionado and gave me good tips in driving at night and on icy roads. I joined the AAA (American Automobile Club), which provided the vital car starting and towing services during the sub-zero winters. As there was no covered parking behind our townhouse, I had to use a big broom to sweep off the snow that buried the car after blizzards. At least my three roommates and I had the luxury of not having to carry the heavy groceries through the snow every week.

There was no parking for students on campus, so I still had to walk eight long blocks to my office in Elliott Hall, the Psychology Department building. Every winter evening when I had to brave the bitter wind and snow flurries to trod back to my townhouse, I kept recalling the Chinese literature essay that I learned in Form 1 at St. Paul's Co-ed called "Peking in the Wind and Snow"

(風雪中的北平 *Fengxue zhong de beiping*). The author Jin Zhaozi 金兆梓 described how he struggled through the blizzard, being blown back one step as he advanced two steps. When we were in sub-tropical Hong Kong, we could not have empathized with the author's experience. Before coming to Minnesota, I naively thought when it froze, I would just get cold and numb. I had no prior concept of the big difference between what was freezing and what was minus seventy degrees Fahrenheit with wind chill. Needless to say, I did not know there were reportedly fifty words for snow or hundreds of ways of describing snow in the Eskimo language.

Having the car gave me the comfort and security I needed. To solve the campus parking problem, I adjusted my work schedule when I started writing my dissertation in my last year. Every evening, I came home a bit earlier to eat dinner and then took a nap before driving back to campus at 10 p.m., when there were no parking restrictions. I could park overnight right behind Elliott Hall, where I had my office. There, I could also borrow the electric typewriter with correction function from the general office after office hours to type my draft manuscript. I would work until 5:30 a.m. and then drive home and sleep for a few hours before going back for my teaching assistant duties. At that young age, my body was easily adaptable.

My greatest feat with my car was the one-month car journey I took right after I graduated. Before I flew home, I thought I should take a grand tour of the national parks and famous tourist sites in North America. I figured once I started working, I wouldn't have that leisurely opportunity. Another Hong Kong student, MC, who had just got her master's degree in social work, enthusiastically invited two more girlfriends to join.

In the age before there was GPS, we consulted AAA, which provided a ringed booklet of maps outlining the itinerary touring the midwest states, the Canadian Rockies, Vancouver, then the Grand Canyon and Bryce Canyon, before swinging through Las Vegas and Los Angeles to reach our destination, San Francisco. Oblivious to potential risks and ignorant of car mechanics, we were as game as "newborn calves who are not afraid of tigers" (初生之犢不畏虎 *Chusheng zhi du buwei hu*). I soon learned that I was the most experienced driver among them all, and I had to take up the major responsibility except when I needed a break. We embarked on our adventure, checking in first at the Badlands and Mount Rushmore in the Dakotas. Every day, we drove until dusk, whereupon MC would go into a roadside motel and try to convince the sympathetic manager to give us two adjoining rooms for the price of one.

My used Pontiac was taking the brunt of the wearing trip. One early evening, as I was driving longer than usual through the dim and winding mountain roads after visiting the Grand Teton National Park in Wyoming, I was enchanted by the bright moonlight shining in the summer night sky. As we wanted to stretch our distance for the day, we kept driving until it got really dark. As soon as we saw the first motel sign in the next town, we drove in and stopped at the reception building. After MC got us the rooms, the car would not start again when we wanted to drive down to the building where our rooms were. I then realized with hindsight that my headlights were losing electricity, and we were relying on the enchanting moonlight to illuminate the road. We were too tired to reflect on the danger or do anything about the car. We just needed to have a good night's sleep. When we got up the next morning, we could not believe our eyes. There was a big Pontiac maintenance garage across the street. It was a Godsend. The mechanic told us that it was a faulty alternator and had it fixed in the morning. We couldn't have been luckier. One up for the women drivers!

Another time in the outskirts of Seattle, one of our drivers got lost near the railway tracks and the car became stuck in the tracks. We were all scared that a train might arrive and hit us. There was nobody around and we had to save ourselves. It was futile for the girls to push the heavy car. I tried my luck using the skill of winter driving in Minnesota when the car was stuck in snow. Rocking the car forward and backward repeatedly, I finally freed the car from the tracks and was heralded as the heroine.

By the time we got to Las Vegas, the car was getting worn out. We lost the air conditioning before crossing the desert in Death Valley. The typical summer daytime temperature in Death Valley was over 100 degrees Fahrenheit. We were prepared to bite the bullet and endure the scorching heat. As I drove across town along Las Vegas Strip, I saw the sign "Dry Ice" at many roadside stalls. As the Chinese idiom says, "Quick wits pop up during emergencies" (人急智生 *Renji zhisheng*). I decided that we could at least cool ourselves down a bit by sitting on packs of dry ice. As the driver, I had the luxury of having a pack on my back and one under my seat, which would be shifted every now and then by the front seat passenger just so I wouldn't get glued to the ice. We left the window slightly ajar to make sure we did not get suffocated by the carbon dioxide. After four hours, when our homemade air-conditioning was almost sublimated, we were jubilant that we survived the Mohave Desert in good shape.

When we finally parted in San Francisco, my work horse Pontiac had served its valiant mission. It managed to survive the junk yard a bit longer when it was taken over by a relative as her first car. Back in Hong Kong, our travel mates had a couple of reunions recounting how these exciting adventures had added sparkles to our American sojourns. Hurray to us celebrated women drivers!

Return to Hong Kong

I decided to return to Hong Kong right after graduation and did not look for a job in the United States. At that time, when most of the other Chinese students tried to find ways to settle in America, I did not share their life plan. I reckoned that if I stayed in the U.S., I could always find a counselling job in the Asian-American community if I wanted to, as there was such a need among the ethnic minorities. On the other hand, I watched my Chinese relatives and friends confined to their own minority network, visiting one another on weekends for barbeques, during which time the women prepared food in the kitchen and the men laid around the couch watching American football with their beers. Otherwise, visiting shopping malls with the family was the common pastime. Collecting discount coupons to get the weekly bargain at supermarkets was a source of satisfaction. I could not envision spending my whole life like this in middle-class consumerist America.

More importantly, I believed that I would always remain a second-class citizen in a predominantly White America no matter how accomplished I became in my own profession. Blatant and implicit racial discrimination still exists even now. Especially after COVID-19 half a century later, Asian bashing and racial hate crimes surged. Every time I passed through the immigration counter at American airports, I could not help feeling unwelcomed if not intimidated by the hostile interrogations. I'd rather return to a place I could call home. I was confident that I could make more contributions to the fledging profession of psychology in Hong Kong, whereas my service would be superfluous to the well-established workforce in the United States.

Without a second thought, I got on the plane to return home after my adventurous car journey. I had not anticipated or planned for the meaningful life that awaited me there.

BROKEN SILENCE

Many people float through life in auto cruise mode. They live day by day according to social conventions, fulfilling expectations for each age without question. Day in, day out, we watch people packing the buses and subways, or cars trapped in traffic jams commuting to work in the morning, repeating the travel routine in the evening. Parents rush to herd their sleepy young children with bulky school bags on their backs onto school buses. At the wet markets, the fresh produce venders haul their loads of fish, meat and vegetables into the stalls before dawn in time for the homemakers to pick up the daily provisions for their families. These daily schedules program our lives. Most people devote much of their whole lives making a living to support their families and raising their children. At the end of the day, their gratification comes from watching their children raise the next generation. This life cycle is part of nature and recurrent in our world. All animals go through birth, growth, reproduction, and eventually death, perpetuating the history of evolution. What human beings do to fill in the time and space from cradle to grave during the life cycle provides them with meaning of life. A savvy few are more ambitious and plan schematically to strive toward specific targets they have set out for themselves (and for their children). In this generation of single-child families, overprotective parents often design a life course programmed for their children from the time they are born. The children live out their parents' goals, often mirroring what their parents missed out in their parents' own lives. The younger generations of millennials and beyond may seek personal happiness and forego children for pets. Making money and having work-life balance are still among the top priorities in their life goals. For people struggling to survive in the war zones or refugee camps in different parts of the world, talking about life goals beyond staying alive is a sad luxury.

In the Cheung family of my generation, we children followed the conventional path of schooling in our early life. Getting an education as far as we were willing to go until university or further seemed to be our only life goal at that time. Beyond that, we were left to our own. Growing up without having to worry about money might be the reason why I did not have any inclination towards a financial goal for myself, even though this rationale did not necessarily apply to all my other siblings and cousins. Where did this disinclination come from? Was it the imprint of traditional virtues propagated by ancient scholars, as in the saying, "Learning is the noblest of human pursuits above everything else" (萬般皆下品，惟有讀書高 *Wanban jie xiapin, weiyou dushu gao*)? Education equipped me with the capacity to learn from, to think about, and to create my life. Or was it the privilege of affluence in my early life that bred my neglect of material pursuits? Remembering the lessons on frugality from my grandmother, I did not acquire extravagant spending habits. Having a professional career provided me with the security of a steady paycheck that was automatically deposited into my bank account without my attention. (After I was married, my casual notion of money that lost track when the number of zeroes exceeded six digits amused and flustered my husband, who took up the responsibility of investment to ensure we would have a comfortable retirement.) Appreciative of my blessings, which gave me a head start and freedom from worries, I could commit myself to repaying society for the benefits I had reaped. Being able to contribute to the social good and helping others in need has brought deeper meaning to my life.

Unlike the generation of millennials hopping jobs to grow and gain new skills, I settled in the same workplace for over forty years. Somehow, I could always find new things to learn or something good from the things I was doing.

That gave me job satisfaction and tenure. The only job changes occurred when new opportunities knocked hard at my door and only when I considered them to be contributing to a greater cause. I did not like change and was totally satisfied with what I had done in all my jobs. Such complacency might seem to be a lack of aspiration. On the other hand, I would not hesitate to make changes when I witnessed a faulty system that affected the people around me and the disadvantaged groups in society. It's then and only then that I would consider transitioning to another vantage point where I could make such changes to benefit the larger society. Not wanting changes for myself but making changes in the society around me seemed to be an apparent paradox in my life. In my long career spanning close to fifty years, I merely held three fulfilling jobs but gained rich experiences from the many spinoffs in community services beyond my paid employment. Within each job, coming across challenges along the way prompted me to seek new solutions to the problems I encountered, without the constraints of bureaucracy. I learned to find my voice and break the silence. It was just doing the right thing at the right time. However, without shedding the baggage of Number 8 and being initiated under a liberal environment when I first started my career, I wouldn't have been able to break new ground.

Incubation at United Christian Hospital

Upon my return to Hong Kong in 1975, my first job was in the Psychiatry Department of the United Christian Hospital (UCH), which had opened just two years earlier. Founded by the Hong Kong Christian Council, the new general hospital was housed in the working-class district of Kwun Tong, which was populated by factory buildings, hostels for factory workers, and first-generation public housing estates. The plastic flower and textile manufacturing industry in Hong Kong, which started in the 1950s, expanded into electronics in the 1970s, when small- and medium-sized factories sprouted up to produce simple but labor-intensive components for radios, televisions, and electronic watches. The industry later advanced to more high-tech components for circuit boards and producing new electronic toys, LCD monitors and mobile phones until the vast majority of the factories in Hong Kong were relocated to southern China in the 1990s after the economic open-door policy in China.

Kwun Tong was one of the earliest urban developments in Hong Kong where factories and the low-cost public housing estates were built in the 1960s. The early public housing estates were primitive. The tiny units did not have their own bathrooms. Public baths and toilets were located at the end of the corridor on each floor. Water was drawn in common standpipe rooms. Residents cooked outside their units and washed their laundry in the communal washroom. Although some families living in such close proximity managed to build a sense of community, the men in the house often had to stand guard when the women went to the bathroom. School classrooms were set up by church groups on the rooftops of some of these housing estates to provide schooling for the residents. Compulsory primary education was legislated in 1971, which ensured that children would have six years of primary education. After primary school, young girls from poor families would start working in the factories to support their family while their brothers could continue their education. They filled the labor demand for the local factories.

Getting Acquainted with Kwun Tong

Having lived in Number 8 in the Mid-Levels and then around university campuses in the United States in my early life, Kwun Tong was a totally alien world to me. Every morning, I drove from Macdonnell Road to the vehicle ferry pier in North Point to take the ferry ride across the harbor to UCH, passing through the factory district and the housing estates. This route saved me the hassle of driving through the congestion at the newly-opened Cross-Harbour Tunnel and the busy traffic across eastern Kowloon. I could take a quick nap and rest up in my locked car. However, it still took me over an hour commuting each way.

I soon obtained permission to stay in a single room in the doctors' quarters. At that time special permission was needed to allocate staff quarters to women in the public sector. Equal pay for women and men in the civil service

At the Kwun Tong market stall (far left) with
United Christian Hospital colleagues , 1976.

was just adopted in 1975 when I started my first job. Prior to that, women in
the public sector received merely 75 percent of men's pay. Under the patriarchal
system in the colonial government, unequal pay for women was justified under
the assumption that men were the major breadwinners and women would be
supported by their husbands. Women civil servants might receive a "dowry"
from the government when they got married, but they were not entitled to
a pension upon retirement. The handful of educated women who joined the
civil service and rose to become senior officers formed their own Association
of Female Senior Government Officers in the early 1970s and lobbied the
government for equal pay and work benefits. While equal pay came into effect
in 1975, equal benefits such as housing and education allowance for children
were only achieved in 1980 for the public sector. It was not until 1995 when
the Sex Discrimination Ordinance was enacted that women in the private sector
could enjoy equal rights in employment and education.

Staying at the UCH quarters afforded me the convenience of getting to
know Kwun Tong. This gave me a glimpse of the lives of people in Hong Kong
who were disadvantaged and marginalized, in a setting which was much more

down-to-earth than Number 8 Macdonnell Road. My Psychiatry Department head invited me to join his committee on a female halfway house for psychiatric rehabilitation located in a rental flat in the crowded urban residential area of Kwun Tong. I visited the halfway house twice a month to support the residents' efforts to reintegrate into the community after their hospitalization. These women mostly did not have a home where they could return. With little public funding, the New Life Psychiatric Rehabilitation Association, which ran the halfway house, had to rely on donations and volunteers like me to run the professional services. After fifty-five years, New Life has become the largest provider of mental health services in Hong Kong today.

Once a week, I joined the other young doctors in the UCH quarters on their excursions to the night food markets in Kwun Tong town center. I quickly learned the casual style of dining by picking up any available wooden stools to form our own table at the food stalls, while individual diners might squat on a wooden bench in front of the food stall kitchen. We had to call out our order to the cook. The only waiter would be too busy to attend to us and asked us to just throw water we used to rinse our eating utensils on the ground. Even the doctors did not mind the hygiene conditions because the food was cheap and tasty. Here, I discovered that dinners could be fun without the stifling ceremonial rituals at Number 8.

Shaping the Psychologist Role

The first medical superintendent of UCH, Dr. Edward Paterson, an English missionary doctor, had the vision of building the hospital into a "health care system without walls." With the foresight that the capacity of UCH would fall short of the population demand in the catchment area in a short time, he set up the Kwun Tong Community Health Project to provide primary health care services. He deployed community nurses to take care of the medical needs of geriatric patients at home so that they would not be abandoned by their stressed-out families after being sent to the hospital. He was a progressive administrator who was supportive of staff initiatives.

As the first clinical psychologist at the new Department of Psychiatry, I had to educate the referring doctors on how I could assist them other than taking

With United Christian Hospital Superintendent Dr. Edward Paterson (left)
and physiotherapist Maggie Walker, 1977.

up the standard referral of "IQ test please," which was based on their limited knowledge of a psychologist's role. Besides attending to individual and group therapy for psychiatric patients, I offered my psychological services to the rest of the general hospital: group therapy to motivate geriatric patients to engage in their physical rehabilitation after their stroke; counselling for pediatric patients and their parents to alleviate their fear and anxiety about hospitalization while waiting for or recovering from their surgery; support groups for infertile wives in the obstetrics and gynecology department who felt dejected like "a hen that could not lay eggs," as well as mental health education to the general public for the Kwun Tong Community Health Project. I remember the time when I walked into my first community mental health talk and found a group of elderly residents sitting restlessly in rows of chairs, calling out to their friends across the room. I had not previously realized that 26 percent of elderly men and 82 percent of elderly women did not have any schooling according to the 1976 census in Hong Kong. I quickly discarded my well-prepared notes and transparencies on the different types of mental health problems in old age. Instead, I chatted with the audience about their daily lives, and asked them what they liked and disliked, their problems relating to the younger generation, and how their physical ailments affected their moods. The participants appeared to be attentive. At the end of the session, two elderly women came up and held my hand, saying how much I understood them. I was glad I did not use my original lecture notes.

Dr. Paterson had arranged for young medical doctors at UCH to rotate through different departments in the general hospital to broaden their exposure. Curious to learn and keen to try out novel approaches to patient care, these young doctors who rotated to the Psychiatry Department livened up our team. Whereas the senior psychiatrists were orthodox and serious, these young mavericks often raised refreshing questions about basic assumptions in diagnosis and treatment. One of them later volunteered to help me resolve the delusion of a pestering admirer who kept writing to me.

This farcical episode started after I received the first letter from a self-anointed knight proclaiming that he would bestow a British noble title on me, using stationery bearing the drawing of the royal coat of arms. My community mental health education efforts on television and radio had raised my public profile. I supposed this exposure had attracted the attention of someone with mental derangement. As he was not a patient at the hospital, I just shrugged off the letter with a giggle. After ignoring the first few letters, I received a copy of the letter the "knight" had sent to the Government Marriage Registry together with a handwritten marriage certificate of my marriage to him. An officer from the Marriage Registry later called me up at the hospital and asked if this "knight" was my patient. After confirming that he was not and that I did not know who he was, the officer sent a formal reply to him copied to me, in the most efficient bureaucratic language, simply stating that according to the marriage ordinance in Hong Kong, his marriage certificate was invalid.

The illegitimacy of the marriage did not deter him from sending more letters addressing me as his wife. Then he started to look me up in my department in the hospital. The "knight" turned out to be a pathetic middle-aged man with a hunchback. Of course, staff at our reception did not entertain his request to see me and he left after sitting in the waiting room for a few hours. During our tea breaks, the senior psychiatrists shared their encounters with female patients acting out their delusional courtship, but they usually settled down after receiving medication. As far as we knew, this suitor was not a registered patient in any hospital or clinic. There was no recourse to deal with this non-patient officially through the senior psychiatrists. I had to come up with a practical solution before his delusion escalated. Judging from his actions so far that he did not seem like a violent person, I cooked up a plot with the young doctors. One of them volunteered to pose as my husband and summoned the knight into his office the next time he showed up at our clinic. Startled upon meeting my "husband," the knight apologized profusely, saying that he did not know I had a husband, and quietly disappeared. We did not hear from him again. The young doctor was jubilant with the success of his acting, and our lively team shared this joke for years, including with our respective spouses in real life when we ran into each other many years later.

All in all, the permissive and progressive culture at UCH offered me the platform to launch the War on Rape Campaign.

Breaking the Taboo

The War on Rape (WoR) Campaign broke the taboo on the hidden issue of rape in Hong Kong. It gave women a voice to break the silence to counter the trauma and fear of sexual violence. It also showed how the collective voices of women could make social changes. As for myself, the WoR initiated me into feminism, and opened my world to the passion of philanthropy shared by the many volunteers who dedicated their life to give Hong Kong a heart beyond materialism. It put me in touch with humanity, and a sense of community beyond my individual self.

Learning from Female Patients

Being the first female therapist in the Psychiatry Department, I built up good rapport with the female patients. Many started to reveal to me their past or recent trauma of sexual assault. These patients had been hospitalized under various diagnoses and manifested psychiatric disorders such as anxiety, suicidal thoughts and attempts, depression, and schizophrenia. One girl with catatonic schizophrenic symptoms, who otherwise appeared expressionless and mute, only muttered "rotten sludge" to herself when prompted to speak. Another teenage girl was admitted to the emergency room multiple times after mutilating her wrist in her repeated suicide attempts. A young woman suffered from panic attack whenever she began to develop an intimate romantic relationship. A middle-aged woman's sexual inhibitions led to her marital and emotional breakdown. A hospitalized patient in the terminal stage of cancer asked the nurse in the ward for a newspaper, which she used to scribble in tiny handwriting her life story along the blank edges of the newspaper, recalling her trauma of being raped by soldiers during the Japanese occupation of Hong Kong. Losing her virginity and self-worth, she hastily entered an unhappy marriage. At the end of her life, she felt impelled to reveal her trauma in the fear that her daughter might suffer a similar fate as hers in the future. Her story brought the ward nurses to tears. At least we were able to partially relieve her psychological burden before she passed away. These patients had not told anyone before about their early sexual trauma for fear of the social stigma and the shame they would bring to themselves and their families. The ones who told their family would have been scolded as if it were their fault, especially if the perpetrator was a member of her family. None of them had reported to the police. They had to carry the burden throughout their lives.

As I engaged these patients to work through their long-term trauma in individual therapy, I could not help wondering why we could not address the systemic problem of violence against women and provide crisis intervention so that they did not have to endure their lifelong suffering. In those days, when the emergency number 999 was dialed, reporters often would be the first to arrive at the scene before the police. They snapped photos of the distraught victims, which were then flashed in newspaper headlines, with enough details of the victims' names and home addresses to be identified by their neighbors and friends. There were no aftercare services, such as medical examinations for pregnancy and venereal disease, access to the morning-after pill or abortion, or crisis intervention counseling. Those who reported to the police had to suffer the secondary trauma of criminal investigation by insensitive or even chauvinistic male officers, as there were very few female officers in the police force in those days. The first batch of ten female police constables was recruited in 1951. The demand for women officers increased after the 1967 riots when there was a high proportion of female protesters, during which time the effectiveness of the women officers in deterring the escalation of violence and disorder was demonstrated. The supporting role of women officers expanded in the 1970s from office duties to frontline positions. In 1990, there was still less than 10 percent of women in the police force. By 2023, the number of female officers had increased to about 4,900, 18 percent of the police force. One expatriate police officer we were working with during the campaign remarked jokingly that "if the woman could not fight it [the rape] off, she might as well lie back and enjoy it!" Such was the implicit bias to which victims were exposed.

If the police decided to indict the rapist, then the victim would be subject to abusive grilling in court by the defense lawyer while being confronted by the perpetrator face to face. Typically, she would be challenged that the act was consensual, that by going out late at night she was a promiscuous woman, or that her prior sexual history would discredit her veracity. These atrocities deterred victims from reporting. With the low rate of report, police and the public did not regard rape as a social problem or serious crime.

Hong Kong Council of Women

As an individual therapist trying to patch up the survivors' wounds manifested in psychiatric symptoms, I could never meet the demand, which was just the tip of the iceberg. How long did victims have to suffer from their trauma before ending up in a psychiatric clinic like my patients at UCH? What happened to those victims who developed other problems? What was the actual prevalence of sexual violence in Hong Kong? Why did men rape? What could be done about it? I was impelled by the dire need to address the social injustice at its core. I first raised the issue of rape in the community newspaper and then television interviews in 1976. Subsequent reporting in the *South China Morning Post*, the major English newspaper in Hong Kong, attracted the attention of a group of expatriate women from the Hong Kong Council of Women. They were excited to find a Chinese voice on women's issues, as there were few local feminists at the time.

The Hong Kong Council of Women (HKCW) 香港婦女協會 was established in 1947 by a group of local women with high social status, including Mrs. Ellen Li, who had served as president of the YWCA. She was appointed as the first woman to the Legislative Council in 1965 and proposed the amendment to the marriage ordinance in 1971 to abolish polygamy. The wife of the colonial governor was invited to serve as a patron of HKCW in the early years. In the 1960s, its members lobbied the government to advance the social, economic, and political rights of women in Hong Kong, including equal pay and benefits in the civil service, as well as marriage and inheritance rights.

In 1975, a group of feminist expatriate women who had formed the International Feminist League to promote personal growth and consciousness raising joined the HKCW. After the mid-1970s, most of the active advocates remaining in HKCW were expatriate women. They continued to raise issues in the English newspapers on separate taxation for married women who had to file their taxes under their husbands (it was only from the year of assessment 1990 onwards that a married person could elect for personal assessment separately from or jointly with his/her spouse), paid maternity leave for pregnant women (statutory maternity leave at two-thirds of pay was first introduced in 1981), and violence against women. Without a Chinese voice, there was little coverage in the Chinese media and the issues did not arouse public concern.

Through the introduction of a member of the hospital's missionary board, three English women visited me at my UCH office. They were wives of expatriates working in Hong Kong for short periods, and one of them, Dr. Edith Horsfall, nee Waldmann, was a medical doctor herself. We had a spirited discussion about the problem of rape and what needed to be done. After several meetings, we decided to launch a War on Rape Campaign. I agreed to join the membership of the HKCW to spearhead the campaign in 1977.

Ideological divergence from Western feminism emerged. Mindful that "rape" was a taboo word in the Chinese community, I recommended that

Interviewing Mrs. Ellen Li at the Hong Kong Sanitorium, 1998.

we refrained from using a direct Chinese translation of the War on Rape Campaign. Instead, we adopted the Chinese title of "Protection of Women Campaign" (保護婦女運動 *Baohu funü yundong*) to appeal to the general public. While the feminist analysis of rape more as a violent crime underlined by power and control than merely a sexual act could broaden the understanding of rape, the Western feminist pitch, which conceptualized rape in a dichotomous framework of men's oppression of women, would alienate half of the population unnecessarily. This dichotomous mental framework of "us versus them" was inherent in Western thinking as is evident in their geopolitical mindset throughout modern history. I convinced the expatriate feminists that men also had mothers, wives and daughters who might be subject to rape. We needed to rally women and men alike in the whole community to work together to fight against rape, an orientation that permeated my lifelong pursuit of gender equality. I was not sure if the expatriate women saw me as too soft to take up the war or found the Chinese approach too conservative for eradicating patriarchy. Nonetheless, I appreciated that they recognized the cultural context and conceded to this inclusive stance.

At a War on Rape campaign meeting with Edith Waldmann (far left) in 1979.

The War on Rape (WoR) Campaign

The WoR Campaign we designed demonstrated a community psychological approach towards rape in which service, education, social action, and research were integrated. The objectives were to present rape as a community issue, to remove the stigma of rape and change public attitudes, coordinate aftercare services with sensitivity, and advocate legal reform to protect the rights of the victims. With limited resources, we liaised with existing service providers to introduce aftercare services for survivors. In addition to the HKCW and the UCH Kwun Tong Community Health Project, the Samaritan Befrienders and the Hong Kong Family Planning Association were invited to join as partners. The engagement with these dedicated service providers and volunteers impressed me, as did the fact that there were so many warm-hearted people in Hong Kong who tirelessly contributed their time and resources to take care of people in need, in contrast to the transactional charity work of socialites who donated money mostly for the sake of fame and recognition. This pleasant discovery of heralded as well as unsung heroes and heroines in society erased my prior skeptical image of mercantile and materialistic Hong Kong before returning from America. Getting to know these people and their deeds as well as working with them enriched my understanding of how Hong Kong was built.

Attending to the Aftercare Needs

One of the key partners of the campaign was The Samaritan Befrienders, which was founded by Mr. Andrew Hsueh-Kwei Tu 杜學魁 in 1960 under the name of the Suicide Prevention Society. Commonly known as the suicide prevention hotline, its mission was to help people facing difficulties, loneliness, and despair to regain confidence in life through providing support and emotional counselling. In addition to the Samaritans, Andrew co-founded the Mu Kuang English Primary School in 1958 to provide education for the underprivileged with Mrs. Elsie Elliot 葉錫恩, a divorced British missionary to China who later became his wife in 1985. Classes in the first few years at Mu Kuang were held under makeshift canopies in a former British Army tent in Kai Tak for thirty poor and refugee children living in squatters. To support the inadequate finances of the school, Elsie taught English part-time in other schools while Andrew served as the school principal. Through their relentless efforts, the school secured donations and government loans and eventually expanded into a regular secondary school for 1,400 students, with a purpose-built school in Kwun Tong in 1972. I met Andrew in the Kwun Tong community mental health promotion activities, and was impressed with the mission of the school. I volunteered to offer mental health programs in their School Parents and Teachers Association. I also helped to provide training on listening skills to the Samaritan volunteers. I had great respect for both Andrew and Elsie, who were staunch defenders of public justice in Hong Kong and Asia throughout their lives. Among other things, Andrew founded the Chinese Alliance for Commemoration of the Sino-Japanese War Victims in Hong Kong. Every year, he and the veterans organized a rally to urge the Japanese government to own up to its war crimes and responsibilities so that the succeeding generations never

With Elsie Tu in 2000.

forgot this bloody page of history. Unfortunately, the size of the rally became smaller by the year as the veterans began to die off. The recalcitrant Japanese government had still failed to publicly admit and properly apologize for its war atrocities. It also rejected the demand by people in Hong Kong for redemption of or compensation for the nullified Japanese Military Yen, which was forcibly exchanged for the Hong Kong Dollar during the Japanese occupation in World War II.

Realizing that the WoR Campaign lacked resources, Andrew provided access to a room in the Homantin Centre of the Samaritan Befrienders as office space for our committee. He generously extended the suicide prevention hotline to rape victims, arranged rape crisis counselling training to their volunteers, and promoted the new hotline service in public announcements. The hotline provided the first stop for victims to seek help without having to report to the police. If not for the existing mechanism of the Samaritan Befrienders, it would have taken more time and resources beyond our means to set up a new telephone hotline.

Medical and psychological aftercare for rape victims was another major service that was non-existent in Hong Kong in the 1970s. The costs required for such a rape crisis intervention center was a major challenge that required

With Peggy Lam in 2005.

extensive fundraising. Through the HKCW, I met Mrs. Peggy Lam Pei Yu-dja 林貝聿嘉, who was an old-time member in 1977. Peggy was the Executive Director of The Family Planning Association (FPA) of Hong Kong, which provided birth control through education and reproductive health services. She later became a leader in community services, politics, and women's affairs, serving as the chairman of the Wanchai District Board for almost twenty years from 1985. She founded the Hong Kong Federation of Women with other prominent women in 1993 to unite women and women's groups across the traditional spectrum in Hong Kong and served as its council chairperson for over twenty-five years. Even after her final retirement from community services at age ninety, she continues to lead a buoyant and zesty life. Although her views were considered conservative and pro-government by contemporary women activists, she was a jaunty and unconventional woman during her early days. She came from a well-off family related to the renowned international architect, I. M. Pei, who was her cousin, and was among the minority of Chinese women who received a university degree in Shanghai in the 1940s. She defied the restrictive attitude of her husband's wealthy family towards the role of a daughter-in-law and launched a life-long career of her own. Her feisty spirit in pushing her cause had brought success to the many ventures she led. Her family planning slogan "Two is enough" was a household word from the 1970s until the 2000s, when the low fertility rate in Hong Kong prompted a reversal in the FPA campaign to promote "Family Big or Small, Family Planning is Best for All."

The sexual health clinic of the FPA offered medical examination for venereal disease, pregnancy, emergency contraception, and referral for legal termination of pregnancy. In the 1970s, a Youth Health Advisory Service was set up under the sexual health clinic. Conscious of the costs and stigma involved in setting a standalone rape crisis intervention center, I approached Peggy to deploy the counsellors in the sex counselling service to offer crisis counselling and provide access to the sexual health clinic to rape victims. In 1978, FPA set up a special unit under the Youth Health Advisory Service to provide crisis intervention aftercare for rape victims in Hong Kong for the first time.

The service continued until 2000 when a group of feminist volunteers set up RainLily, a one-stop crisis intervention service for rape survivors. The RainLily counsellors answered a telephone hotline, accompanied the victims to the hospital and police reporting, and provided aftercare counselling and forensic examination by the government forensic pathologists at the RainLily premises. Running on donations only, the first executive director took a pay cut from her former social worker job to save the finances of RainLily. As the only comprehensive service that catered to rape victims, RainLily continued to appeal to the government for financial subsidy. Disfavoring the vocal feminist stance of the association, in 2007 the government deflected its funding support to the Tung Wah Group of Hospitals to set up the CEASE Crisis Centre to offer an alternative support service for victims of both sexual and domestic violence. Vocal feminism was still regarded with skepticism and resistance by the establishment.

At the time of the WoR Campaign, we had to design all the services from scratch without any help from the government. We all contributed input from the perspective of our professional experiences with rape victims. Dr. Edith Waldmann set up a medical subcommittee to survey the facilities for the treatment of rape victims in hospitals. Victims who were injured were sent to the hospital emergency departments, where treatment varied vastly. To ensure that the rape victims were handled with sensitivity and proficiency, the

With the RainLily committee members at the opening ceremony, 2002.

subcommittee designed a medical kit with instructions for examining victims with the cooperation of the government forensic pathologist. The kit was sent to every doctor and every hospital so that they would pay attention to the medical and forensic needs of the victims.

Even though the sexist attitude of some police officers was appalling, we found the Police Department generally supportive of the campaign to fight rape as a crime. Rather than condemning the macho police culture, the WoR Committee liaised closely with the department from the onset to discuss the needs of rape victims and the role of the police. As a result, the Police Department set up a working procedure for rape complainants. With only a handful of woman officers who might not always be available in each police station, the police agreed to assign one female officer to work with the rape victim throughout the case and accompany the victim to the FPA for aftercare service. In 1978, the police mounted a Hong Kong-wide fight-crime campaign on rape. Posters and leaflets were distributed in the community to arouse public awareness on the issues, encourage reporting, and inform about services. In working with the police, we learned to put aside differences and prejudices to strike a chord with strategic partners to achieve pragmatic outcomes. Just as in any profession or any community, there were good cops and there were bad cops.

Training Frontline Workers

Despite the frontline workers' good will and favorable responses to the campaign, they nevertheless felt unprepared and requested more training that was not provided in their professional education. The target groups of professionals and paraprofessionals most likely to be working with rape victims included nurses, doctors, teachers, social workers, and other mental health professionals. To acquaint frontline workers with background information and approaches in working with the rape victim, we compiled a bilingual manual for counsellors of rape victims. The manual collected information on medical, legal, and psychological aspects of rape, and provided guidelines on the physical and psychological assistance for rape victims.

We designed training workshops with content adapted according to the specific needs of the target groups. The core program included information on existing procedures and resources, sensitization to the needs of victims, existing rape myths, and practice on relationship skills in helping the victim. Talks were given by an interdisciplinary team including a nurse, a lawyer, a police officer, a social worker, and a psychologist. Discussion, exercises, and role play were used to increase personal sharing and participation. Developing these training modes subsequently informed and improved my own teaching method at the university by adopting a more interactive mode.

Promoting Awareness and Attitude Change

To promote public awareness of rape, dispel rape myths, and destigmatize rape victims, mass programs and talks were launched in cooperation with schools and community groups. In those days, non-governmental press conferences were uncommon. Publicity on social issues often relied on press coverage following invited talks to lunch meetings of service organizations like the Rotary Club and the Lion's Club. At that time, the members of these clubs were all male businessmen or professionals who formed social networks in a mission to contribute to community services. Their regular lunch gatherings were more social events, and the talks were just part of the pro forma agenda. Nevertheless, the press interviews arranged after the talks provided publicity coverage in the media.

Talking to an all-male uninformed audience about rape was a novel experience for me. Away from the hospital, being the only woman in meetings and committees soon became a norm in my early career. I remember one luncheon talk at the Lion's Club during which the club president was apparently embarrassed about the topic. After introducing me as the speaker, he added a remark: "Rape is a matter that concerns only women but not us men…" I could not help interjecting: "I beg your pardon, Mr. President. Without men, there would be no rape. (Under the definition of rape in Hong Kong law, rape could only be committed by a man upon a woman when she did not or could not consent to the intercourse.) Besides, all men have mothers or other family members who may become victims of rape." At that point, the other Lions roared with laughter and teased the president, who had to pay a fine as donation to the club to make amends. Such was the community attitude with which we had to contend and which we needed to change continuously.

Mass media played a major role in promoting the campaign. Being the Chinese face of the campaign, I accepted many radio and television interviews to raise public consciousness. Besides widespread coverage of our activities, newspaper articles and letters to the editor were written by our members and supporters. Given public interest, television and radio programs were produced to discuss the issues. The government's Radio Television Hong Kong (RTHK) decided to produce a three-episode television program on a rape victim in their highly rated docudrama series "Under the Lion Rock" (獅子山下 *Shizishanxia*) to depict the psychological and social problems faced by victims, and to reflect positive and negative public attitudes. A popular television actress, Louise Lee Si-kee 李司棋, played my role as a psychologist counseling the victim, with my coaching during the shooting. Given the popularity of the series, our message was able to reach many Chinese homes.

Appearing on television at that time was a big deal and put me in the limelight. While I eschew personal publicity, the exposure was a necessary price to pay for promoting a cause. At Number 8, my home, my prime-time media appearance as the messenger rather than my message itself received more attention. My mother complained to Sister Ten that it was an embarrassment for her that her daughter would be speaking about this sexual taboo so openly in public. However, she dared not mention anything to me. Aunt Four often casually remarked to me, not sure whether as a compliment or a sneer, that she saw my appearance again on television. I just grinned back. To understand how the older generation would react to rape in the family, I once posed a question to my mother: what would she say to her daughter if she, her daughter, had been raped? She hesitated for a few seconds to think of a politically correct answer and then replied timidly: "Oh, of course I will not blame her." I pressed her what she would say then. "I will just tell her not to do it again in the future!" The ludicrous response reflected the deep-seated prejudice that rape was the fault of a woman. I was abashed by my failure to educate my mother. I could imagine how other parents would respond.

Advocacy and Legal Reform

With heightened public awareness and support, the assertive expatriate women successfully lobbied the Attorney General to investigate legal reforms to protect the rights of rape victims. In 1978, the government gazetted the Crimes (Amendment) (No. 2) Ordinance, which safeguarded the anonymity of rape victims and provided that the previous sexual history of the victim would not be adduced in evidence. Court provisions were made for the rape victim's testimony to be heard in camera or behind a screen. In 1981, legal abortion was also extended to rape victims. Eligibility for compensation from the Criminal and Law Enforcement Injuries Compensation Boards specifically included rape victims as victims of violent crime. Applications for the compensation scheme were encouraged not only for the sake of monetary award, but more importantly, for the symbolic recognition of rape in the same way as other violent crimes. Even with the passage of the laws, we constantly monitored the press coverage and arranged expatriate volunteers to observe the trials (which were conducted only in English during the colonial days), to keep our vigilance on violations and flaws in criminal justice concerning rape. At last, the identity of victims has disappeared from news coverage on rape and rape trials nowadays.

Fact-Finding Research

When the WoR Campaign began, little was known about the pattern of rape in Hong Kong. Facts were needed to substantiate the veracity and credibility of an issue and to dispel myths. To build up our local knowledge on rape, we compiled the pattern of rape, locations of dangerous areas, as well as profiles of rape victims and typical perpetrators presented in police reports and at the FPA aftercare service. Even though reported rape only provided an incomplete picture, that was a first start. Without access to individual cases of victims and perpetrators, more in-depth analysis of their profiles could not be conducted.

Meanwhile, we started with studies on public attitudes towards about rape, as well as attitude changes following training and public education. These preliminary studies showed the prevalence of rape myths in the community, especially among men, similar to what had been found in Western studies. These rape myths typically put the blame on women for their behavior or the way they dressed, and the responsibility on women to physically resist the attack. Such myths reinforced the social stigma of rape and pointed to the importance of reframing rape in a wider socio-cultural perspective of violence against women with the essential notion of the woman's consent. Built-in evaluation studies helped us to assess the effectiveness of the training programs for professionals and their various formats in improving the trainees' attitudes, skills, information, and confidence in taking care of rape victims.

Research on rape is continuing to improve services. After the RainLily crisis intervention service for rape survivors began operation at the end of 2000, I helped the new group to conduct research to evaluate their training programs for frontline service providers and to assess the needs and outcomes of the survivors after receiving the services. Pre- and post-training surveys demonstrated positive attitude changes among the trainees to justify the cost-effectiveness of the educational programs. Follow-up assessment of the survivors illuminated their psychological adjustment at different phases after the sexual assault incident as well as their satisfaction with the service. These studies provided the empirical evidence to validate and further improve their programs, which had helped to strengthen their appeal for public funding.

Not until 1998 when the Correctional Service Department set up the Sex Offenders Evaluation and Treatment Unit (ETU) to help sex offenders in custody would there be more understanding on the psychological profile of offenders. Clinical psychology services were first introduced to the prison system in Hong Kong in 1976. In 1982, the "Prisons Department" was renamed the "Correctional Services Department" to reflect the new emphasis on offenders' rehabilitation instead of punishment, changing the culture and image of the department. The department's psychologists helped to set up the ETU located at Siu Lam Psychiatric Centre in 1998 to provide comprehensive psychological services, including thorough assessment and specialized treatment to sex offenders who had been screened for their suitability. Trained as scientist-practitioners, the psychologists in the ETU were committed to backing up their service with research. They invited me to lead a team from the Department of Psychology at The Chinese University of Hong Kong to undertake a commissioned study to construct a local risk assessment tool and an attitude scale to assess the cognitive distortions in sex attitudes of the sex offenders. A follow-up study in 2009 demonstrated the validity of these tools in predicting recidivism among sex offenders. In 2008 and 2018, I served as a member of the International Treatment Advisory Panel to evaluate the ETU services based on international guidelines for sex offender treatment programs. The other international experts were impressed with the professionalism and standard of the ETU, which set a role model in Asia. The commitment of the Correctional Service Department to evidence-based practice and research had been instrumental in improving the effectiveness of the rehabilitation program of sex offenders. It was gratifying to see training and research built into the mechanism of rape prevention services, as well as other future infrastructures on gender equality, outside of academia.

Postscript

The WoR campaign marked the first time that a taboo topic on violence against women broke the silence and received widespread public support. The community psychology concept adopted in the WoR Campaign demonstrated the value of a comprehensive approach that integrated service, education, advocacy, and research. In reaching out to multiple partners and stakeholders in the community to join the common cause and leveraging on their existing services, we put aside ideological divergence. Through relentless lobbying, laws were changed to protect victims' rights. We initiated research to guide our actions and provided training and publicity to destigmatize rape. With limited resources, the campaign's success was built on the passion of volunteerism, which characterized the role of civil society's contributions to social services and societal development in Hong Kong. While the WoR Campaign succeeded in bringing rape into public consciousness, attitude change remained a slow and long-term process that involved addressing the underlying structures and dynamics of gender relationships. This realization led me into my lifelong journey of promoting women's rights and well-being.

Shortly after the WoR Campaign was launched in 1977, I was recruited to join the faculty of the psychology minor program under the Sociology Department at CUHK. I was reluctant to leave UCH, which had opened my eyes to the social realities of Hong Kong. Yet, given there were only two academic psychology units in Hong Kong universities at that time, the opportunity could not be missed. Psychology was a novel subject in Hong Kong and there was a lack of psychologists and training in psychology. As one of the few local Chinese with a doctoral degree, I believed that I could contribute to the development of the field. I had already initiated research on psychological assessment and on rape on my own at UCH, even though the hospital setting was not equipped for research support. An academic setting would pave the path for the development of the psychology profession. I weighed the loss in my commitment to clinical services against the broader vision for the field of psychology. I was certain that moving to an academic position would not curtail my community engagement. Still harboring the feeling of reluctance to leave, I went up to bid farewell to Dr. Paterson and thanked him for his inspiration and staunch support for my community campaigns.

Universities in Hong Kong provided a laissez-faire environment for me to pursue my community engagements. In the 1970s to 1980s, the cutthroat "publish-or-perish" culture did not exist yet. Government research funding was not introduced until the 1990s. So long as faculty members met the basic demands of teaching and publications, they were free to engage in their own interests, be it happy hours at the senior staff club, stock market investments, Mahjong and card games, or other leisure activities. My free-time activity was my community engagement. Contrary to the skeptical attitudes of my senior male colleagues, my community engagement was more than leisure. It enriched my teaching and research. When I met some of my former students decades later, they told me how my sharing of these experiences had inspired their learning.

The First Community Women's Centre

After three years of the WoR Campaign, our committee considered the long-term development of our efforts and deliberated the need to set up a designated rape crisis intervention center on our own to consolidate aftercare services for rape victims and to continue the efforts of the campaign. Discussion with stakeholders in the local community convinced us that the time was not ripe as the prevailing social stigma would deter rape survivors from coming to the center. Listening to the voices of our target users, we concurred on the priority to empower women to help themselves, and to address women's needs and development in a more holistic approach. The WoR Committee evolved into a steering group for the establishment of a community women's center.

From Idea to Action

The idea of the Women's Centre grew out of two groups functioning under the Council of Women: The War on Rape Committee and the Women's Health Group. In the early 1980s, social and medical services did not cater to the specific needs of women. No government department held a portfolio on women's affairs. Bureaucrats insisted that all their services were catered to everyone in the community and women's social needs were covered under the family services, implying that women's identities were subsumed under the family. The compartmentalized government services were designed to fit the bureaucracy without bearing the unique needs of users in mind. Oftentimes women were unclear about what services they required in the first place or where to find such services. There was a need for a place from which women could obtain women-focused information and assistance.

Early studies of Hong Kong women had shown a lack of awareness of their own bodies and their health needs. Women experiencing emotional distress were ignorant about mental health problems and resources. Before the internet was introduced in the 1990s, access to information was limited to the better educated and the well-connected. According to the Census and Statistics Department of Hong Kong, only 23.9 percent of the female population in 1976 attended secondary school, matriculation, and technical institutes, compared to 32.2 percent of the males. The percentage who attained postsecondary or university education was a mere 2.1 percent for females and 4.5 percent for males. Related to lower educational attainment was the lower level of economic participation among women. At that time, the percentage of women in the labor force was 43.6 percent, and the job status of women workers remained low. With half of the population living in public housing estates, working-class housewives stayed home most of the day taking care of their children and household chores. The public housing policy that allocated units to the nuclear family meant that the housewives were isolated from their extended families. In the 1980s, young families were relocated to new public housing estates in remote parts of the New Territories. Poor transportation access in these new towns resulted in many husbands who had to work long hours in the urban area staying away from home during the week, leaving the wives with young children to cope with hardships on their own. A series of tragic cases of women jumping off the high-rise buildings in these new housing estates, sometimes with their young children, shocked society. The sheer provision of a roof above one's head without consideration of community building and social support reflected the siloed planning practice of the government bureaucracy, which ignored the intersectional nature of daily needs.

The steering group of the Women's Centre decided to pay special attention to the needs of women at the grassroots level. Learning from the experience of the WoR Campaign, a holistic approach was adopted to engage community stakeholders to improve community resources to serve women without espousing Western feminist rhetoric that condemned men as the primary source of women's problems. With cultural sensitivity to the predominance of the target users being ethnic Chinese, the steering committee agreed that more local women should be involved in the leadership, while the expatriate women who did not speak Chinese would focus on the planning instead of frontline service. I was nominated to be the Chair of the steering committee and later the Chair of the Women's Centre when it was established in 1981.

Telephone Helpline

Without funding and premises, our steering group members decided to start off with a telephone information and referral service run by volunteers as a first stop for women who needed help. We all chipped in to compile a database using hand-written index cards (before Word or Excel files were available) on resources for women's legal, medical, and social needs. In the days before mobile phones, the telephone helpline had to be answered by volunteers at a physical location. Mrs. Elsie Elliot, partner of Mr. Andrew Tu of the Samaritan Befrienders, came forth by offering a small room in her Urban Councilor's office in Homantin, Kowloon.

Elsie came to Hong Kong with her then missionary husband in 1949 after the Communist Party expelled all foreign missionaries from mainland China. Shocked by the poverty, injustice, and corruption she witnessed in the squatter community where she was staying, she stood up to speak her conscience. She left the church, which prohibited her social activism, and later divorced her husband for his rigid religious faith. In 1985, she married Andrew, her long-time partner in the Mu Kuang School and her comrade in social activism. Elsie was respected by the public in our generation as "Hongkong's most widely admired personality" for good reasons. From the 1960s to the 1980s, she actively fought for gay rights, better housing, welfare services, bus routes, hawker licenses, recognition of Chinese as an official language and many other social problems. She became known for her strong antipathy towards colonialism and corruption, as well as for her work for the underprivileged. The creation of the Independent Commission Against Corruption (ICAC) in Hong Kong was attributed to her relentless advocacy. First elected to the Urban Council in 1963 and to the Legislative Council in 1988 through the indirect election under the constituency of the Urban Council as an electoral college, she became the most popular voice of the common people.

Before Hong Kong's return to Chinese sovereignty in 1997, the colonial government sped up the process of democratization by introducing direct election to the Legislative Council and enlarging the electoral colleges. With her seasoned experience of over thirty years in politics and her heart in what was more important to Hong Kong, Elsie opposed the electoral reforms of the last colonial governor, Chris Patten, and the fast-paced democratization reforms advocated by many politicians from the democrat camp. She challenged the hypocrisy of the British colonial government, which had refused to give Hong Kong democracy for over a century but then accelerated such reforms only in the final few years of what she labelled as the "disgraceful colonial era" without cultivating democratic literacy in the generally uninformed electorate. She advocated a gradual pace of democratization that was also preferred by the Chinese government, which led her critics to brand her with the unpopular label of a pro-Beijing politician, and eventually losing her direct election to the Urban Council and later the Legislative Council to the candidate of the upcoming Democratic Party. In the run-up to 1997, the media painted a negative image of anyone who was considered pro-Beijing. Even upon her retirement from politics after 1997, Elsie continued to voice her conscience on issues of social injustice and unfair government policies. When I visited Elsie on her 100th birthday, she still spoke in her gentle voice about her social concerns with sharp mental clarity despite being physically frail. She corrected me that the room in Homantin she lent to the Women's Centre was a real office despite its small size and not a storeroom that I thought it was. Elsie passed away in 2015 at age 103.

Elsie's Urban Council office room gave us the launch pad for the Women's Centre. We trained up Chinese volunteers for the telephone helpline, which operated on Tuesday and Thursday mornings and evenings every week. We recruited women doctors and lawyers to provide special advice on the helpline once a month. The telephone helpline began operation in 1981.

Keeping up with continuous publicity, the helpline had a high rate of utilization. Most of the callers' initial enquiries were about how they could get a divorce, which was more a call for help with their marital problems. Rather than jumping to a legal referral, the volunteers talked them through their problems of family discords and explored multiple resources before resorting to the break-up, which was not what they really wanted. By building up their access to information and resources, we helped to empower women to take charge of their lives.

While we were grateful for the use of the Homantin premises, which were situated behind the gas stations on Princess Margaret Road not far from the Cross-Harbour Tunnel, it was not an ideal location at night. A major route for cars, there was no easy access to public transportation. The dedicated night volunteers had to walk through a dark alley to get to the back entrance of the building. Some of the professional women who served as volunteers in the evenings joked about the risk of twisting their ankles in their high heels when stepping over the ditch behind the gate in darkness. Still, the team of committed women volunteers persisted for over five years in this location.

Since its launch in 1981, the telephone helpline has been maintained until now, with more sessions on the weekdays. Many of the current helpline counsellors had experienced similar troubles in their lives and had benefited from the helpline before. With professional training from the center's social workers, the volunteer counsellors enhanced their competence, analytic skills, and knowledge of social resources. Modern technology in mobile networks now enables the volunteers to answer the calls at home without having to be physically present at the center.

A Center of Our Own

Finding our own premises for the Women's Centre was an arduous priority. Location and funding were the key challenges in setting up the physical premises

At the Women's Centre opening exhibition, 1986. Fanny is on the right.

of the Women's Centre. Although Hong Kong is relatively small in geographical terms, access to public transportation was a major consideration if we wanted to attract users to come to the center. The property value of commercial buildings in central locations rendered them beyond the reach of welfare organizations. Most government-subsidized housing estates are situated in outlying areas. Only when the mass transit railway (MTR) system was completed in 1983 was it feasible to consider premises in these noncentral locations.

To qualify for a concessionary rent rate on premises in the public housing estates, it was necessary to obtain the government's support. Without a government policy on women, it took over a year to pass through the different units in the government bureaucracy before the Social Welfare Department finally agreed to certify that a women's centre, which aimed at promoting women's development rather than the direct delivery of welfare services, qualified for their support. Even with the certification from the government, there was a long waiting list for office space at public housing estates in the urban areas.

In 1983, I was appointed as a member of the Shatin District Board, which gave me access to different government officials attending the District Board meetings. After lobbying the Housing Department representative over the next few years, we were finally offered in 1985 an office unit in the Lai Kok Public Housing Estate in Cheung Sha Wan, a low-income industrial district in East Kowloon with easy access to the MTR. The new center housed the telephone inquiry service, a resource library, and meeting rooms for educational programs. We hired the first staff members, an executive secretary and a part-time office assistant, in 1986. The Women's Centre of the Hong Kong Council of Women, the first community-based center for women in Hong Kong, began operation in 1986.

Lack of funding continued to be a greater barrier to overcome. It was difficult to convince local funding agencies to sponsor projects exclusively designed for women, especially those who were not "victims" or "destitute." Women's development was not perceived as welfare services. Instead, donations for welfare projects were more readily given to children and the disabled.

Overseas funding was initially sought from the 1975–1985 United Nations Decade for Women Project Funds. Although there was initial support and encouragement from the Southeast Asian office, the application was turned down because Hong Kong was no longer considered a low income region by the United Nations. Unfortunately, economic development in Hong Kong had not benefited all sectors of the population. The market Gini coefficient, which measures household income inequality prior to taxes and transfers, remained over 40 percent since the 1970s, reaching close to 50 percent in 2016. Studies have shown a large rise in income inequality since the 1980s. We continued to try other funding opportunities. With the help of an expatriate member from a missionary family, small grants were finally obtained after years of proposal writing from two overseas church organizations that had designated women's development as one of their priorities. With the grants, we were able to launch our programs.

One of the objectives of the Women's Centre was to empower underprivileged women by developing their competence so that they could gain control of their lives. Acquiring a repertoire of alternatives and skills, women could choose from a position of strength. We planned our educational programs with the aim of increasing access to information and resources, promoting self-awareness and self-confidence, as well as fostering self-help and mutual help.

Research was built into our planning and evaluation process. Before we designed the educational programs, we surveyed the women living in the neighborhood on their needs and interests. Self-improvement was one of the requests of the housewives who stayed home most of the day. Contrary to the feminist idea of political and economic empowerment, we were surprised that most of the housewives requested to learn English. At first, we thought some of them were contemplating emigration in view of the reunification with China in 1997. After talking to the housewives personally, we realized that they felt inadequate when coaching their children with their homework without knowledge of English. Children's education was the mother's priority. It verified the saying that "when you educate a woman, you educate the whole family."

We convinced the expatriate feminist members not to belittle the mundane English lessons; English literacy would enhance the housewives' self-confidence and esteem in front of their children. Instead, we nudged them to design teaching materials using examples of women's issues and possible solutions which would be discussed during class. The expatriate members invited local women advocates to write short essays sharing their experiences on social causes in Hong Kong, which were later compiled into a reader for women to learn English. The English classes remained one of the popular basic courses for women at the Women's Centre.

Inching Women's Empowerment

The Women's Centre became a hub for the aspirational housewives to gather during their free time. They became interested in other self-empowering programs like health care, self-understanding, and self-defense. Without promoting explicit feminist themes that might threaten the participants' comfort zone, conscientization of women's perspective was raised indirectly in talks and classes through discussions and reflections. For example, in a discussion series on choosing television programs for children, the group leader brought up the topic of the sexist portrayal of women in the mass media. Similarly, in English conversation tutorials, expatriate women talked about women in their home countries and shared an international perspective on women. After a year, regular subscribers of the resource library and participants in the educational programs became comfortable enough with the center to venture into such relatively unfamiliar issues as civil rights and social participation. Many of them signed up to be trained as volunteers to assist the center's activities and help other women. This gradual approach proved more effective in stimulating the interest of women who would not otherwise expose themselves to nontraditional ideas. Volunteerism itself proved to be an effective way of promoting women's empowerment.

During the planning of a field trip to Taiwan to learn about housewives' efforts in environmental protection there, one of the active members who was keen to join sadly announced she had to withdraw. Her husband was concerned that there would be nobody at home to take care of the housework. Other members came forth to offer help and look after her teenage children. The husband was still reluctant. After several rounds of negotiations that tried to resolve what purportedly were household chores to no avail, it finally turned out that her husband found it hard to accept that his wife would have gone on an overseas trip ahead of him and become superior to him as he had never been abroad. How could he face his neighbors?

While the husbands of the center's participants and volunteers were pleased to see the overall benefits brought by the women's development and competence to the whole family, the men's engagement became an important consideration. The center started to invite the husbands and children to join family activities. Some of the husbands soon got involved and assisted the center with the heavy work during these events. They reckoned that the center did not turn their wives into feminists as feared.

It was important for women's development to be complemented and synchronized with men's enlightenment. Men could and should be rallied as allies and not be put down as competitors, oppressors, or a nemesis of the women's movement. In my advocacy on women's rights, I had often called for men's own enlightenment and "liberation" in the twenty-first century, after women had been "liberated" in the twentieth century. With women's advancement and modernized gender roles, men need to keep up so as not to be left behind or blame the liberated women for creating conflict between the sexes. Whereas Chinese culture emphasizes harmony, the confrontational style

The Yin Ngai Society opening with Shelley Lee
(seated second from the right), Carrie Yau (seated first from the left)
and Fanny (seated second from the left), 1985.

of the feminist movement that originated in the West has been perceived as inciting conflicts between genders. We are conscious of the need to avoid anti-feminism backlashes that are spreading globally and silencing women activists in many countries.

The Women's Centre Coming of Age

The idea of the Women's Centre had resonated with the then-Secretary for City and New Territories Administration, David Akers-Jones, to take similar action to address the multiple suicide tragedies of women isolated in the remote housing estates in the new towns. He recalled his trekking trip with his wife, Jane, in the Himalayas, during which they came up with the idea of organizing non-working women in the new towns to get together for mutual help and self-improvement. He invited me, several women professionals, and a few talented and promising female administrative officers working under him, including Shelley Lee 李麗娟 and Carrie Yau 尤曾家麗, to brainstorm possible mechanisms. The name Yin Ngai Societies 賢毅社 was chosen, as it symbolized women's traditional virtues (*yin* 賢) and determination (*ngai*毅), which also characterized the conventional orientation of these groups. The first three Yin Ngai Societies were launched in Shatin, Tsuen Wan, and Tuen Mun in the New Territories in 1983 and expanded into other districts later with the support of the government bureau for district administration. These networks focused more on the needs of women in their family life, such as cooking, housekeeping, crafts, and English lessons. Although these women's groups did not engage in advocacy of women's rights, they provided the mechanism to build up women's competence and confidence and became an important constituent in the government's community development policy in district administration. Some of the early leaders of Yin Ngai Societies told me a few years later how they had grown beyond the confines of their family roles through their engagement with other women in the community. They had found their own voices and witnessed their personal transformation from diffident and unkempt housewives to self-assured and poised big sisters taking charge of planning and action. It demonstrated how women's empowerment could enhance the human capital in community building through diverse approaches.

By 1991, the Hong Kong Council of Women decided to dissolve. With the turnover of the expatriate women who left Hong Kong after their short stay, and others getting involved with the council's spinoff services, few members remained active in the council itself. HKCW, which had been instrumental in initiating services to address the basic needs of women in Hong Kong, had accomplished its historical mission. Its two successful spinoff services—the Women's Centre and Harmony House 和諧之家 for battered wives—had been operating in autonomy and became independently registered.

Harmony House was established in 1985 as the first shelter for abused women and their children in Hong Kong. Like rape, domestic violence was a taboo topic, and battered wives did not have a voice or recourse to protection. In traditional Chinese culture, marital problems were kept under wraps within the family. After the issue was first raised by Mr. Tom Mulvey, the director of a family service organization, three expatriate members of the HKCW, Ms. Pam Baker, a human rights lawyer, Dr. Judith Mackay, a medical doctor, and Ms. Joanna Leung, an Australian educational administrator married to a local Chinese man, joined forces to break the silence. Without existing services,

With Judith and John Mackay at their
Double Golden Anniversary celebration in 2017.

and thus no central record of cases, victims of domestic violence were invisible to the government's Social Welfare Department, which denied there was any problem of domestic violence in Hong Kong at that time.

Judith Mackay, who was working at the United Christian Hospital in the late 1970s to early 1980s, took the government to task. She compiled the daily statistics on cases at the hospital's accident and emergency department of women who came in inflicted with bruises, contusions, abrasions, lacerations, scalds, fractures, and other injuries indicative of battering. The data demonstrated that even at one hospital in Kwun Tong, there were at least one case or more each day. Interviews with the fifty women claiming to be assaulted by their husbands or cohabitees revealed profiles of domestic violence similar to those found in Western literature. The government could not ignore the problem.

Arriving from Scotland in 1967 to join her husband who had a group medical practice in Hong Kong, Judith encountered sex discrimination at her first government hospital job in 1971, being given 75 percent of the male doctors' pay. This transformed her into a committed feminist fighting for equal terms and benefits for women throughout her life. Judith is a life-long advocate on public health, especially on health issues related to women and tobacco control. Realizing how women were exploited by cigarette advertisements and were dying from smoking—which became a form of bondage instead of the promised emancipation for women—she has been a zealous campaigner for over four decades since 1984 to reduce tobacco use in low- and middle-income countries. In her fight with big tobacco companies over policy control, laws, and tax systems, she has been vilified, threatened with lawsuits, and received death threats. Among the numerous professional honors and awards that she has received, Judith proudly touts her "accolade" of being named as "one of the three most dangerous people in the world" by the tobacco industry.

Pam Baker was recruited to Hong Kong from Scotland to work as a lawyer in the government Legal Aid Department in the early 1980s. She soon got involved in the movement to establish the first shelter for battered women in 1985. As a founder of the family law association, she lobbied successfully for legislation against domestic violence. In the 1990s, she fought for the rights of Vietnamese refugees and left her position after being reprimanded by the colonial government for granting legal aid to Vietnamese boat people, who were protesting the government for poor conditions in their detention camps. She set up her own law firm to continue to fight for the human rights of refugees and was hailed as the "Florence Nightingale" of Hong Kong's refugee camps. She made no money from her work, which was basically driven by her irritation at injustice. Her fight for the human rights of refugees persisted till shortly before her death in 2002.

Such was the courage, bellicosity, and tenacity of the expatriate members of the Hong Kong Council of Women (HKCW) who advocated for Harmony House, the operation of which was then taken over by the local members, who diverged from the Western feminist stance to avoid the service image of breaking up the family system under traditional Chinese culture. This ideological tension reflected the cultural context in which feminists had to navigate in order to gain community acceptance. Providing indispensable services to women in need gained more traction in the Chinese community at the beginning. Starting with providing free short-term refuge for battered women who ran away from home, Harmony House has since developed into a one-stop anti-domestic violence service agency, offering preventive, therapeutic, and developmental programs to help families affected by domestic violence. It also promotes community education on healthy family relationships, provides training to multi-disciplinary professionals, and advocates the government for policies and laws on domestic violence.

After the dissolution of HKCW, its two spin-off services flourished on their own. The Women's Centre renamed itself as the Hong Kong Federation of Women's Centres (HKFWC) 香港婦女中心協會 in 1992. HKFWC acquired membership in the Hong Kong Council of Social Services as well as the Community Chest of Hong Kong, which qualified us for the Chest's annual funding allocations. It has since expanded into ten centers across different regions in Hong Kong, providing a broad range of services including counselling and legal support, training and employment support, gender education, caring for the carers' program, women's wellness program, continuing education, childcare and after-school care, social participation, social enterprise, and handicraft workshops. HKFWC also became active in advocacy to promote gender equality.

Succession planning is essential for the continuity of voluntary organizations. New leadership can bring refreshing ideas to steer the further development of and avoid stagnation in these organizations. Recruitment of the next generation of leaders is often neglected by many non-governmental organizations (NGOs), which dedicate their attention to their services at the expense of corporate governance. Mindful that I had served as the Chair of the Executive Committee for ten years since we first started the telephone helpline, I passed my role to another active member who commanded the support of other volunteers, while I took up the honorary position of President of the HKFWC until 1996 when I had to resign to become the founding Chairperson of the Equal Opportunities Commission to avoid the perception of conflict of interest.

Women's Advocacy

In a way, the HKFWC played a role in the formation of the EOC. The 1980s saw the rise of feminist activism among local Chinese women, who had benefitted from mass education and were influenced by Western feminism ideology, including the Association for the Advancement of Feminism 新婦女協進會 and the Hong Kong Women Workers' Association 香港婦女勞工協會. These local women's concern groups became politically active and joined forces in advocacy efforts on gender equality. In 1989, HKFWC joined eleven other women's concern groups to form a Women's Joint Political Platform to urge the British colonial government to extend to Hong Kong as its colony the United Nations Convention on the Elimination of All Forms of Discrimination Against Women (CEDAW), and to create a Working Group on women's policies in the government. CEDAW was adopted by the UN General Assembly in 1979 to urge its member states to set up an agenda for national action to end what constituted discrimination against women. Both China and the UK had ratified CEDAW in 1980 and 1986, respectively. By 2023, 189 of the 193 UN Member States have ratified CEDAW (the only six UN member states that have not ratified or acceded to the convention are Iran, Palau, Somalia, Sudan, Tonga, and, interestingly, the United States, despite its constant criticisms of other countries on human rights issues).

After the introduction of a handful of elected members for the first time to the Legislative Council in 1991 by the colonial government in its effort to speed up democratization before Hong Kong's return to China, women's groups took up more political tactics to lobby Legco members to pay attention to women's concerns. At the Women's Centre annual meeting in 1990, we invited a popular pro-democracy LegCo Member to give an address as the guest of honor, which nudged him to look up on women's issues for his speech. We further raised an unexpected question following his speech, asking whether he would bring the issue related to the advancement of the status of women back to the Legislative Council, to which he had no choice but to agree after a short hesitation. In 1991, he invited another female LegCo member to raise the question with him, to which the Secretary of Home Affairs responded that women were not being discriminated against in Hong Kong. Other female legislative members then set up an ad hoc group to study the need for a women's commission.

In 1992, a coalition of fourteen women's concern groups, including HKFWC, rallied the government to set up a women's committee in the government to address women's concerns. One of the issues was the lack of land inheritance rights of rural indigenous women living in the New Territories. Even up to the 1990s, the colonial government maintained the Qing-dynasty customary law in the indigenous villages in the New Territories which was leased to Britain, unlike the rest of urban Hong Kong which was ceded as a colony where the British colonial government's laws were applied. Even without any brothers, the women villagers had no right to inherit their father's land if their father died without a will. They could be expelled from their family home if other male relatives took over. Encouraged by the activism of local women's groups, some rural women villagers called for protection of their inheritance rights. In 1993, HKFWC helped to set up the "New Territories Indigenous Women's Committee" in support of the demand for equal rights of female indigenous residents in the New Territories. The rural women protesters wore masks of crying faces and paper shackles hanging from their necks to symbolize the unfair Chinese customary law. The protests stirred strong opposition from the traditional rural leaders and villagers, including some women, who argued that the family's properties should remain under the control of the patrilineage. Daughters were regarded as marginal lineage members whose ties with the natal families would be terminated once they married out to other families. They condemned the protesters for being selfish and troublemaking, bringing in Westernized outsiders to disrupt the traditional Chinese kinship system.

With the media coverage and the public outcry, an appointed Legislative Councilor, Christine Loh 陸恭蕙, took up the cause. Christine was a former Chairperson of the Hong Kong Observers, a middle class-based pressure group in Hong Kong that was vocal in influencing public opinion and pressuring the government through objective research and newspaper articles during the 1970s and 80s. An investigative journalist in the UK revealed in a 1980 article in a political news magazine that the colonial government had set up a secret committee called the Standing Committee on Pressure Groups to infiltrate pressure groups in Hong Kong and monitor their activities. While the Hong Kong Observers was considered a friendly opposition, it still bore the brunt of these pressure tactics. Although the colonial government denied its infiltrating activities, it was forced to admit the existence of both this Standing Committee as well as a Special Branch under the Police Force as an anti-Communist and anti-subversion squad. After the Hong Kong Observers' middle-class members considered its future role under the new politicized environment, they decided that they were not ready to plunge into election politics and discontinued its activities as the group in 1983.

Christine was one of Chris Patten's appointees to the Legislative Council who was supportive of human rights and democratic reforms. In response to the New Territories indigenous women's protests, she made use of the government's move to introduce an unrelated New Territories Land Exemption Bill which was originally intended simply for changed land use by the government. In the review of this bill, she proposed an amendment to the bill to lift the ban on female inheritance of rural land within the same bill. This amendment was passed by Legco in 1994, giving indigenous rural women the right to land inheritance. In 1995, women villagers were also given equal rights to participate in elections like their urban counterparts.

The success of the campaign for New Territories indigenous women encouraged the HKFWC and other women's concern groups to continue to lobby the government to protect other women's rights. The opening up of the political system in Hong Kong offered women's groups greater access to advocacy apart from lobbying the government. To gain popular support, the budding political parties jostling for electoral support were keen to be identified as "pro-human rights" and "anti-establishment," which fit the rhetoric of freedom and democracy. Women's concern groups began to demand candidates to include women's issues in their election platforms.

The Fourth World Conference on Women in Beijing

The United Nations Fourth World Conference on Women met in Beijing in September 1995. The ten-day conference was attended by 17,000 representatives from 189 countries and territories, the UN organizations and its specialized agencies as well as government and non-governmental organizations. The Secretary for Home Affairs represented the Hong Kong Government to attend the conference under the auspices of the British colonial delegation. The

Beijing conference was considered the most successful world conference on women, which was not held again after 1995, except for the various anniversary commemoration events of Beijing +5. Beijing +10, up to Beijing +25 in 2020. The Beijing Declaration and the Platform for Action, which identified twelve areas of critical concern in an agenda for women's empowerment adopted unanimously by 189 countries, was considered the pivotal and most progressive global policy document on gender equality, until gender equality was incorporated as Goal #5 in the seventeen UN Sustainable Development Goals (SDGs) of the 2030 Agenda for Sustainable Development in 2015.

In conjunction with the Fourth World Conference on Women, the Non-Governmental Women's Forum was held in Huairou, a rural town sixty kilometers north of Beijing. It was rumored that the Chinese government was wary of the potential protests by feminist groups, who might strip themselves naked in Beijing's Tianamen Square and security officers would have to prepare blankets to wrap them up if that happened. To move the potential chaos out of central Beijing, facilities were quickly constructed in rural Huairou up to the last minute to accommodate the 31,549 participants who attended the forum. Under the general theme of "Equality, Development, and Peace," 39,000 discussion sessions in addition to street-level talks and skit shows were held at the Huairou Forum to address various issues of concern to women. For many feminists, attendance at the Beijing conference and the NGO forum was likened to having been to the Mecca of gender equality.

The local organization of the Beijing conference was undertaken by the All-China Women's Federation (ACWF), the largest women's NGO in China, founded in 1949 with the dual role of bridging the Chinese Communist Party (CCP) and the government with women. The ACWF has an umbrella-like network from provincial, municipal, county, district and village branches throughout the country reaching out to grassroots women. Its mission is to represent and safeguard women's rights and interests as well as to promote gender equality. Despite the ideological commitment to women's emancipation by the CCP, which stipulated the equality of women as full citizens in the 1949 People's Republic of China Constitution, gender inequality persists under the patriarchal system of the state and the family, which holds on to the Confucian values of gender norms. The ACWF played a central role in navigating the state apparatus to pursue gender equality under the Party's ideological framework.

I was appointed as one of the special delegates from Hong Kong to the 7th to 11th ACWF's National Congress of Chinese Women between 1994 and 2017, which gave me a closer view into the work and development of ACWF since the Beijing conference. Every five years, around 1,600 provincial and regional delegates from all parts of China attended the National Women's Congress in Beijing. Everyone stayed in the large government guest house compound where we held group meetings, ate, and slept. Transporting the delegates to the opening and closing ceremonies in the Great Hall of the People was organized like clockwork. The election of the president and executive committee members of the ACWF at the plenary closing session was a miniature version of the National People's Congress, during which the delegates would cast their vote into the ballot boxes one by one. The votes were recorded by the ballot boxes electronically and the results would be tabulated and announced shortly after the voting process. Chinese organizations were experienced in mobilizing human resources to coordinate these formal activities.

On the other hand, the logistics of running the UN Conference were much more demanding. This was the first time after the 1989 Tiananmen Square incident that a large-scale international event was held in Beijing. The ACWF faced extraordinary pressure to ensure that the conference would meet up to international scrutiny. The stately Chairwoman of the ACWF, Madam Chen Muhua 陳慕華, who as Vice-Premier of the State Council was one of the highest-ranking women in China's top decision-making body, was the head of the Chinese delegation, and State Councilor Madam Peng Peiyun 彭珮雲, who later succeeded Chen as Chairwoman of ACWF, headed the Chinese Organizing Committee. The actual work of the local organization of the conference was undertaken by Madam Huang Qizao 黃启璪, Vice-chairwoman and First Secretary of the Secretariat of ACWF. I have great admiration and respect for these women leaders, who have contributed enormously to the advancement of Chinese women. In particular, Big Sister Qizao, as she was fondly remembered, dedicated her life and health to the successful hosting of the UN Conference.

With the All-China Women's Federation's Chen Muhua (middle) and Huang Qichao (second from the left) on a visit to the Equal Opportunities Commission in Hong Kong, 1997.

Feminine, soft spoken, and mild mannered, Qizao defied the Western stereotype of autocratic Party cadres caricatured by the image of Jiang Qing 江青, the wife of Chairman Mao and who was identified as one of the radical Gang of Four during the Cultural Revolution. Qizao attended to the details of the conference organization with great care. In the run-up to the reunification of Hong Kong with China, she had designated a central location for the Hong Kong Pavilion at the NGO Forum. The newly formed Hong Kong Federation of Women, chaired by Peggy Lam, would head the Hong Kong delegation and host the Pavilion. When Qizao visited Hong Kong in 1993 to attend the inaugural conference of the Hong Kong Federation of Women, she took me aside to discuss how to organize a united front of all women's groups from Hong Kong to form the Hong Kong delegation. Being trusted by both camps, I was in the position to explain to her candidly that the local feminists and activists who had fought for women's rights for over a decade would be unwilling to compromise and subjugate their groups under the newly formed federation, which they perceived to be too elitist, traditional, and pro-Beijing.

In the run-up to the reunification with China in 1997, being "pro-Beijing" was branded in a negative light by the local media and pro-democracy camp. I showed Qizao that women's groups worldwide had always been diverse, and there was no need to forge a united front in Hong Kong. Just let "a hundred flowers bloom and a hundred schools contend" (百花齊放, 百家爭鳴 *Baihua qifang, baijia zhengming*) as Chairman Mao once said. She graciously accepted my suggestion that unlike China, women in Hong Kong could have multiple voices. Qizao worked tirelessly before and after the conference, which was much larger in scale and in terms of attendance than the previous three UN congresses in Mexico City, Copenhagen and Naibori. After the conference, she was diagnosed in 1998 with late stage Mesothelioma cancer. Her health deteriorated until she passed away in 2000. Unfortunately, she was too sick by then to attend the Beijing +5 anniversary commemorations.

As I shuttled between central Beijing and Huairou during the 1995 Women's Conference, I witnessed the ceremonial grandeur of the opening at the Great Hall of the People, the mega-scale coordination of logistics, and the dynamism of global participation. Hundreds of buses efficiently transported delegates between the Workers' Stadium in central Beijing and the Huairou station. Women from all over the world voiced their experiences of common concerns in gender inequality and brought women's issues into the international agenda. Despite the heavy rain flooding the muddy streets of Huairou, women flocked in line to get into venues to hear celebrities like Hillary Clinton, who was the First Lady of the United States at the time, to promulgate "women's rights are human rights" at the NGO Forum.

The landmark UN World Conference on Women in Beijing contributed epoch-making historical significance to women's development and gender equality in China as well as across the world. Critical areas of concern and concrete strategic action were identified, presenting a pertinent agenda for national governments to follow up on. The collective voice of women reverberated for the next few decades. In addition, it provided ACWF an unprecedented opportunity to develop with an increase of overall available resources, as well as access to dialogues with upper-level Party committees. In the 1980s, helping poor women out of poverty was ACWF's main task.

The Beijing Declaration and Platform for Action adopted at the conference provided ACWF a much broader-based mandate for taking action on women's concerns, including assisting laid-off women workers with re-employment and engagement in small economic entities, eliminating illiteracy in women, improving the competence and talent of women, and promoting women's participation in politics, government, and the scientific community. The conference gave a boost to the legitimacy of women's issues within the traditional political and academic structures, providing a louder collective voice to women. It also gave rise to women's and gender studies in China as well as in many other middle- and low-income countries.

LEARNING
ABOUT WOMEN

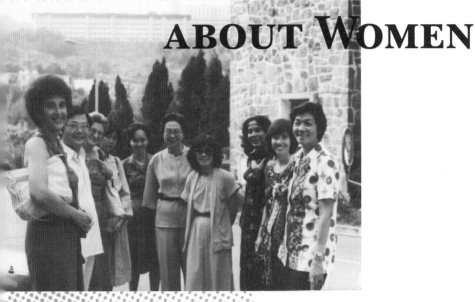

The United Board for Christian Higher
Education's Women for Development Network
on a visit to Chung Chi College, 1981.
Fanny is fourth from the right.

4

Women are diverse. On the other hand, being a woman entails commonalities of womanhood based on biological sex and the social construction of gender. From the moment we are born, our identity as male and female shapes our destiny. In many cultures, when the nurse or midwife congratulates the new parent, saying "It's a girl," the mother cries with disappointment in her failure to produce a male offspring to continue the patriarchal line. With modern medical technology, the revelation of the baby's sex is now advanced to the prenatal stage, which may lead to early sex-selective abortion of the fetus. This was one of the allegations against China's one-child policy implemented from 1979 to 2015. Although the practice was denied officially and female infanticide was illegal, the disparity in the sex ratio at birth had risen to as high as 122 rural males and 120 urban males to 100 females respectively by 2010, with long-term social implications, including a large proportion of wifeless men, sex trafficking of women, and propensity to violence against women. One of the unintended benefits of the one-child policy to gender equality was the higher educational attainment of the female single child, especially in urban families in the twenty-first century.

We seldom reflect on our identity as women and men. Most people just assume the identity as it is assigned in our birth certificate or as prescribed by how others treat us. Gender norms, expectations, and implicit bias persist throughout the life cycle. Baby girls receive gifts of pink outfits and dolls or kitchenware playsets as toys, while boys receive blue outfits and cars or guns as toys. Males and females are steered into different life courses, including choice of subjects in school, occupational choices, career trajectories, and family responsibilities. Gender differences prevail in educational level, employment rate, median income, and leadership positions.

Why do we need to learn about women or men if that is a fact of life? I only began to examine the subject out of the need to understand and persuade what I was advocating. I remember attending a hearing in the Legislative Council on the establishment of the Equal Opportunities Commission in the early 1990s, when a skeptical male LegCo member challenged the need for advancing women's rights. He claimed in his sweeping generalization: "All the senior government officials are women; we don't need a commission to protect women; we need one to protect men instead." At that time, Mrs. Anson Chan 陳方安生 was the most senior government official after the colonial governor. As the first Chinese and female Chief Secretary in Hong Kong, she projected a strong image of women power. Having prepared myself with the gender statistics in the civil service, I replied to the Honorable LegCo Member: "I have checked the number of women in the civil service. They only constitute less than 10 percent of the directorate grade or above in the Government in 1992, although that is already a big increase from the 1 percent in 1971. This is not yet one-quarter, and far below what you consider as 'all' the senior government officials. Even in the Legislative Council, there are only 11 percent female councilors. It baffles me how your honor came up to the calculation of ALL in the upper echelon of the Government are women." The Honorable LegCo Member had nothing more to say.

This type of overgeneralization based on single cases is commonly found in biases and prejudices, not only in Hong Kong. To substantiate the demands for gender equality, we needed to support our advocacy with facts, evidence, and research demonstrating discrimination against women. Even when citing research literature, gender issues had been discredited for being Western imports, which would be irrelevant to Chinese culture. When I tried to convince a tycoon to appoint more women on his company's board, by citing international research that showed corporations with more women on the board of directors were more profitable, he just brushed it off and said that those were Western studies that did not apply to Hong Kong. It was essential for us to build up our local knowledge base in order to design more culturally sensitive policies and practices for women in Hong Kong. Knowledge brings out women's voices to break the silence in the many invisible domains of their lives. Personally, I gained more understanding of womanhood after I started to study and research into women issues.

Women's Voice in Asia

Upon joining The Chinese University of Hong Kong in 1977, I brought the gender awareness gained in my community engagements into my own academic career. In my overseas university education, gender courses were not part of my curriculum. It was not until I was asked to meet members of the network of Asian women scholars from the United Board for Christian Higher Education, which was visiting the University in 1981, that I came across the field of women's studies. Although my assignment to the welcoming party as one of the few women faculty members at the university was only intended for courtesy, I struck a chord with the Asian women scholars. We shared our mutual concerns about the lack of available materials and resources to understand the issues of women across Asia. Subsequently, we formed the Committee of Women's Studies in Asia as a loose network from eight Asian countries or regions, including Hong Kong, India, Indonesia, Japan, Korea, Pakistan, the Philippines, and Thailand. Together, we published several resource books on Asian women's studies. In the process, I found common roots of women's studies in different locations from the need to provide women's movements with theoretical and empirical foundations. Women's studies evolved from the lives of women whose voices had not been heard previously.

Asian women shared many mutual concerns. In the early 1990s, when we invited authors from around Asia to contribute book chapters on topics of violence against women in their countries, we discovered that most of the authors independently converged on the common problem of domestic violence. Apparently, domestic violence had been swept under the carpet all along across Asian cultures, as it was regarded a private family matter. The centrality of marriage and family had muffled the call for help from battered wives. Wife beating was minimized and normalized by the authorities as well as by their own family members as private affairs, and often seen as the women's fault. There could be specific cultural contexts to spousal violence in different regions, such as the dissatisfaction of the husband and his family with the inadequacy of the wife's dowry in India or the illegal practice of child marriages in South Asia, but the types of violent acts and the responses were common across the regions. It took alarming tragedies to attract national attention, like the case of a Chinese husband in Changsha city hurling his battered wife from a six-story balcony to the ground for running away to her maternal home and asking for divorce. As illustrated in our edited book on violence against women in Asia[1], the silence was finally broken through the collective efforts of the local women's movements. It was important to give women their voice.

Another thing I learned personally about women's voice from one of the senior scholars in our network was that my own voice needed to be empowered too—I used to speak in a soft voice which did not carry weight, and I could hardly be heard in meetings. Even after practicing diaphragmatic breathing, I still had to use the microphone to speak in meetings and lectures. No matter how soft or subtle, we just need to find our own ways to project our voice and be heard.

These confident and poised senior women academics in Asia provided inspiring role models. Some of our group of seasoned scholars later assumed leadership locally and globally, one becoming the Minister of Education of her country, another the Chair of the UN Commission on the Status of Women, and a few others, university presidents. Working with the committee encouraged me to build up the vacant knowledge base on Chinese women.

---

1   Fanny M. Cheung, Malavika Karlekar, Aurora De Dios, Juree Vichit-Vadakan and Lourdes R. Quisumbing, eds., *Breaking the Silence: Violence Against Women in Asia* (Hong Kong: Equal Opportunities Commission, 1999.)

Launching Gender Studies in Hong Kong

Universities are supposed to be at the forefront of knowledge advancing humanity. Whereas its members are free to explore their own research ideas, the university structure is highly hierarchical and resistant to bottom-up initiatives in new disciplines. Academic merit is scrutinized by senior academics, who are predominantly men. Demonstration of student demand and funding resources are some of the hurdles. A strong case must be made as to how the academic mission of the university could not have been advanced without this new discipline. Having served on university committees for a few years taught me the foot-in-the-door tactic. Setting up research units was much more flexible in the system than proposing a new major subject or department. Criteria for considering new research centers included having a critical mass of academic staff, research activities, external funding sources, identifiable benefits, and impact. Having champions and allies in the university's review process would be very helpful. A new research program focused on specific topics under an existing research center was considered a temporary internal unit. This required fewer administrative hurdles and could be a steppingstone in getting started.

Based on years of experience in community engagement with limited resources, I learned to navigate the organizational matrix and identify windows of opportunity at CUHK. When I became the Associate Director of the small Centre for Hong Kong Studies under the Institute of Social Studies, I took the opportunity to propose setting up a Gender Research Programme in 1985. The institute director held conservative views on gender equality. He was unenthusiastic but did not want to be seen as a reactionary by rejecting this initiative, especially coming from his junior deputies. To insert his authoritative guidance, he suggested it was more appropriate to call it a "Women's Research Programme." Gender was usually erroneously equated with women, and since the proposal came from me, a woman, it would be "a woman's thing." I disagreed, to his surprise. I argued that women's issues were embedded in their gender roles and relationship with men, and that a broader and forward-looking academic framework would avoid the marginalization of research on women. Even though I expected there would be mostly female colleagues participating in the program, the term "gender" would be more inclusive and could enlist interested male colleagues to join. With the promise that the new program would not be asking for funding from the center, there was no reason to reject this bottom-up research initiative. My insistence was vindicated as a few male colleagues had become keen members and supporters from the beginning. In 2016, a Sexualities Research Programme to study sexuality and sexual minorities, another first of its kind in Hong Kong, was established under the enlarged Gender Research Centre.

The Gender Research Programme was the first research unit on gender and women's issues in Hong Kong. We later found that two other women's research units were coincidentally established in Taiwan and in China in the same year, although ours was the first one in Greater China to cover the broader perspective of gender research. Our three units held cross-strait collaborative conferences to boost mutual support in the early years. With its steady growth and scope of its vibrant activities, our program was later renamed the Gender Research Centre (GRC) in 2000 under the restructured Hong Kong Institute of Asia Pacific Studies.

When we began back in 1985, a few of our colleagues from the faculties of Arts, Business Administration, and Social Science gathered under a virtual hub to share common interests and concerns, even though there was no financial support. We started with compiling a bibliography of local studies (before the days of easy Internet search) and encouraging empirical research on gender-related issues in our own disciplines. Instead of staying in the ivosry tower, we aimed at influencing policies and practices affecting gender equality and women's development through consultancy, advice, community liaison and advocacy. In addition to academic conferences, we hosted annual gender workshops bringing together researchers, policy makers and community stakeholders in dialogue on current issues concerning women. The societal and policy impact built into the research activities of the GRC was the forerunner in university research, which had been characterized by academic silos until recent years. The requirement for researchers to demonstrate their research impact in the academic research assessment exercises of universities was introduced in the UK and Australia in the 2010s and adopted in Hong Kong since 2019. Now our universities have begun to support and emphasize demonstration of

The Gender Research Centre's Annual Workshop government guest speaker
Shelley Lee, 1995.

the societal impact of research. Why do academic institutions have to wait for
external requirements to do what is right for society?

Faculty members affiliated with the GRC incorporated their research
interests in their teaching and began to offer courses on women and gender
in their own departments. When I became Dean of Social Science in 1995, I
discovered that the range and number of courses available in CUHK sufficed
to offer an interdisciplinary Minor Programme in Gender Studies (GRS)
that did not require extra funding from the university. Without the hurdle of
central budget allocation for a major department, getting the University Senate
to approve the academic minor program only required the demonstration of
academic merit and student interest. Even during my leave from CUHK from
1996 to 1999 to launch the Equal Opportunities Commission, I continued
to help colleagues with the planning and lobbying for the new curriculum.
Starting the GRS Minor Programme in 1997 was another foot-in-the-door
tactic in navigating academic inertia.

The next move was to introduce an interdisciplinary postgraduate research
master's degree program, which also involved little additional funding. We

took advantage of the government's policy to increase postgraduate research training to convince the academic departments to partner with the GRS Minor Programme, through which faculty members could take up supervision of postgraduate students who would get a joint degree between gender studies and their home discipline. The joint degree could also provide more flexibility for graduates in their career development given the novelty of a gender studies degree in Hong Kong. In 1998, CUHK offered the first MPhil Programme in Gender Studies in Hong Kong, followed by a PhD program in 2002. The stepwise pragmatic approach we patiently undertook bore fruit.

Although I was hailed by the first cohort of graduates of the program as the "Mother of Gender Studies in Hong Kong," the program could not have materialized without the passion and dedication of our female colleagues. It was a common characteristic for the early generation of women academics to sacrifice themselves with hard work without jostling for personal gains. Upon my return to the university after three years at the EOC, I was alarmed to learn that the two co-convenors of the fledgling GRS Programme had to cough up money out of their own pockets to print the promotional posters during the admissions application exercise. Without any champion and attention from the university administration, the meager budget allocation for the program was released in arrears only one year after the students' admission, leaving no surplus funding available for student recruitment in the current year. Whereas my demure colleagues accepted the prescribed financial policy, I considered the university's bureaucracy to be unacceptable. How could our university turn our precious human capital into images of "pitiful daughters-in-law trying to make ends meet to feed the family by digging into their own pockets"? I brought the two co-convenors to meet the then University President, Prof. Arthur Li, who had earlier proudly announced his support for interdisciplinary studies. I could tell it was certainly not Gender Studies that was in his original plan, as it was off his radar. Prof. Li's strong leadership style had earned him the reputation as "King Arthur" while he carried his stately image with diplomatic suaveness. He was embarrassed to face these women colleagues, who were contributing their sweat and tears to interdisciplinary studies. I gently asked him how he could showcase his support for interdisciplinary studies given what these pioneering

The Gender Research Centre's Globalization and Women's Health Conference opening remarks by President Arthur Lee, 2000.

Gender Research Centre members on a visit to the Heritage Museum's Women's Exhibition, 2002.

colleagues had to put up with. King Arthur reiterated the importance of interdisciplinary studies in the university. The advanced funding was released shortly after the meeting.

A Home for Women Academics

Apart from its academic contributions, the GRC provided a home for our female faculty members who felt marginalized and invisible in their home departments. As junior and minority members in all departments, they faced common concerns and difficulties that were not recognized by their seniors. Tenure timetable coincided with their own life cycle of childbirth and baby care without special considerations. They were excluded from the social networks of their male colleagues and were off the radar screen of their senior male administrators for promotion, resource allocation, and nominations to awards or prizes. Their disadvantages were typically explained away by the special circumstances of each individual case. If they could not get ahead, it was based on their underachievement or lack of competence, thus rewards were not warranted.

In the 1990s, only a couple of heads among the sixty departments were women at CUHK. Up until then, there had only been two female faculty deans among the eight faculties, and none in more senior administration. We checked the data from other universities in Hong Kong, and the situation was very similar. When I joined CUHK, female students constituted less than one third of the undergraduate student population. Nobody considered that to be an issue. By 2000, when over 50 percent of the undergraduates were women, the general impression was that gender equality had been achieved in universities. The fact that women were still in the minority among graduate students and faculty members was ignored. Some senior male faculty members even lamented that with more female graduates, the university would become less competitive, as fewer of our alumni would become leaders in society. They did not consider it our mission and responsibility to train leadership qualities and skills in all our students regardless of sex. It was particularly important to sensitize our students to the gender nuances in the workplace.

Even with more women faculty members being recruited into junior ranks since the twenty-first century, the leaking pipeline to senior level prevailed over the past two decades. Women continued to remain at 10 percent or less for senior or chair professors for another two decades. By 2023, ten years after we started to show the gender statistics at the University, only 15 percent of chair professors are female while full professors had reached 25 percent. At several STEM (Science, Technology, Engineering and Mathematics) departments, there was still not a single woman faculty member in the tenure professorial track. One department head was surprised when I showed him the graph depicting the absence of any female faculty member in his department over the decades. He had never realized there was such a gender imbalance. He said he would look harder at the applicant list next time. Unfortunately, this individual effort could not solve the systemic problem of bias against women academics, and the culture the minority of women would encounter after they were recruited.

This was a common phenomenon across academia everywhere. In 1999, sixteen female faculty members from the Faculty of Science at the Massachusetts Institute of Technology (MIT) collected and analyzed the differences in salary, space, awards, resources, and response to outside offers between male and female professors, with women receiving less despite their professional accomplishment being equal to those of their male counterparts. Many tenured women professors felt marginalized and excluded from a significant role in their departments. This pattern of gender disparity was repeated in successive generations of women professors. With the support of their male dean, a committee on women faculty members was set up to compile a report which demonstrated the effects of decades of discrimination and made recommendations for change. While it was acknowledged that the discrimination was mainly unconscious, the effects were real. At MIT, the Dean of Science and the University President were committed to making long-term changes. This top-level commitment was critical. In 2023, a quarter of a century later, the MIT President, Provost, Chancellor, and

Vice-President for Research were all women, a remarkable achievement at a STEM-dominant ivy-league institute.

At CUHK, concerns about gender imbalance were sidelined without top-level administrative support. It was not until I became the first female Vice-President for Research in its fifty-year history in 2013 when we could bring gender consciousness into the university administration. Efforts were made to support the needs of and empower women academics. However, there was still no institutional commitment to comprehensive and systemic changes even when the annual statistics on gender imbalance were compiled.

Meanwhile, the GRC provided our network of female faculty members a haven where they offered one another mutual support and encouragement. We shared experience and advice on coping with work-life interface, workplace isolation, unfair work assignment, and sexist attitudes. Decades of research had demonstrated the importance of social support in the workplace to promoting psychological well-being and job satisfaction, as well as mitigating the effects of adverse conditions. In contrast to male-dominated research units, where the senior male director usually made all the decisions on research directions and resource allocations, the GRC demonstrated the collective decision-making process reported in studies of female leadership style. We ensured that men were not excluded even though a founding member with radical feminist views initially rejected men's participation. Despite most of the members being women, we wanted to demonstrate inclusivity and recruited men as allies on gender issues. I ensured that we would be sensitive to the minority men in this female-dominated environment and not repeat the oppression that women had faced as the minority. With the expansion of gender research into sexualities, male and female researchers interested in masculinities, fatherhood, and LGBTQIA (Lesbian, Gay, Bisexual, Transgender, Queer, Intersex, and Asexual) issues joined the network. Up to ten academics from different fields volunteered each year to share responsibilities as members of the executive committee of the research unit, all on top of their work at their own home department. Given the camaraderie at GRC, members did not mind the slight from their own departmental administrators on their time and contributions to the GRC, which were considered peripheral and did not earn them any credit in their performance evaluation.

Promoting Women Leadership at CUHK

Before my appointment as the first female Vice-President at CUHK in 2013, senior management was overwhelmingly men in dark suits. At the university's 50th anniversary celebration that year, I was the only woman, adding some color to the line-up of senior officials hosting the toast on stage. A picture is worth a thousand words. The glaring scene also caught the attention of some of the more gender-sensitive guests from international partner universities, whereas most of the others in the audience were oblivious to the symbolic image.

Members of the GRC were elated with my appointment, hopeful that I could bring a woman's voice to senior management. As the first woman leader at the university, I could be seen as a role model and an advocate. However, we needed to promote women leadership at the organizational level by transforming the mindset and institutional culture, introducing gender-sensitive policies and practices, and mainstreaming an inclusion framework with top level commitment.

I pondered how to project women onto the radar screen of the administration. As the Vice-President for Research, I organized the first luncheon gathering for women researchers to celebrate International Women's Day in March 2014. I invited the University President, Prof. Joseph Sung, to come and greet our female colleagues. I told him that with his busy schedule, it would be nice to at least come at the beginning to welcome our colleagues. With insider information about his presence, members of the GRC came prepared with a list of challenges faced by women faculty. Joseph stayed through the whole lunch, and at the end, was persuaded to set up a Task Force on Women & Family-friendly Policies. One year later, Prof. Sung told me that with my inspiration, he has decided to appoint Prof. Isabella Poon to be the second Pro-Vice-Chancellor. In 2025, Prof. Poon was appointed as Provost of the University.

Naturally, Joseph asked me to chair this task force. I deliberately broadened its remit with an aim to promote a working environment that is responsive to the needs of women and colleagues with family responsibilities, so that it would not become marginalized to the sideline, as another "Fanny's thrust." I insisted that the task force should be co-chaired by both a female

The lone woman at the CUHK 50th anniversary banquet toast, 2013.

At CUHK's International Women's Day celebration, 2019.
Fanny is second from left, front row.

and male vice-president and included representatives from faculties, colleges and administration. We surveyed the needs of our female colleagues, which revealed the dire plight of the lack of breastfeeding facilities on campus. We learned that female staff without their own offices had to pump their milk in storerooms or the toilet. My task force co-chair was a professor in pediatrics and his expertise was called to the fore to design the nursing rooms. We garnered resources for this purpose by nudging different colleges and offices to set up these rooms at convenient locations. There are now seven nursing rooms accessible across campus. To raise awareness, we compiled gender statistics on our website to show the low representation of female faculty members in senior ranks. We reviewed and enhanced gender-sensitive policies. To empower our female colleagues, we set up a support network matching junior women faculty with senior professors, and organized women leadership training. Both structural changes and capacity building are needed in the promotion of women leadership.

The underrepresentation of women in senior leadership positions in higher education was not confined to CUHK, or even Hong Kong. In solidarity with the newly-appointed female vice presidents of the University of Hong Kong and the Hong Kong University of Science and Technology, we went on a roving road show to raise gender awareness in the local universities. We compared ourselves, the three female VPs, to the Three Tenors, whose successful concert performances around the world in the 1990s promoted opera to a wider global audience. I was also invited to join other international forums to share our experiences of addressing these issues, including the British Council Going Global Conferences, the European Women Rectors Association, and the World Women University Presidents Forum.

In a 2020 special issue of the *International Brief on Higher Education* published by the American Council of Education, I wrote an introductory article summarizing the disappointing state of women's leadership in higher education across the world. Even among the more advanced Anglo-based countries, women university presidents only reach as high as 30 percent. The percentage in other parts of the world are far lower. The gender gap in academia is not confined to the top level. There is a leaking pipeline that shows a

At the CUHK-HKU-HKUST Tri-university Women's
Leadership Training Workshop, 2017.

At the 5th European Women's Rectors Association
conference in Brussels, 2017.

decreasing proportion of women at the senior professoriate level. International gender research has shown detriments for women in tenure rate, pay, and publications. These detriments are heightened by the internationalization and commodification of universities emphasizing KPIs (key performance indicators), ranking and h-index. The COVID-19 pandemic and working from home restrictions have exacerbated women's handicaps, which will affect the gender trend in the coming decade. Apparently, the culture of gender is a dominant theme that is still resistant to change in higher education.

It is gratifying that gender consciousness has become institutionalized at CUHK, and that the GRC continued to contribute to gender-sensitive policies and practices at CUHK in the Sub-Committee on Women Academics under the Diversity and Inclusion Steering Committee, which was established in January 2022, taking over the function of the temporary task force, to support women academics and empowering their leadership development and promoting a supportive workplace. I will talk about the Diversity and Inclusion Committee at CUHK in Chapter 8.

Advancing Gender Equality

Beyond the university, the GRC played a key role in advancing gender equality in Hong Kong. In the run-up to 1997 when Hong Kong was to be reunited with China, the British colonial government started to introduce democracy to Hong Kong during its last decade of colonial rule. Whereas the British appointed governors since World War II were mostly colonial administrators or diplomats with Chinese backgrounds, the last governor, Chris Patton, was a politician and the Chairman of the Conservative Party. He lost his parliamentary seat in Bath in 1992, and Prime Minister John Major appointed him as the twenty-eighth and last governor of Hong Kong in the same year. With his political skills vastly different from the previous colonial administrators, he quickly gained popularity and started political reforms in Hong Kong, five years before the reunification.

With increasing active campaigns from women's groups for gender equality in the early 1990s, coupled with the pro-human rights stance of the politicians and the pro-democracy stance of the governor, the government bureaucracy finally responded. In 1993, the government conducted the first public consultation on sex discrimination in Hong Kong with the *Green Paper on Equal Opportunities for Women and Men*. As there was no central government repository on gender issues, the Principal Assistant Secretary from the Home Affairs Bureau had to rely on the resources of the university's GRC to draft the background of her policy paper. This was the first time the Hong Kong government had compiled any data focusing on the status of women. In the Green Paper, the government acknowledged persistent earning gaps between men and women but tried to evade the problem of discrimination by explaining these differences with non-discriminatory variables, including differences in education, capabilities, and experience. The women's concern groups and Legco members did not accept the government's conclusion and pressured the government to examine the extent of sex discrimination in Hong Kong using an empirical survey.

In 1994, the GRC was commissioned by the government to conduct this survey. We were glad to be able to win the bid and shape the research design. We realized that if we asked public respondents simply whether they believed there was sex discrimination in Hong Kong, the answer would likely be "no" as the concept of discrimination was foreign to the public at that time. Many public opinion polls were designed with such simplistic questions. Instead, we designed more sensitive questions that addressed specific areas where women were treated less favorably than men in a variety of domains in employment, education, and social roles. By anchoring the questions in real life situations, more distinct answers were obtained which demonstrated public consensus on the existence of discrimination against women in many domains in Hong Kong, including less favorable treatment in employment, education, leadership positions, and social image. The government could no longer evade acting on sex discrimination.

Meanwhile, the political scene in Hong Kong in the run-up to 1997 became more pronounced. Appointed LegCo member Ms. Anna Wu 胡紅玉, a human rights lawyer, introduced her private member's bills to cover a broad range of equal opportunities protection under a Human Rights & Equal

Opportunities Commission. This comprehensive human rights framework was resisted by the colonial government as too radical. In response to the demands of women's concern groups, and the parallel demands of groups representing people with disabilities for protection against discrimination, the colonial government opted for a more gradual approach by creating an Equal Opportunities Commission with a circumscribed scope to combat sex discrimination, and disability discrimination under the first two anti-discrimination ordinances proposed by the government and passed by the Legislative Council in 1995. The Family Discrimination Ordinance was added in 1996, and the Race Discrimination Ordinance was added much later in 2009. I will talk more about my involvement with the EOC in Chapter 5.

Combating Sexual Harassment

Even before the Sex Discrimination Ordinance came into effect, the GRC took the lead in addressing the issue of sexual harassment in education and employment. The legal concept of sexual harassment was first raised in the United States in the 1970s by women's groups in universities and in books on sexual harassment of working women. The MIT was one of the first major institutions in the U.S. to develop specific policies and procedures aimed at stopping sexual harassment as a form of sex discrimination in the early 1970s. Sexual harassment gained international attention in 1991 during the U.S. Supreme Court nomination in Congress, when Lawyer Anita Hill accused the nominee, Clarence Thomas, her former supervisor at the U.S. Department of Education and the Equal Employment Opportunity Commission, of sexual harassment. During the highly politicized hearing, Hill's credibility was repeatedly challenged, and Thomas's appointment as Supreme Court Judge was eventually confirmed by the U.S. Congress with a narrow margin. The televised hearing had pushed the issue of sexual harassment beyond academic and legal circles into the national and global consciousness. Even with this heightened awareness, sexual harassment has prevailed across the world, while victims suffer in silence. It took another twenty-five years before another surge in attention across the world reignited public concern. Following the exposure of numerous sexual-abuse allegations against American film producer Harvey Weinstein by actresses and models in October 2017, the MeToo movement began to spread virally as a hashtag on social media, raising awareness on the prevalence of sexual abuse especially in the workplace, and empowered vulnerable women through empathy and collective strength. The hashtag and campaign trended in over eighty countries.

Back in 1994, we learned from several GRC members about incidences of sexual harassment on the CUHK campus. Instead of relying just on anecdotal reports, we decided to conduct the first study of students' awareness, experiences, responses, and expectations of institutional intervention to sexual harassment at the university. With little resources, we managed to collect close to 1,000 returns from students attending the weekly or monthly assemblies in their colleges. We found that one in four students indicated they had experienced sexual harassment in various forms, with 1 percent having been coerced into sexual activities by their peers or teachers in the university. Between 13 and 30 percent of the female students experienced peers' sexist remarks about their bodies and various unwelcome intimate seductive behaviors such as kissing and caressing hands, whereas 12 percent of them reported experiencing teachers' misogynistic remarks about the female gender as well as unwanted physical contacts such as leaning over, cornering, putting arms around shoulders, or taking hands. The rates of various forms of sexual harassment experienced by male students were much lower at less than 10 percent and were usually from male peers. Two female students reported being bribed into sex by their teachers and one woman was a victim of coercive sexual activity. The students only resorted to avoiding or ignoring the harassers to protect themselves. The majority concurred that the university should take up an active role to combat sexual harassment. This survey provided the facts to bring the issue to the attention of the university's senior management.

The then University President, Prof. Charles Kao 高錕, who later received the 2009 Nobel Prize in Physics for his work on fiber optic communications, was an open-minded scientist with liberal views. Sadly, his Nobel Prize came after he was afflicted with Alzheimer's disease, and his wife, Gwen, had to read his acceptance speech on his behalf. Gwen took care of him through different

At Charles Kao's 80th birthday, with Gwen Kao (left), at CUHK, 2013.

stages of his illness until he passed away in 2018, and set up a foundation to relentlessly promote public understanding of dementia.

Prof. Kao was a most caring president. Conscious of the isolation of the campus community, he and Gwen initiated a women's club at CUHK to provide social support and networking for wives of expatriate faculty members, many of whom were recruited from overseas and unfamiliar with the local culture and environment. The network was later extended to female staff members. Cognizant of the issues of sexual harassment in American campuses and companies where he had previously worked, Prof. Kao immediately agreed that CUHK should take up the responsibility to protect its students and staff. He asked me to join an ad hoc committee to set up a policy to address sexual harassment. Had it not been Prof. Kao at the helm, others would not have been as forthcoming.

In 1995, CUHK became the first university in Hong Kong to adopt a Policy Against Sexual Harassment. A committee was set up to handle complaint investigation as well as promote education and training. To prevent sexual harassment, the committee promoted awareness and understanding of what constituted unwanted sexual advances and hostile sexual environments through circulars, leaflets, weblinks, seminars, and workshops. In setting up the committee to implement the policy, we ensured there was gender balance among committee members and resource persons to gain broad-based support across different sectors in the university. This presented a unified stance and avoided the perception of bias against men. We developed training programs for administrators and later, for all teaching staff. Based on our experience, we rallied other universities in Hong Kong to develop similar policies.

The CUHK policy was adopted as the model for promoting public awareness and prevention of sexual harassment in education and employment by the EOC when I became its chairperson in 1996. After I returned to the university, I continued to share the CUHK policy and mechanism with higher education institutions in Macau and mainland China and provided training workshops. At CUHK, students, faculty and administrative staff now have to participate in online training modules on the prevention and handling of sexual harassment.

Having policies in place does not mean that the problem will be solved. Unfortunately, we continue to witness cohorts of university freshmen across Hong Kong being subjected to sexual harassment and exploitation during the student-run orientation camps. Where did this begin and where is it going to end? I hope we have the answer and solution.

Disaggregated Gender Statistics

Although disputed, the nineteenth-century British Prime Minister Benjamin Disraeli was attributed by Mark Twain as having coined the phrase: "There are three kinds of lies: lies, damned lies, and statistics." This mistrust of statistics reflected how statistics could be manipulated to support almost any position. When I taught students about poorly designed surveys, I cited the case of a survey conducted in the early 1980s during the residents' protest against the government's plan to set up the first psychiatric halfway house in a Shatin housing estate. Frightened by the stigma about psychiatric disorders, the "not-in-my-backyard" sentiment among the residents was fanned by pro-democracy elected district board members who pandered to their fear. In 1984, the two politicians showed the results of a survey in which they asked the residents with a leading question: if they would "object if the government insisted to impose the halfway house in their housing estate." As expected, 98 percent of the respondents said they would object. The biased questions and the timing of the survey produced results that served the need of the politicians to show that they were the people's champions. They argued that the Shatin District Board should reject the government's plan. I was an appointed district board member at that time. I considered the halfway house to be a safe and much-needed facility where there would be supervised rehabilitation care before mental patients in recovery would be reintegrated into the community. To counter the two politicians' argument, I designed another equally biased survey for the Shatin District Board. We surveyed a broader sample of Shatin residents and asked if they cared about their own and their family's mental health, and whether they would like the government to install more mental health facilities in the community. Framed in a positive tone, most of the respondents said yes to these questions. These divergent results showed how statistics could be manipulated for different purposes. Blind references to these simple statistics without considering the methodology or analyzing the results would not lead us to better understanding of problems or formulation of policies. Unfortunately, the media in Hong Kong tended to report sensational survey results as presented without scrutiny.

Even with scientifically conducted surveys, how the results are interpreted can affect the conclusions. With the government census demographic statistics, which were based on strong methodological design, the use of combined average data often masked the discrepancies between different subgroups in the population. Given the differences between women and men in many life domains, using average data of the whole population could not illustrate important disparities.

At the 1995 Fourth World Conference of Women in Beijing, the concept of gender statistics was incorporated in the Beijing Platform for Action, the defining framework for change, with comprehensive commitments under twelve critical areas of concern related to women's rights. One of the actions to be taken up by national governments was the collection, analysis and use of data disaggregated by sex and age, and other established demographic criteria and socio-economic variables, in policymaking, planning, monitoring and evaluation. Sex-disaggregated data could reflect areas of inequality, problems, and issues related to women and men in society so that governments could identify actions to advance gender equality and women's empowerment.

Prior to the introduction of women's studies, academic research in many fields had been gender blind. Academic research claimed to be neutral and scientifically unbiased, but early research samples were often limited to male participants and conclusions were generalized as if it could be applicable to everyone. Beyond biological differences, there are differences in every society between what is expected and allowed in women and in men, resulting in differential impact in their lives. Although the female sex is considered the stronger biological sex due to lower prevalence of sex-related genetic diseases and longer life expectancy, early research on many diseases did not include women, resulting in inaccurate diagnosis and treatment. For example, the lack of gender analysis and representation of women in medical research has resulted in flaws in evidence-based medicine, affecting diagnostic accuracy and treatment efficacy in heart diseases, chronic pain, bleeding disorders, and autoimmune conditions. Research findings that were pertinent to men might be irrelevant or even harmful to women in areas of health, mental health, business, education, and social science.

Economic policies that do not consider gender differences in labor force participation, which further intersect with marital status and education, would be off target. The 2023 Nobel Prize in Economics recognized the trailblazing research of Prof. Claudia Goldin at Harvard University on women in the labor force. She traced the history of women's participation in the labor market in the United States, which increased in the later part of the twentieth century due to women's higher educational attainment and the availability of birth control pills. However, the earnings gap persisted, which could be traced to women's role in parenting, corresponding with the birth of their first child. Goldin offered a recipe for narrowing the pay gap between men and women: more government funding of childcare and more jobs in which people could share duties.

Likewise, the low female labor force participation in Hong Kong concentrates in married women with low educational levels. Single women with tertiary education are as actively engaged in the labor force as men. The gender differences reflect the family responsibilities undertaken by married women, especially among those who could not afford hired domestic help. Governments that are now promoting high fertility rates in developed economies must consider these gendered contexts and design policies to entice fertility such as the provision of affordable quality childcare for families and promoting gender equity in family responsibilities.

In awarding Claudia Goldin the 2023 Nobel Prize, the chair of the prize committee said, "Understanding women's role in labor is important for society." He lauded Goldin's groundbreaking research for illuminating the key drivers of gender differences in the labor market and the barriers that need to be addressed in society. The recognition of Goldin's gender research in economics not only pointed to her achievements in conferring the "greatest benefit to humankind," but it also authenticated the academic standing of women's studies and answered many queries on why we study women.

Until 2001, the annual statistics published by the Hong Kong Census and Statistics Department had not provided breakdown by sex, which made it difficult to identify areas of gender disparity. The GRC decided to take the lead to demonstrate the value of compiling statistics disaggregated by sex. In 1995, we published the first gender profile in Hong Kong.[2] Based on key social indicators in the annual census, we showed how women and men differed in areas of education, work and employment, marriage and family, health and welfare, crime and punishment, as well as political participation over a period of two decades since 1971. These statistical trends showed how educational attainment, especially among girls, increased after the policy of mandatory and compulsory education up to Form 3 or junior high school came into effect in 1978. Prior to that, many girls from poor families had to quit secondary school to start working to support their brothers to go on to college. With the increase in university places in the early 1990s from 2 percent to 18 percent of the secondary school graduates, the percentage of university students reached parity in the late 1990s. By 2020, the increase in female university students stabilized, with women making up 54 percent of the undergraduate population.

---

2   Robert Westwood, Toni Mehrain and Fanny M. Cheung, *Gender and Society in Hong Kong: A Statistical Profile* (Hong Kong: Hong Kong Institute of Asia-Pacific Studies, The Chinese University of Hong Kong, 1995).

Sex-disaggregated data in economic activities showed the disparity in men's and women's medium income, with women earning only eighty-five cents to the dollar of men's income, even when industry and job level were considered. Marital status demographic trends from 1966 to 1991 showed that the percentage of never-married men and women at age twenty-five to thirty-four increased about 200 percent and 950 percent respectively. Whereas more men entered marriage later in life, more women remained single throughout their lives. Overall divorce rates had increased about 510 percent for men and 590 percent for women, with more women heading single families. Gender divide in demography was able to reveal areas of concern that should be considered in policy planning, including the declining fertility rate and social services for single families.

Over the years, the GRC lobbied the Census and Statistical Department to adopt sex disaggregated data in presenting its annual statistics. The bureaucracy was resistant to change. It was only after the Women's Commission (WoC) was established in 2001 as the government's central mechanism for women's advancement that sex disaggregated data was published by the department. Our 1995 statistical profile of gender and society provided the blueprint for the Department's annual edition of Women and Men in Hong Kong— Key Statistics.

Internationally, gender disparity began to be incorporated in global measures of human development in the 1990s. The United Nations Human Development Program (UNDP) introduced in 1995 a Gender Development Index (GDI) and a Gender Empowerment Measure (GEM) using sex disaggregated data and as a compendium to the Human Development Index (HDI) in its annual Human Development Report. The HDI is a statistical composite index that includes life expectancy to represent a long and healthy life, mean years and expected years of schooling, which represent education and knowledge, and gross national income per capita of a country, representing the decent standard of living of the people in that country. The HDI is used to rank countries' development into four tiers of human development, with the Western developed countries in the top ranks. The GDI is a composite index which measures development within a country and then negatively corrects for gender inequality based on gender-gaps in life expectancy, education, and incomes. The GEM measures women's access to attaining power in economics, politics, and decision-making positions. These indices of the relative ranking of countries allow international comparisons on the status of women. For example, in 1995, Japan ranked the ninth in the world in its HDI, the highest among Asian countries, but its GDI rank dropped to thirteen and its GEM rank was even lower at thirty-eight. For South Korea, its HDI rank was thirty, GDI rank was thirty-eight, and GEM rank was eighty-three.

Small differences in the rankings between GDI and HDI suggest gender parity, whereas large differences reflect likely gender discrimination in those countries. However, with the components of GDI riding on the coattail of the income level of the country—which also affects indices covering health and schooling provided in the country—the difference between the GDI and HDI was artificially small. These early gender indices were heavily criticized by experts for their inability to accurately capture gender disparities. In the 2010 Human Development Report, the UNDP introduced an independent Gender Inequality Index (GII) to capture the loss of achievement due to gender inequality based on three dimensions: reproductive health (maternity mortality rate and adolescent fertility rate), empowerment (share of parliamentary seats and post-secondary educational attainment), and labor market participation (women's participation in the paid and unpaid workforce), excluding income level of the country. With a separate value and ranking from that of the HDI, the GII may be interpreted as the percentage of potential human development lost due to gender inequality. In 2023, the Nordic countries were in the top ranks, with Iceland leading with a GII at .91, which showed less than 10 percent loss of human development due to gender inequality. The best GII in Asia was the Philippines at .79, followed by Singapore at .73. South Korea, China, and Japan trailed behind at .68, .67, and .64, respectively. The gaps showed that gender inequality in these countries had usurped potential human development by around 20 to 30 percent.

As can be seen from the methodological challenges of the UN indices, compiling accurate data of gender disparities is a demanding task. Yet, it is only the first step to assess areas of gender inequality to be addressed. We must bear in mind that differences between the two sexes per se may not indicate sex discrimination. For example, women's longer life expectancy compared to that of men is a biological fact based on sex differences in genetics as well as lifestyle. On the other hand, the under-representation of women in leadership positions is underlined by unequal access to opportunities, gender-based norms and stereotypes, as well as biased attitudes against women. Even for the minority of women who have made it to the top, many have remained single and/or childless in contrast to male leaders. The gender divides in career track and in the interface between work and family reveal the societal backdrop under which the inequality unfolded. While gender statistics pointed us to the direction, further analyses and research would be needed to uncover the reasons for the inequality which may indicate direct or indirect, as well as deliberate or unconscious discrimination. The complexity of gender discrimination demonstrates it is not easy to give a simple conclusion as to whether gender differences would be an indication of sex discrimination, and whether the same or different treatments of men and women may result in discrimination or the resolution thereof.

Learning about Women's Leadership beyond Statistical Studies

Trained in the empirical tradition in psychology at the University of Minnesota, my research had always adopted quantitative methods, which were deemed more scientific under the positivistic orientation in modern science. The academic counting game of citations in high-impact top-tier journals had shaped research in psychology and other fields of science and social science with prescribed research methodology, statistical analysis, and report format. To control for confounding factors that might affect the outcome of the studies, the research conditions were dissected into simple variables that could be manipulated to illustrate the direct relationships. On the other hand, given its interdisciplinary nature, gender research adopts multiple methods, including ethnographic and descriptive approaches which deviate from this positivistic approach. As a result, it suffers from the slight of the scientific elite circle. This has hampered the status and recognition of gender studies and gender scholars in academia. Yet, most quantitative studies reported average values of a sample that illustrated the characteristics of the majority but paid little attention to the outliers. To deconstruct the nuanced meaning of gender differences, qualitative research can help in contextualizing the objective data with more in-depth analysis of the circumstances and experiences that led to these differences. The qualitative approach can provide much richer information to understand the outlying minority who do not fit into the average, such as the handful of successful women leaders who stood out among other women.

Even though I was regarded as a gender expert in the community, gender issues had been on the periphery of my mainstream academic research in psychology, which focused on cultural perspectives in personality and assessment. My studies and publications on women's issues rode on my involvement in advocating women's status, using quantitative surveys to understand violence against women or health risks of women with multiple roles at work and at home. These quantitative studies were insufficient to understand the complex contexts of women's experience.

As I contemplated on my own research on gender issues, I saw the need to expand into women as agents of change and not only women as victims. Why are there so few women reaching leadership positions? Nobel Economics Laureate Claudia Goldin found that the bulk of the earnings difference between men and women in the same occupation arose largely when they have children, given the unequal division of unpaid caregiving and household labor between couples in the family. Thus, they had less time to dedicate to their careers.

Early research on the gender earnings gap focused on women's deficits and disadvantages under traditional norms and systemic barriers. Studies talked about the double burden for professional women without illuminating solutions. Western feminist values that promote women's autonomy and empowerment were regarded by Asian men (as well as some conservative women) as threats to the family or social harmony. Little attention was paid to the need to promote men's role in sharing caregiving and household chores in the family. Is it possible for women to succeed in bridging the gender gap despite these social norms and barriers to have both a successful career as well as a happy family? I wanted to learn about the resilience and agency of the rare cases of women leaders with children who defied all odds to overcome the barriers to reach the highest levels of their careers.

I reckoned it would have been difficult to get a research proposal for such a qualitative study past the reviewers in the field of psychology from the Hong Kong Research Grants Council. Qualitative and exploratory studies without rigorously designed methods to test hypotheses would be deemed preliminary. The opportunity for launching such a study arose when I was selected as one of thirty-one international scholars in the 2004 Fulbright New Century Scholars Program with the theme of that year being "Toward Equality: The Global Empowerment of Women." With the project grant, I could spend a year interviewing women leaders from China and Hong Kong on their work-family interface. One requirement for the Fulbright grant was to include an American perspective and an American collaborator. I decided to expand the study into a cross-cultural comparison with American women leaders and invited Prof. Diane Halpern at Claremont McKenna College to collaborate with me on the project.

Diane is a distinguished psychologist who specializes in cognitive development and cognitive differences between men and women. In 2004, she was elected President of the American Psychological Association. One of the central themes of her presidential priorities was the issue of combining work and family. We met in an unusual circumstance, being at opposite sides of the historic sex discrimination lawsuit in Hong Kong between the EOC and the Education Department on the controversial secondary school places allocation system. Before I finished my term as Chairperson of the EOC, I had launched a special investigation into the system, which was found to be discriminatory. The EOC recommended the Education Department to revise the allocation system in line with nondiscriminatory and modern pedagogic practices. I discussed with the then Director of Education on the way forward on changes to the system. Unfortunately, both of us left our positions shortly thereafter. When the new Director of the Education Department refused to make the change, my successor at the EOC initiated a lawsuit and won the case. Diane was the government's expert witness on sex differences on the development of cognitive abilities of boys and girls. After the Education Department lost the

Dinner with Diane and Sheldon Halpern in Beijing, 2004.

lawsuit, Diane worked as the government's consultant to help revise the system for secondary school placement.

As psychologists, we agreed on almost everything related to the secondary school places allocation system as well as the preference for an amicable resolution instead of the costly and bitter legal battle. Since our initial meeting at an American Psychological Association conference, before she came out to Hong Kong as the government's consultant, we have become close friends and admirers of each other's work. Diane is a rigorous researcher with gender and cultural sensitivity. For the Fulbright project, she was much more than a research collaborator. She and her university hosted my sabbatical visit in the U.S. when I conducted my interviews with American women leaders. We worked together seamlessly to interpret the findings from the interviews, bring out the cultural contexts, tie in the relevant research literature, and write up the report and later a book.[3] When we exchanged our drafts of the book

---

3   Diane F. Halpern and Fanny M. Cheung, *Women at the Top: Powerful Leaders Tell Us How to Combine Work and Family* (Chichester, UK: Wiley-Blackwell, 2008).

manuscript, we often could not recognize which of us had written those parts of the chapters, as our thoughts converged. During this truly collaborative process, we discovered our mutual styles of doing our best for our work while our husbands gave us relentless support throughout the entire process. When I spent my two-month sabbatical at Claremont McKenna College, my husband Japhet took leave from the university to travel with me in the U.S. and assisted me with the study. Likewise, Diane's husband Sheldon has been a champion of her career. When Diane later came out to Hong Kong for three months to work with me on the manuscript for the book, Sheldon supported her separation from the family and came along initially to help her settle in Hong Kong before returning to his attorney work in California.

Between 2004 and 2005, I successfully interviewed sixty-two women with families and prominent leadership positions, about twenty each in the U.S., China, and Hong Kong. The group of women leaders included government officials, politicians, corporate CEOs, entrepreneurs, university presidents, professionals, and philanthropists. In the U.S., most of my interviewees were contacted through the California, New York, and Texas chapters of the International Women's Forum (IWF), an organization of pre-eminent women at the top of their professions, of which I am a member of the Hong Kong chapter. In China, I contacted women leaders in Beijing and Shanghai through contacts at the All-China Women's Association, the China Association of Women Entrepreneurs, as well as universities and personal networks of the leaders. In Hong Kong, I knew most of the top women leaders in the public and private sectors through the IWF Hong Kong chapter and my previous position at the EOC and other public engagements.

The stories of the women leaders in my study enriched our understanding of their early life course, and how they evolved into their leadership positions while managing their family responsibilities at the same time. Their narratives illuminated their leadership styles and the challenges they had overcome along the way. They showed how women could combine babies and briefcases for dually successful lives by adopting effective time management strategies and redefining the normative roles for good mothers and good leaders. They did not create stressful expectations of "supermoms" for themselves, but they were conscious of their family being their priority. They were not typical women. What stood them apart was how they had all built a strong sense of self-efficacy and commitment. More importantly, they concurred that it was essential that the husband or partner was supportive, not only in sharing the household responsibilities, but also the emotional support, encouragement and coaching for their career development. Their husbands were self-confident and regarded their wives' accomplishments not as their own failures, but as the success and pride of the whole family. While there was a lot of give and take, the family built a strong emotional bond. The revision of the mindset from the zero-sum game that "when women gain, men will lose" to the notion of mutual benefit could help remove one of the major barriers and resistance to women's leadership.

At first, I thought there might be more cultural differences between the American and Chinese women leaders. The Western women's movement, as well as affirmative action and family-friendly policies in U.S. corporations, would have afforded American women a more liberating context. Under the more individualistic orientation in Anglo culture, success at work would be seen as a source of self-actualization. In the Western dualistic polarity's perspective, women's commitment to their work poses a challenge to work-family balance when time is taken away from the family. This challenge does not seem to apply to men. Thus, we find more women in leadership positions to be single, divorced, or childless. Other women drop out in the leaking pipeline.

In Chinese culture, traditional Confucian values can place women in a more restrictive role. This subservient role of women has changed gradually with modern economic development, when more women need to work outside the home to support the family. In collectivistic cultures, the needs of the self are subsumed under the needs of the family. The extended family, usually the grandmother, plays an important role by providing support on childcare and household chores. In the early days of centralized economy in China, work allocations often separated the couple to different geographical locations. The care of their children was entrusted to their own parents. Many of the mainland Chinese women endured hardships during the early days of poverty and then disruption to their studies during the Cultural Revolution. However, these women leaders did not harbor bitterness toward their suffering but understood their life course in the context of the country's developmental process. Several of them who had gone through the turmoil of wars and famine said that without a country, there would not have been a family. The self was voluntarily subsumed under the collective. Their resilience and positive attitude in life underlined their current success in reaching the top of their careers.

From the experiences of the group of American and Chinese women leaders who were mothers in the study, we were surprised to find more cultural similarities in the shared culture of gender being women, which overrode the differences in their historical, socioeconomical and cultural backgrounds. Gender roles were similarly prescribed, and sexism existed across cultures, even though they might be expressed in distinct forms in the different cultures. While all the women leaders regarded their motherhood role to be more important than their career, the expression of what were important tasks for a mother diverged between the American and Chinese mothers. American mothers emphasized the importance of never missing their children's school play or soccer game, while Hong Kong mothers emphasized helping their children with their schoolwork. Chinese mothers in both the mainland and Hong Kong considered it a priority to eat their dinners together with their children and family first before going out on their own business dinners or going back to work in the office at night. The concept of the family dinner was much looser in American dual career families. When I was visiting Diane, I saw her often just taking out what was conveniently available from the refrigerator and eating whatever and whenever time was available. I always prefer to have a sit-down dinner when everyone is home.

With their sense of self-efficacy and personalized strategies of work-to-family transitions, the women leaders in our study were able to make it to the top while combining work and family. They demonstrated confidence in developing their own leadership style that combined caring for colleagues and demonstrating competence in leading the organization. They did not have to be cloned into the masculine stereotype of authoritative and hierarchical leadership. Instead, many of them promoted a more inclusive style. These dually successful women leaders provided role models to other women, showing that they did not have to choose between work or family. Their stories underpinned research that demonstrated better corporate performance in organizations with women's representation in senior management. Their success further dispelled the dualistic zero-sum dichotomy in gender equality, that women had to choose between work or family, and that women's success meant men's loss.

This study was by no means representative of Chinese or American women leaders, as they were a special group of women who were successful in combining work with family. Their experiences showed other women that it was possible, although it was hard work to be dually successful. These women leaders not only aspired to succeed, but they also had developed a sense of self-confidence in their competence to do so, climbing one rung at a time. In preparation for motherhood, they got their husbands involved in making the decision and participating in the preparation for life as a family. In so doing, they redefined the normative roles for good mothers and good leaders and rejected self-imposed or unconscious guilt. They found creative ways to integrate work and family and make work-to-family transitions easier with the use of pre-planned personal rules. From their successes, we compiled a checklist of practical ideas for combining work and family and making it to the top.

Women and women leaders are diverse, and their leadership styles are not uniform. The social, economic, political, and cultural contexts that women need to navigate are also different. We are conscious of the increasing heterogeneity in the norms of gender and leadership which underline our future scholarship in studying women. Despite the increase in representation of women in leadership positions in the business world, and the occasional breakthrough of women in the political arena, many of them still share the traditional barriers and challenges. There is so much more to learn about women and women leadership.

Beyond Western Perspectives on Gender Studies

Womanhood was shaped not only by the biological and evolutionary foundations of men and women, but also by the sociocultural contexts across time. The international and regional conferences hosted by the GRC brought together Western and Asian gender scholars to share their research on women's issues. While women across the world share many experiences under the culture of gender, the epistemology of gender studies had been dominated by Western perspectives, which may not fully represent women from the Global South and non-Western countries. We needed to strengthen our local scholarship to understand women in the context of Chinese culture.

In the 1980s, female scholars in different disciplines in mainland China began to meet and discuss their common concerns on women's issues. Research groups and associations on women's studies sprouted spontaneously. Women's studies provided Chinese women the support for their struggle to break away from the grip of class theory, highlighting women as a distinct category deserving scientific and scholarly research. The 1995 Fourth World Congress of Women in Beijing further legitimized the conceptual framework of gender introduced in contemporary Western feminism. Promoting a gender consciousness as well as women's voluntary participation in women's own cause was incorporated into the agenda of the All-China Women's Federation, which began to advocate for the adoption of gender analysis in all levels of decision making. The Chinese Women's Research Society was formed in 1999 as a national academic network under the umbrella of the All-China Women's Association, to organize and coordinate women's/gender studies academics in order to establish Chinese women's studies with its own cultural and socialist characteristic.

Like Hong Kong, there were few Chinese scholars in the new field who were formally trained in gender or women's studies at the beginning. Through the enthusiastic initiative of a Chinese-American scholar at the University of Michigan, collaborative projects had been established between the university and women's studies scholars in China since 2000, including the University of Michigan-Fudan Joint Institute for Gender Studies at Fudan University, Shanghai. Through my contacts with colleagues at the University of Michigan Institute for Research on Women and Gender, we came up with a joint proposal between our two universities to co-train the young gender scholars and professionals as trainers in different Chinese universities, to prepare women faculty and to expand programs in the emerging area of women's studies. With the funding support of the Henry Luce Foundation, we proposed seven courses in 2002, with a postgraduate diploma in women's studies offered

At the China Gender Studies diploma graduation ceremony, 2004.
Fanny is on the far right.

by The Chinese University of Hong Kong over two summers to be held at the Chinese Women's College (CWC). (The second year was delayed by the disruption of the SARS epidemic.) The decision to choose the CWC, rather than a more prestigious university, as the site for the program was based on several considerations. Conscious of the potential risks of creating this new field in China, the involvement of the CWC, a branch of the official All-China Women's Federation, legitimized the establishment of women's studies as an academic field, and in turn, helped to mainstream feminist scholarship in the official educational system of the federation which consisted of twenty-six other cadre schools. This international graduate program helped to raise the academic standards and credentials of women's studies faculty in the CWC, which had designated women's studies as the specialty of their college.

The four teachers from the U.S. and Hong Kong provided the introduction to Western feminism, with cultural adaptations and cross-cultural perspectives based on our experience in Hong Kong. Three mainland Chinese scholars offered the historical and social perspectives of women in China. The transnational learning community also exposed the American feminist scholars to the Chinese cultural contexts of women's concerns. The class of twenty-two trainees graduated in 2004 with a celebration in a typical style among Chinese women's groups—a singing and dance performance by the teachers and students. I wondered how the Western feminists perceived the awakening of gender consciousness among these Chinese scholars. Similarly, the Chinese scholars were intrigued by the pressing inquiries from one of the American professors when she checked into the hotel, asking where she could find the Starbucks Coffee Shop. She was worried that she would be deprived of her daily dose of caffeine in China. She was amazed to find two, not just one close by her hotel. Nowadays, gender studies has begun to flourish in many universities in China, helping to build up the knowledge base on Chinese women's issues. Transnational exchange and collaboration in gender studies have become more common. The study of gender has also expanded beyond simple categories of womanhood and manhood.

Women's and men's experiences are contextualized in multiple dimensions in terms of gender, class, age, ethnicity, and other social dimensions. Research highlights the importance of recognizing the intersectionality between gender and culture or other social locations, which affects the socialization and development of women from different parts of the world. Yet, most books on the psychology of women include research on Western women only, raising questions about the validity and cultural relevance of the theories and practices in gender studies.

When I was attending an international conference in Milan, Italy in 2015, I was approached by the Commissioning Editor of psychology books at the Cambridge University Press, Janka Romero, to write a book on cultural psychology or psychology of women for the press. At that time, I was busy with my administrative work as the Pro-Vice-Chancellor of my university, and I was hesitant to take up a major publication task. Janka was persistent and followed up with me during the next few months, exploring the idea of an edited handbook or a written textbook on the psychology of women. Despite my hesitancy, the idea of the handbook fit my mission of promoting women's development by building up scientific evidence, as well as bringing the cultural perspective in the psychology of women. I immediately thought of my good friend and collaborator, Diane Halpern, as my co-editor for an edited handbook that would provide an international perspective on the psychology of women. As a prolific author, Diane was efficient and thoughtful about the options for this handbook. In no time, we came up with a list of ideas for the book. I checked out these ideas with Janka when she caught me in between my meetings at the 2016 international conference in Yokohama, Japan. She was keen to prompt us to go ahead. Without such a supportive and trusting editor, I would not have embarked on this editorial journey.

Why do we need to study the psychology of women? Early psychological research had tended to ignore the lives of women, who remained invisible. The perception of women's attributes and behaviors were often affected by myths, biases, and unfounded beliefs. Scientific research on the psychology of women helped to fill the gaps, debunk popular myths, and deconstruct the similarities and differences between women and men, as well as among the diversity of women, before gender inequality could be addressed. Diane and I drew up a comprehensive list of topics based on the general domains that were critical to understanding the gendered lives of women. We covered the theoretical and methodological underpinnings of sex differences, the life-span development of women, cognitive and social factors, work and family issues, inequality and social injustice, as well as health and well-being. To ensure the incorporation of international perspectives in each chapter, we identified a lead author and at least one or more co-author from or familiar with a different region or culture in the world. The final version of the *Cambridge Handbook of the International Psychology of Women*[4] consists of thirty-eight chapters and over 560 pages, with over 100 authors (of whom twelve were men) from all continents of the world. The rich materials covered in the chapters broadened our horizon of evidence on the diversity of women's experience beyond Western textbooks.

While we found many universals in the lives of women across the world, such as the common problems of domestic and sexual abuse, body esteem, and barriers to career development, their experiences varied due to geopolitical and historical developments, such as racial and caste segregation, one-child policy, migration, and post-colonial struggles. In the Global South, child marriages,

---

4 Fanny M. Cheung and Diane F. Halpern, eds., *The Cambridge Handbook of the International Psychology of Women* (Cambridge, UK: Cambridge University Press, 2020).

bride price, and polygamy underline the ecological context of domestic violence. Despite child marriage and domestic violence being criminalized in all countries, many families remain unaware of the law. Sociocultural norms in Africa and South Asia normalized and justified wife beating, restricting the impact of legal changes. In North, East and West Africa, female genital mutilation (in which the external female genital is partially or completely removed) persists even though this cultural practice is legally banned. Mothers concerned about their daughters' marriageability would subject them to be cut before puberty. This reminds me of the Chinese cultural practice of foot binding imposed on young girls since the tenth century until it was outlawed in the early twentieth century.

The international perspective also challenged some existing theories that were assumed to be universal. Previous suicidality theory in the English-language literature were primarily dominated by American studies, which conceptualized suicide in a mental disorder paradigm in which suicide was regarded as a form of mental illness. Risk factors in these Anglo-centric cultures based on studies of men of European descent were attributed to the perception of being a burden to others, and the act of suicide was a distorted call for interpersonal belongingness. Studies of suicide among women in Muslim-majority communities and in China challenged the assumed connection to mental illness. Instead, by attending to the socio-economic and cultural contexts, women's suicidal behavior could be seen as a desperate rebellion against the suffocating environment of inequality and abusive life conditions. Listening to the diverse voices of women supports a much-needed paradigm shift for the field of suicidality.

Many scholars editing a big handbook often lament about the taxing chore of managing chapter authors on deadlines, delays, missing information, and other mechanical details of academic writing. For me, the experience of editing and writing for the *Cambridge Handbook of the International Psychology of Women* was gratifying, not only professionally. The camaraderie among the authors during the process made it worthwhile. Many of us shared life events of medical conditions, family illness, childbirth, loss of loved ones, and other challenges in the critical stages of our personal lives during our joint journeys. We got to understand and appreciate the culture and contexts from which we all came. Despite our diverse backgrounds and orientations, we shared a common vision for science and the passion for gender equity. The lived experience made writing for this handbook much more passionate and compassionate than the mechanical paper chase in which researchers had to churn out journal publications to fulfill their academic performance requirements. Our only regret was that the COVID-19 epidemic in 2020, when our handbook was published, had usurped our plan for the authors to meet and share the insights from the various important topics at several international conferences.

Expanding the Gender Binary

As I continued to learn about women, I became more educated about the disruptions to our traditional concepts on gender which, in the past, were presented in the binary categories of men and women. We divide the population into two halves based on the biological sex, with which they are assigned at birth based on the shape of their genitals. As we discard our assumptions that women are homogenous, we need to consider the intersections of socioeconomic status, race, sexuality, religion, age, geographical location, and other demographic variables. In different contexts, racism, classism, ageism, heterosexism, and various combinations of these biases affect the realities of women from different backgrounds. For example, young women in the lower caste in India are more at risk for poor sexual health outcomes and death due to pregnancy or childbirth. In America, poor, black and minority-status women experience more brutality and violence than White and middle-class women. Furthermore, we can no longer restrict ourselves to the two normative categories of male and female when we begin to understand more about the diversity in gender identities, including lesbian, gay, bisexual, transexual, intersex, queer, gender-less, and other variations. The marginalization of these sexual minorities who experience greater victimization reflects the complexity in our understanding of gender equity.

Recognition of these diversities challenges the way we collect data about the participants in our studies. We used to ask our participants to indicate their sex or gender under two categories. I remember when I was conducting a survey for my doctoral thesis back in 1974, asking for the "sex" of the participant was a standard item. I quickly changed the open-ended question to "gender" with a choice of male and female after a male participant filled in the answer "YES" to the question of "sex."

Nowadays, this binary choice is being challenged, and there are objections to reducing the self-declared gender identity to the three categories of "male," "female," and "others." Gender scholars are still pondering how to address this question with sensitivity and respect. Some public toilets have added a neutral option apart from the conventional designation of men and women toilets. These contentions prompt us to contemplate more deeply into our understanding of gender equality. Learning about women and men is an ongoing learning process through continuously listening to different voices.

BREAKING
NEW
GROUND

The EOC senior directorate team in 1999.
From the right: Angela Ho, Fred Tong, Fanny,
Michael Chan, and Alexandra Papadopoulis.

5

The year 1996 may be considered a watershed in anti-discrimination efforts in Hong Kong. With the establishment of the Equal Opportunities Commission in May, a central mechanism came into being for the first time to protect the rights of women and persons with disabilities with statutory powers. The United Nations Convention on All Forms of Discrimination Against Women was extended by the British Government to Hong Kong in October with the consent of China that year. The first sets of anti-discrimination laws, the Sex Discrimination Ordinance (SDO) and the Disability Discrimination Ordinance (DDO), came into full operation in the same year.

Established under the SDO that passed in 1995, the EOC consists of a full-time chairperson and sixteen members from different backgrounds appointed by the government to represent diverse interests of the community. The design of the powers and functions of the EOC was modelled after the Equal Opportunities Commission in the UK and the Victorian Equal Opportunity and Human Rights Commission in Australia. The members of the Commission formed the governing body with statutory authority to perform the functions and exercise the powers of the commission as stipulated by the ordinance. Although fully funded by the government, the EOC was not considered an agent of the government and acted independently as a body corporate. Yet, the degree of control and influence that the government could exercise through its appointments, funding, and accountability to the Home Affairs Bureau (HAB) was a point of tension and had been criticized by human rights activists for undermining the independence and governance of the EOC. There were high expectations from the civil society, countered by great anxiety and resistance from the business community. Coming in amidst an increasingly politicized climate as Hong Kong edged toward reunification with China, politicians and journalists quickly jumped on the bandwagon as protectors of human rights. To the public, the concept of equal opportunities was novel, confounded with myths, and confused with equality, sameness, and fairness. This was the hot kitchen that I entered when I became the founding Chairperson of the EOC in May 1996.

The Appointment Knocked at My Door

In 1995, I was elected Dean of the Faculty of Social Science at CUHK. Busy with my new responsibilities, I had not followed closely the debate on the passage of the anti-discrimination ordinances. I was certainly happy to see the establishment of the EOC after years of campaigning for a Women's Committee under the government. Given my long-standing involvement with the women's movement and with rehabilitation services, as well as my track record of serving in many governmental advisory committees, I reckoned I was likely to be appointed as one of its members. I had not considered the chairperson position of the EOC because it was a full-time position which meant that I had to leave the university and my deanship. As the new dean, I was committed to guiding the directions for the seven departments of the Social Science Faculty at that time with many new and innovative (at least for my university at that time) initiatives at the planning stage. I was just interested in being able to contribute to the directions of the EOC as a member.

Many people perceived public offices in terms of power, status, and privileges. The EOC Chairperson position was set at a high status, comparable to the ministerial level Bureau Secretaries of the Hong Kong government. In the civil service hierarchy, it was pitched at D8, the highest directorate grade just below the three principal officers of Chief Secretary, Financial Secretary, and Attorney General. Other than the salary, there was the provision of an executive car with a chauffeur. The grade also afforded first class air travel (before 1997, which was subsequently changed to business class travel after the reunification). I was told later that the D8 level and structure of the EOC was matched with the Office of the Ombudsman to reflect the importance of the commission and its power to take legal action on the government if necessary.

As I had not been keeping track of the government's preparation for the EOC, I was oblivious to the political wrestling on this potentially sensitive position. Human rights activists were pushing their advocates to make rapid social transformations, while the business community leaders were wary of litigious mavericks. Apparently, I was considered a balanced and safe choice by the government. Having served on the Shatin District Board, the Regional Council, and many governmental advisory committees with a progressive, pragmatic, and steady style for over a decade, I had gained the trust of senior officials, especially in the Home Affairs Bureau in charge of setting up the EOC. The Deputy Secretary of the Bureau approached me to apply for the chairperson position.

I was reluctant, very reluctant. I truly enjoyed my academic work and did not want a career in public office. Apart from having to resign from my deanship less than a year after my election and leave the CUHK, taking up this demanding job meant that I would have less time for my family. Both my husband, Japhet Law, and I were professors at the university. Though we were busy with our teaching, research, and administrative work, we lived on campus and could spend our free time together.

However, it was Japhet who convinced me to go ahead to take up the new position. Japhet had all along teased me for being the natural-born romantic volunteer who kept serving for the sake of serving, without looking at the impact or return. Being trained in mathematics and operations research, he had a sharp, analytic, and logical mind. Having joined the Business School at CUHK and serving as the Associate Dean of the Business School at that time, he had always been more pragmatic in his approach, strategic in his planning, and tactical in action. He pointed out to me that being just a member would not be able to steer the direction of the EOC in the same way as the founding Chairperson. Having spent all my life advocating for the advancement of women and protecting the disadvantaged, I should take this opportunity to elevate my mission to the next level. He understood and supported my cause and commitment.

Japhet was not only true to his word; after I took up the new position, he became the self-appointed advocate on many informal occasions to inculcate in other skeptical males, including businessmen and public officials, the meaning and value of equal opportunities. He was much more articulate and vigorous and would have been more effective than me in the man-to-man talk. He accompanied me to official social functions and was often the only man amidst hundreds of women in those events. He boasted that no other man in Hong Kong had had this credential.

Coming close to the application deadline, the government official urged me again. I finally agreed to put forward my application and attend the selection interview. Upon being offered the position for a three-year term, I told the Secretary of Home Affairs, Mr. Michael Suen, that I would only accept it if I did not have to resign from the university. In the government, there was a practice called "secondment" by which officials would be temporarily transferred to another position while retaining their original employment. There was no such practice of temporary absence at CUHK. Mr. Suen offered to discuss this with our Vice-Chancellor, Prof. Charles Kao. Charles was open-minded and supportive of my service to the EOC. Eventually, the university set the precedent by granting me a three-year no pay leave to serve the government, after which I could return to my original position. This new personnel policy later paved the way for other colleagues to take up short-term government appointments.

The transition to the new position took the next few weeks as the government was under pressure to set up the EOC. I had to inform my colleagues and department chairs, work on the handover with an interim Dean of Social Science, arrange caretaker supervisors for my doctoral students, as well as resign from all my NGO positions to avoid perceived conflict of interest. I got special approval for informally guiding my students on their thesis during my spare time, which turned out to be odd hours in the evenings or weekends. I had to do a crash course to comprehend the provisions of two discrimination ordinances, consulting legal experts along the way. I assumed the new position at the end of May in 1996.

There was a change in lifestyle when I had to leave the bucolic work setting at CUHK and commute through the traffic jam in early hours to the office tower at the Convention Centre in Wanchai. Throughout my work life, I had avoided commuting and had lived close to where I worked. I even preferred staying in the simple stripped-down single room at the United Christian Hospital in industrial Kwun Tong over my comfortable home at Number 8 Macdonnell Road during my first job in Hong Kong. The time and energy that I saved provided a much better quality of life. The only compensation for the EOC commute was the provision of a chauffeur that came with my position, who drove me to work every day. Even though I was embarrassed by the D8 status symbol of the executive class of vehicle with a personal chauffeur, which was likened to the pecking order in Number 8, I appreciated the convenience of being driven through the traffic jam during the long commute when I could read my documents and catch up with EOC-relevant issues in the daily newspapers.

Laying the Foundation of the EOC

My first task as the Founding Chairperson was the mundane chore of designing the layout and ordering furniture for the EOC office. The Home Affairs Bureau (HAB) had seconded six executive officers and clerks to help me to set up the office and run the members' meetings. Before the commission could start operation, I had to hire my management team and the key operational staff for the complaints handling, the legal, and the administrative and promotion divisions. The structure and staff strength of sixty had been designed by HAB in its original proposal submitted to the Legislative Council to set up the EOC. Over the first three months, I conducted over a hundred recruitment

At the EOC's senior management morning press briefing
with Angela Ho, 1997.

interviews shortlisted by the administrative staff to fill the thirty officer-grade staff positions, with the participation of some of the other EOC members. Although the attractive remuneration packages resulted in many applicants, the challenge was to identify the right candidates who were committed to the cause. The concept of equal opportunities was novel in Hong Kong, and few of the candidates understood the work of the EOC. We had to screen out those who were only interested in the pay from those who were genuinely interested in the new challenges. One candidate simply said she was no longer interested when being told that her civil service pension would be suspended when working in the EOC, which was a statutory body. We were glad we did not need to waste our time interviewing her further. When the division heads were in place, they took up the duty to recruit the remaining supporting staff. As this was a brand-new initiative, intensive staff training had to be quickly organized for the new officers and staff on the two ordinances, issues of discrimination and operating procedures for handling enquiries and complaints.

One of my best recruits was Mrs. Angela Ho Choi Wai Yee 何蔡慧兒, an Assistant Commissioner of the Labour Department, who filled the Chief Executive position. Although she admitted to not being familiar with equal opportunities issues before, she had been engaged with employment laws and selective placement services for job seekers with disabilities. She later told me she was impressed by my vision during the interview and in our follow-up personal meeting, which raised her enthusiasm about the new challenge. It was worth waiting three months for her to move over to the EOC. With her experience as a seasoned administrator and a popular official with the labor groups, she was a dynamic pillar to the office, which allowed me to concentrate on the strategic directions of the EOC. Over the next three years, she competently motivated staff members while managing personnel problems with strong governance and fair procedures. Given her civil service experience, she provided me with timely advice for handling the government bureaucracy and the political arena.

Building Consensus as a Body Corporate

Before the employment provisions of the Sex Discrimination Ordinance and the Disability Discrimination Ordinance could be brought into effect, the legislation required that the EOC issue Codes of Practice on Employment under the two ordinances to facilitate the compliance of the employment sector. It stipulated the EOC to undertake two rounds of public consultation on the codes and vetting by the Legislative Council. As a body corporate, I had to get the disparate EOC members to come to a consensus on the vision, mission, and the strategies of the commission. Members who took a more human rights stance supported a more legal approach, while the more conservative members were concerned about community harmony. We went on a full-day retreat on a luxury yacht generously offered by one of our members to brainstorm our ideas. At the end of the day, the members were happy to settle on a holistic approach

EOC members brainstorming retreat, 1996.

for the EOC to promote equal opportunities and eliminate discrimination with the support of the community. For many members, the cultural concept of social harmony was important, and it was not the intention of the EOC to create animosity and class conflict. We agreed to build a firm foundation based on the guiding values of equality, fairness, integrity, sensitivity, energy, and efficiency.

The consensus between different interests was also achieved later in the selection of the design of the EOC logo. The final decision was to combine two contrasting designs which consisted of the more angular first character of "equal" in Chinese 平 *ping*, which also means "level," in the center, surrounded by silhouettes of heads in circles representing different people. This consolidated design satisfied all the members. Despite their divergent professional backgrounds, political orientations, and personalities, the sixteen members appointed by the government were cooperative and civil during discussions. They contributed to the formulation of policies deliberated in the four committees set up to help steer the operations of the commission: the Administration and Finance Committee, the Community Participation

Committee, the Public Education and Research Committee, and the Legal and Complaints Committee. Many of our dedicated members worked long hours with me to launch our commission into action.

While most of the members who were committed to the cause of equal opportunities were seasoned professionals and experienced in public service, there were individuals who were appointed from various interest groups, including a member of the rising pan-Democrat camp who was vocal in human rights slogans but lacking in true understanding of the subject matter. They would distract the substantive proceedings of the meetings. Despite the confidentiality undertaking and the agreement that any collective EOC decisions should be centrally disseminated via the Chairperson, embargoed documents under preparation were still leaked to political parties and the media. That was the political reality with which we had to tolerate.

How should we carve out the work of the EOC in its first three years? With my knowledge of social psychology, I understood that legislation might at best be able to restrict unlawful behavior, while discriminatory attitudes— which could not be governed by law—had to be changed through long-term educational efforts. Based on my previous experience of social campaigns, I steered a comprehensive promotional strategy of preventing discriminatory acts and changing discriminatory attitudes by reaching out to the community directly. A four-pronged strategy was launched to secure compliance and reform through legislative means, promote education to raise awareness, strengthen communication with community organizations and corporate partners to promote participation and non-discriminatory practices, as well as conduct research to guide our forward direction. This comprehensive approach rallied the members together and was well received by stakeholders.

Animal Farm of Politics

During the three years at the EOC, I learned much more about the animal farm of politics, underscored by hypocrisy and questionable integrity that was antithetical to the values in academia. Democracy in the form of direct election was rushed into center stage by the colonial government, especially the last governor, shortly before the reunification. Even though I could survive in the arena, my close encounter with the immorality of many players raised questions about the proclaimed sanctity of democracy as a universal value, when personal gains and thirst for power subjugated the interests of the people. The rising guises of populism and political kabuki which fanned extremism in Hong Kong and across the world in the twenty-first century reified my disdain for political life.

During the political transition in 1997, junior pan-democrat politicians trying to steal the spotlight often targeted the EOC in political posturing with unfounded criticism to attract media attention. Initially, we reckoned that they were not familiar with the legislation and had a misconstrued notion of the role of the EOC. One ardent political critique had repeatedly blamed the EOC in the media for not prosecuting residents of a private housing estate, who had protested the establishment of a clinic for AIDs patients near their estate. The anti-discrimination ordinances were based on the principle of tort in civil laws, which required claimants who suffered loss or harm to come forth to either file a lawsuit in the district court against a plaintiff for compensation and relief from the wrongful act, or file a complaint with the EOC for investigation and then conciliation. The civil law did not include criminal offenses, which would be prosecuted by the government's law enforcement agencies, and not by the EOC. For the EOC to take action under the statute, an aggrieved person needed to come forth to make a complaint. So far, nobody had been aggrieved yet as the clinic had not been set up yet. At that point, we could only promote public understanding on the acceptance of people with AIDS, prevention of discrimination, and the safety features of the clinic.

To help the rookie politician understand the provisions of the Disability Discrimination Ordinance and the role of the newly founded EOC, I invited him to visit our office for a meeting with our Legal Advisor and the Director of the Disability Division. After over an hour of introduction and legal explanation by the experts, the politician nodded as if he finally understood. However, as soon as he came out to meet the waiting reporters whom he had invited to our office, he blasted the EOC for being intransigent in refusing to prosecute the residents. I was sure it was not the incompetence of my colleagues who failed to educate him, or his lack of intelligence to comprehend the law—which would have been worrisome as he was supposed to be a legislator. Unfortunately, despite my disdain for political theatre, being a public figure drafted me into the kabuki script.

At the same time, the sensational and oversimplified reporting by the media helped to fan misconceptions about the concept of equal opportunities and the role of the EOC. The rise in the popularity of the sensational tabloid, *Apple Daily*, which had become the best-selling newspaper since it was launched in 1995 until it was shut down in 2021, transformed the eco-system of traditional broadsheet newspapers. I was disappointed that our universities had not trained our journalism graduates to be more thorough with their investigation, and more balanced and objective in their reporting. I noticed that many of the reporters attending our press conferences were novices with little experience and low pay. To minimize errors in reporting, we drafted more detailed press statements to be distributed to the reporters after press conferences. We prepared answers to anticipated questions for the question-and-answer sessions. Notwithstanding the contents of the reports, the headlines were designed and decided by editors to capture attention. It did not matter that the caption might be discrepant or unrelated to the substantive report, which might mislead the casual readers.

Given the hostile media reporting during the initial period, some friends who were seasoned executives kindly recommended that I could hire a media consultancy company to help build the EOC image and provide media training for our senior staff. Some of the tips we picked up were helpful, like giving simple answers and keep repeating key messages. I had to learn to discard my habit of attentive listening and responsiveness to questions as a psychological counsellor and become single-minded in getting my message across. In hindsight, I should have stood back and asserted my case irrespective of the accusative remarks of the interviewers. In the early days before the ordinances were brought into effect, one expatriate journalist in a live show kept accusing me for not suing an employer that was reported in the newspaper for its discriminatory practice of requiring its female employees to wear dresses and not pants. Instead of just explaining about the legal framework of dress codes provided by my lawyers, I should have gone on the offensive by making use of her presumptuous blaming attitude before ascertaining the facts and circumstances of the case as an illustration of how prejudices and biases were formed.

At that time, I was still naïve in my expectations of journalistic professionalism in reporting the truth. This continued until twenty years later, when I witnessed the biased media narratives with geopolitical agendas even among well-established and respected western media during the social conflicts unfolding in the region and other parts of the world. Harvard historian Prof. Jill Lepore's bestseller, *These Truths: A History of the United States*, captured ardently the absences and asymmetries in what was assumed to be the truths in historical records, and the ways that media could be and had been manipulated for political causes.

Winning over the Business Sector

The business community had been most opposed to the creation of the EOC during the legislative debate. They were worried that the new anti-discrimination laws would increase labor conflicts and litigation costs. My first official lunch at the EOC was with one of our own members, Mr. Andrew Leung 梁君彥, who was a General Committee member of the Federation of Hong Kong Industries at that time. He later became the President of the Legislative Council in 2016. Andrew invited me to meet with a few representatives from the business sector who expressed their concerns about the role of the EOC.

I reassured them that equal opportunities policies were actually good for business, based on the growing research literature that showed greater profitability among corporations that adopted diversity and inclusion policies. I also offered to work with employers and human resources officers to promote training on best management practices. While international corporations were more knowledgeable of and compliant with anti-discriminatory laws, the local firms—especially the small and medium-sized enterprises (SMEs) (with less than 100 employees in the manufacturing industries and less than fifty employees in other sectors), which made up over 95 percent of the enterprises in Hong Kong—lagged behind. Many of the employers were entrepreneurs starting their business from scratch. They still adopted traditional modes of employment practices, which included blatant stereotypes. Antiquated newspaper advertisements which specified sex-specific positions such as female clerks or receptionist and male managers or sales executives constituted 37 percent of the recruitment advertisements in the print media when the anti-discrimination laws came into effect at the end of 1996.

Under the law, the publishers and advertisers bore the legal responsibility for ensuring that advertisements published did not indicate any intention of discrimination. Before taking legal action on the discriminatory advertisements immediately, the EOC wrote to the publishers, advertisers, and employment agencies to advise them of their legal responsibilities. We also provided examples of proper advertisements that would fulfil their recruitment needs with "genuine occupational qualifications" without reverting to outdated stereotypes. Instead of specifying a woman for the receptionist position, the recruiter could advertise the qualities expected of a receptionist such as language skills and courtesy, or meticulousness and filing skills for a clerk. For the manager position, it was more important to consider training background, communication skills, knowledge of the field, and management experience. We reminded the employment sector that decisions based on stereotypes restricted the range of eligible candidates to be chosen. Initially, the newspapers, which were the majority publishers of the classified ads, were up in arms. Many articles appeared in the newspapers blasting the EOC for its "frivolous" and "disruptive" laws, and for upsetting traditional social norms. Undaunted by the media flurries, we persisted in sending reminders whenever we spotted the unlawful advertisements. After six months of relentless education and monitoring, the number of discriminatory advertisements dropped to less than 1 percent. It had become a non-issue for the media by then—no longer frivolous or disruptive!

Unlike other discriminatory acts, which had to be filed by the aggrieved persons to the EOC for investigation and conciliation, unlawful discriminatory advertisement was one of the few areas where the EOC had direct powers to bring legal proceedings. After the first six months of educational efforts, the EOC took legal action against five newspaper publishers and one advertiser in 1997, who were later given penalties of HK$1,000 to $2,000 fines by the court. The message was clear and discriminatory advertisements became history thereafter.

The most recalcitrant case involved a sexist advertisement for "several pretty female reporters to report on balls and parties" in a Chinese newspaper with a reputation for sensationalism. This aroused widespread public interest and debate. Although the original intention was obvious, and the newspaper initially apologized to the EOC for not scrutinizing the advertisement before it was published, the newspaper picked up on an alternative interpretation in the media debate based on the ambiguity of the Chinese statement. Without punctuation, the statement could mean that they were recruiting reporters to report on pretty girls in the parties. The newspaper presented this as its defense. The District Court originally dismissed the case, as the ambiguous advertisement could have an alternative interpretation. On appeal by the EOC, the Appeals Court concluded that the advertisement was discriminatory.

Employment-related discrimination constituted most of the complaints under the anti-discrimination ordinances. Cognizant of the sexist biases prevalent in the Chinese community at that time, and the lack of awareness among local employers about their statutory responsibility in preventing discrimination in the workplace, the EOC produced pamphlets on Good Management Practices, with practical guidelines on specific areas of concern to accompany the Code of Practice on Employment, as well as training modules with video clippings of what to do and what not to do in various scenarios. The popularity of the free training workshops offered to managers inspired the later formation of the EO Club with individual and corporate membership to promote a diverse and inclusive culture in the workplace. Employers and the human resource personnel had come around to appreciate the benefits of modern management practices. The ethos of diversity, equity and inclusion policies in the workplace had now become recognized as a proud asset of modern corporations.

One of the most contentious issues strongly resisted by the employers initially was the determination of sexual harassment. As employers, they felt it was unfair to them to be responsible for preventing and intervening in sexual harassment in their companies. The employers argued that it was difficult to distinguish sexual harassment from office romance. They claimed that courtship among colleagues was common and given the typical demure behavior of Chinese women, the men had to be more aggressive and persistent to win them over. Given that these interactions occurred in private between individual parties, the management would not be able to judge what happened after the fact. They further believed that these claims often happened after the relationship turned sour or if the women were given unsatisfactory evaluation from their male supervisors. The determination of a "sexually hostile environment" was even more enigmatic, as it did not involve physical contact. How could they know when a funny joke, for example, could be perceived as being hostile?

To help the management to understand the nuanced distinction between sexual harassment and normal human relationship, I shared two related concepts: "respect" and "power differential." Consensual relationship and positive office culture should be based on respect and not aggression. Even though the perpetrators might not intend to be offensive, the recipients might feel offended as compared to an average person under similar situations. However, when there was a power differential between the position of two parties, the onus should be on the person with power to ensure that the absence of overt rejection did not mean an implicit consent. In addition, we produced a special training module on sexual harassment at the workplace with videoed scenarios of sexual harassment and a sexually hostile environment. We presented recommendations for action to be taken with samples of record-keeping notes for the victims and handling procedures for the management. We showed ways in which the victims could convey that the behaviors were unwelcomed. Above all, we encouraged the management to promote awareness and training in the workplace as preventive measures.

Sexual harassment has persisted as a major complaint under the SDO. Originally, the unlawful act was only covered under the employment-related provisions of the SDO. Given my experience in setting up the anti-sexual harassment policy at CUHK, we organized workshops and training programs for universities, which were both employers as well as educational institutions.

The provision involving sexual harassment in education was finally added to the SDO in 2008. As with the worldwide trend after the #MeToo movement, the heightened awareness and continued prevalence of sexual harassment—as revealed by a series of research studies commissioned by the EOC—had led to the establishment of a dedicated resource platform on the commission's website.

The business sector's initial fear of the proliferation of litigation did not materialize. Most of the legitimate complaints were resolved by conciliation. Only a few cases that were not successfully conciliated received support from the EOC to proceed to the District Court with the purpose of illustrating the case law. At the end of my three-year term, a leading legislator from the business sector commented in a radio interview that I had been fair-minded and balanced in leading the EOC. He told me in private, however, that his constituents would still need to be critical in public. According to his analysis, if I were equally criticized by the activists and the conservatives from both ends of the spectrum, I should have been doing things right. Such was the tactic in the political arena.

Reaching Out to the Community

Equal opportunities and discrimination were foreign concepts in the local community when the EOC was established. They involved abstract values with practical implications. Myths arising from misunderstanding abounded when we began to promote these concepts. Popular misconceptions included: "Equality meant that everyone was born alike, and this could not be true"; "Promoting gender equality was denying sexual differences and trying to make men and women the same"; "Equal opportunities meant that everyone should be treated in the same way without any special consideration, which would be considered reverse discrimination."

The English words "equality" and "equity" are translated into the same Chinese term, 平等 pingdeng. In English, "equality" is closer to the meaning of fairness through equal access or treatment, whereas "equity" recognizes the imbalance in the starting point that requires adjustment or accommodation in order to reach a just outcome. In recruitment or school admission, an equal opportunity policy means that everyone with the same capability should be given equal consideration without regard to irrelevant biases such as sex stereotypes or stigma toward disabilities. Under an equity policy, individual differences are recognized, and people who have been disadvantaged at the outset due to disabilities or a history of discrimination may be given special consideration at the starting line so that they could reach the same outcome. In Hong Kong, the discriminatory laws did not include affirmative action or special quotas for disadvantaged groups, a provision which had led to allegations of reverse discrimination in some countries. The only allowance to level the playing field was the special accommodation arrangement to facilitate persons with disabilities to perform the inherent requirements of their jobs under the DDO, such as the provision of special equipment for persons with visual disabilities.

In actual practice, the nuanced interpretations of these concepts were more complex. We needed practical cases and examples to illustrate these concepts to educate the public. To help the public to change attitudes and comply with the laws, we should put ourselves in their shoes and understand their misconceptions and habitual practices. With new laws affecting many sectors of the community, we needed to reach out to address the stakeholders' concerns. This reminds me of the government's new waste charging scheme, originally targeted for implementation in April 2024, to reduce municipal garbage with the use of prepaid, government-approved garbage bags. The public and stakeholders were still confused about the details of the scheme three months before the target date. There were many practical gaps in the implementation process. In response to the public clamor, the Director of Environmental Protection made an unempathetic remark, drawing further public ire. In an interview, he commented that those who wanted to follow the law could have found their ways to understand the law, implying that the onus was on the public to take the initiative to find out about what they should or should not do. Following this public relations fiasco, the government subsequently decided to delay the implementation by another four months and strengthen its promotion and public education efforts. After four months, the scheme was further suspended until an indeterminate date.

In the first three years of the EOC, we collaborated with the media in an all-out front on public education to produce television and radio programs, short advertisements as public announcements, as well as articles in the print media. So far, the *Hong Kong Standard* had been more balanced in its reporting of the work of the EOC. Instead of just reporting negative and sensational stories, the senior editor agreed with our aim to educate the public. We collaborated on publishing fifteen short articles in the newspaper to promote the concepts of equal opportunities, dispel the myths, and illustrate the provisions of the anti-discrimination ordinances, which were later compiled into a bilingual booklet entitled *On Common Ground* (平等檔案室 *Pingdeng danganshi*) and distributed to interest groups. These educational materials were fundamental to the promotion of equality in human development. After the representative of the UN Development Program Office in Beijing read our booklet, she found it to be very helpful in their own work in China and ordered 100 copies of the Chinese version for its distribution.

Our public education strategies aimed at both breadth and depth to reach across the community. Social psychology research showed that in changing attitudes, facts would be less effective than daily-life encounters and storytelling. We could identify better with others' feelings and experiences as we read or watch their stories. Beyond rational understanding, empathy and viewing events from others' perspectives would help to enhance altruism and reduce prejudice. Other than regular publicity messages on radio and television, we worked with the government public broadcaster to produce stories illustrating different forms of discrimination in a TV docu-drama series which was shown on prime time, and in ten drama series on radio which reached an average of 1.3 million listeners. With our community participation funding program, we supported initiatives from over eighty community organizations to launch activities to promote equal opportunities to their stakeholders. Our special Education TV program targeted junior secondary school students. My colleagues and I gave over 700 talks and seminars to companies, educational institutions, labor unions, social service agencies and other stakeholders in the first three years.

For me, that was much more than the psychology lectures that I had to give to my students at the university. To multiply our educational efforts, we produced training modules to train the trainers with case vignettes for human resources personnel, social workers, teachers, and community leaders.

With my strong belief in evidence-based practice, we informed our work through regular surveys about areas of discrimination for people due to their disabilities or their gender. We also conducted periodic evaluation of public attitudes. In the first three years, we launched four surveys on public attitudes toward sex discrimination and disability discrimination to identify obstacles and hindrances, as well as to establish the baseline subjective indicators on attitudes toward equal opportunities and discrimination for future comparison.

These surveys not only guided our directions on areas of concerns, but they also helped us to gauge public awareness and understanding of the work of the EOC. At the launch of the EOC in September 1996, only 35 percent of a representative sample of 2,000 respondents had heard of the concept of equal opportunities. Eighteen months later, the percentage of awareness rose to 87 percent. An overwhelming 98 percent of the respondents supported having an anti-discriminatory body like the EOC. The number of complaints received by the EOC rose by 195 percent in the second year and 109 percent in the third year to a total of more than 1,200 complaints. The success rate for cases that proceeded to conciliation was 66 percent. Another 76 percent of the cases that needed follow-up action were successfully resolved. These success rates were comparable to the rates achieved by the established jurisdictions overseas. These hard figures silenced the cynical administrator from the Home Affairs Bureau monitoring the work of the EOC. She was concerned about the initial critical media reporting and attempted to intrude into our work plans. Our management team simply disregarded the housekeeping mentality of this mid-level administrative officer and forged ahead with our strategic directions.

My good friend in the government, Shelley Lee, whom I had known since the early 1980s when we worked together with David Akers-Jones on the establishment of the Yin Ngai Society, learned about these survey results. She was the first female Director of Home Affairs at that time. She wisely advised me to share the positive survey results within the government establishment as

Introducing the EOC to senior women officials at the Chief Secretary's reception, 1996.

an internal public relations measure, as the other senior government officials merely read the negative reports about the EOC from the media. Shelley was one of the founding members of the Association of Female Senior Government Officers who lobbied the colonial government for equal remuneration terms for married women in the civil service. Fondly nicknamed the "Community Godmother" for her warmth and sincere concern about the underprivileged and disadvantaged, she always took the initiative to help others. She kindly organized an informal gathering for other senior female officials at the residence of the Chief Secretary where I could share my work at the EOC. Many of the senior female officials had become strong allies.

While my educational background had prepared me well for the public education efforts of the EOC, I was less prepared for the highly politicized arena in which the EOC had been pitched. There was a tussle between the push for activism and the pull for stability at the turning point leading up to Hong Kong's reunification with China. With the fledging commission constantly in the public limelight in the first few months, we had to prepare for rapid media responses. During my long commute through the traffic jam to the Wanchai office in the morning, I could listen in to citizens calling up radio programs with their comments while scanning the daily newspapers for news and editorials. This prepared me for the first meeting with senior management at the office, which was dubbed the "morning prayer"; these are meetings that are held in many government departments to review emergent political issues and media responses. I had to get used to media sound bites that did not allow elaborate explanations, and to avoid being quoted out of context. This required a steep learning curve beyond my previous academic endeavors and my personal temperament. In academic research, we always specified the theoretical background and experimental contexts, with caution against over-generalization.

At least one thing that I had learned from an early age was not to be affected by unwarranted criticisms, which preserved my balance. I remembered the guileless advice I once gave to one of the nuns in my American high school when she got depressed by the nasty retorts from my rebellious classmates. I told her the girls were not attacking her personally, but only her position of authority. She should not mind if she believed she was doing the right thing. This detached perspective also served me well throughout my career.

Showcasing Hong Kong on the International Stage

The reunification of Hong Kong with China in 1997 attracted international (Western) scrutiny on human rights in the former British colony. The Western narrative presumed that China would restrict individual freedom and threaten human rights in Hong Kong under its autocratic regime. In 1993, the United Nations had declared that women's rights were human rights. Thus, the EOC had become one of the spotlights in human rights monitoring. Contrary to the doomsday conjecture, the transition of reunification was smooth under the "one country, two systems" policy stipulated in the Basic Law, which serves as the Hong Kong Special Administration Region's mini constitution. In the first twenty years after the transition, the extent of individual freedom and political activism surpassed that which had transpired during the British administration of over a century.

After 1997, many international dignitaries arranged to visit the EOC, including the spouse of the then Deputy President of South Africa (Mr. Thabo Mbeki), the Vice-President of the Paris Economic and Social Council, the governor of a prefecture of Japan, as well as the heads of other human rights or anti-discrimination commissions from Australia, Canada, India, and the U.K. The visitors were most impressed by the comprehensive approach in promoting equal opportunities adopted by the EOC. We later learned from Mrs. Mbeke's office that the EOC publications and training materials were adopted in South Africa's anti-discrimination promotion programs.

In 1998, when U.S. President Clinton visited Hong Kong, the First Lady Hillary Clinton and Secretary of State Madeleine Albright hosted a Women Leaders' Round Table. In addition to speaking at that forum, I helped to prepare the dossier on the status of women in Hong Kong for the wife of the Chief Executive, Mrs. Betty Tung 董趙洪娉, and the Chief Secretary of Administration, Mrs. Anson Chan. The Round Table gave me a glimpse of American political performance, which was filmed for Mrs. Clinton by her press office but left me with a feeling of emptiness. Despite its high profile, it had minimal local impact as only a select few elites were invited to the show, and there was no coverage on the contents of the discussion in the local or international media.

To maintain EOC's active role in the regional network on women's affairs and human rights, I visited counterpart offices or commissions in the U.S., Canada, Australia, and the UK, and attended international forums on human rights, gender equality, and disability rehabilitation. Apart from learning from the forefront experiences of international partners, we were also able to put the Hong Kong SAR on the world map in promoting human rights and eliminating discrimination.

In May 1998, riots broke out in different cities in Indonesia after the police shot and killed four protesters demonstrating against President Suharto's thirty-two-year rule. The mobs then looted and destroyed the shops, factories,

A visit to the EOC by the South African delegation led by
the former first lady of South Africa Zanele Mbeki (sixth from the right),
and Fanny (fifth from the left), 1998.

With Hillary Clinton (to Fanny's right) and Madeleine Albright (to Fanny's left)
at the Hong Kong Women's Forum, 1998.

and homes of Chinese Indonesians, who were stereotyped as rich and the cause of the economic recession. When I learned about the mass violence against ethnic Chinese in Indonesia in the May riot, during which over 100 women were reported to be raped, I was concerned that the Indonesian government initially seemed indifferent to the plight of the ethnic Chinese community. During my attendance of the Asia-Pacific Forum of Human Rights Institutions held in Jakarta later that year, I held a side meeting with one of the members of the Indonesian National Commission on Human Rights, as well as a pioneer of the women's movement in Indonesia, Prof. Saparinah Sadli, and a representative from the United Nations High Commissioner for Human Rights attending the forum. I had previously known Prof. Sadli as a fellow psychologist and a pioneer in the women's movement. I alerted her to the concerns circulating in the overseas Chinese community and urged the Indonesian National Commission together with the UN Human Rights Commission to investigate the matter. I also facilitated contact between Indonesian women's rights leaders and the UN High Commissioner's office so they could pursue the matter. I don't know how much impact these activities achieved, but I felt compelled that I should take the opportunity to contribute whatever I could. These experiences also enriched my exposure to the international human rights community and helped me understand more about the difficulty of fact-finding to discern truth from misinformation. Even though the mass sexual violence was confirmed subsequently by a government investigation, there were allegations of fake photos using unrelated pornographic websites and discrepant numbers of confirmed cases based on different sources of reporting.

The Paradox of Social Justice

Conscious of the gaps between a Western legal system that advocated human rights and the emphasis on harmony and balance in conflict resolution in traditional Chinese culture, I adopted an inclusive approach to rally partnership in promoting equal opportunities and addressing discrimination. We wanted to

At the Asia-Pacific Forum of National Human Rights Institutions
in Jakarta, 1998, on the far left.

recruit the stakeholders on board to review and change discriminatory practices. I considered litigation as a last resort in resolving conflicts.

Beyond the business partners, we provided advice to different government departments on their regulations, policies and practices that might be discriminatory. This advisory process required rounds of persuasion which might not result in immediate changes to the system. On the other hand, legal action could enforce a determination that brought forth changes. In cases where systemic discriminatory practices were grounded on outdated concepts and stereotypic beliefs, the violators would not readily recognize what the wrongdoing was and accept what could be done to change the underlying fundamental problems.

Such was the case of the Secondary School Places Allocation (SSPA) System, which had allocated equal quota of secondary school places to boys and girls in co-educational schools in Hong Kong since 1978. The SSPA was an elaborate system using the individual students' internal school assessment scores, which were standardized on the results of their whole school in a common public examination called the Academic Aptitude Test. Although the scoring adopted rigorous psychometric techniques with good intentions to ensure fairness, the system was based on outmoded entrenched concepts in child development, testing, and selection.

The complexity of the SSPA requires a brief description. For secondary school allocation purposes, Hong Kong was divided into eighteen geographical school nets, in which Primary 6 students were allocated places in the secondary schools in their respective school nets. The Education Department decided not to combine the individual students' internal assessment scores with their own scores on the Academic Aptitude Test because they wanted to reduce public examination pressure. Over the years, average differences were found in the scores for the two sexes, with girls scoring higher on the school's internal assessment, which covered more language abilities, and boys scoring higher on the Academic Aptitude Test, which emphasized reasoning skills. To compensate for boys' disadvantages in the scaled internal assessment scores, separate curves were constructed by psychometric consultants of the Education Department to determine the scores of the male and female students, who were divided into five equal bands in each of the eighteen school nets. School places in each net were then divided into places for boys and girls according to fixed quota. The banding formula in the SSPA was not made public until 1998, whereupon some parents discovered that their children might have scored better in the internal assessments of their school but were given a lower banding than students of the opposite sex in the same school. Due to the lower banding, their children were allocated a place lower on their school preference lists. In addition, the fixed sex quota for admission into the individual co-educational schools restricted the choice for their children.

Given the public uproar on the discriminatory nature of the SSPA system, I approached the Director of Education to examine how the system could be changed. The then Director of Education had collaborated with me on several projects to promote equal opportunities to school children in kindergarten through secondary schools. While she was receptive to the possibility of discrimination in the system, the bureaucrats in her department were adamant about the fairness of their selection method. As the SSPA involved potential systemic discrimination, the EOC decided to invoke its statutory power to conduct a formal investigation into the SSPA system.

We engaged a panel of local and international experts in psychology, education and testing to assist the investigation team and consulted teachers, school principals, and members of educational associations through focus groups. In a survey of over 25,000 parents of Form 1 students, we found that 14 percent of the respondents believed separate placement of boys and girls by sex had made a difference in their children's school places allocation. Using past records, the EOC estimated the difference in allocation by comparing the number of top preferences allocated to boys and girls based on the gender-based methods with simulated figures using gender-free methods. To make the long story short, the formal investigation concluded that the SSPA system was discriminatory.

We recommended the Education Department to revise the SSPA within their major review of the academic system of primary and secondary education, which was underway at the time. This provided the golden opportunity for schools to modify their pedagogic approaches to address individual differences in development and learning styles, such as in language acquisition and reasoning skills. In psychological research, sex differences had been found in cognitive abilities, with girls performing better in verbal and memory tasks and boys performing better in spatial perception and mathematical tasks on the average. However, large-scale analyses of multiple studies found that the differences were negligible. The belief that these sex differences were primarily biologically or genetically determined was not supported in recent research. Biological differences in hormone or brain structure only contributed a small part to the explanation. Many educators in Hong Kong continued to insist on the myth of the "late bloomer" effect for boys who would catch up later in secondary school. Yet, public examination results showed that girls still scored more favorably than boys on different educational indicators up to the university level, refuting the argument that boys would catch up during the adolescent period in secondary school. Instead, early experience, educational policies and culture more strongly affected sex differences in cognitive performance. Even when slight sex differences were found, we should remember that these sex differences were based on averages, while there were greater individual differences among boys themselves and among girls themselves within their own groups, resulting in a wide distribution of overlapping performance scores for the two sexes. The approach to address these sex differences required more fundamental pedagogic considerations in teaching languages and STEM (science, technology, engineering, and mathematics) subjects to stimulate the interests and maximize the potentials of all students. Given the scientific evidence, the Education Department should have worked with the schools to redesign pedagogic methods for teaching different cognitive skills and identify the most appropriate assessment procedure to reflect children's ability within an educational framework. This could have been a win-win position.

Unfortunately, the opportunity to revamp the educational system according to psychological science was missed when both I and the Director of Education left our respective positions shortly after the formal investigation. My successor at the EOC and her successor at the Department of Education did not see eye to eye on the matter. The latter was convinced by the bureaucrats in her department, who were resolute that the current SSPA system was fair and non-discriminatory. Setting equal quota for boys and girls was a necessary special measure to ensure that boys would be given equal opportunities to get into co-educational secondary schools and to maintain a more gender-balanced school population. My successor, being a human rights lawyer, decided to flex the muscle of the EOC and took up legal action to judicially review the government department's SSPA system.

The outcome of the court case was a win–lose decision. The beliefs about the fairness of the SSPA differed among the experts in the court case. But the determination of sex discrimination according to the Sex Discrimination Ordinance was premised on the fact that some students were given less favorable treatment in education based on their sex. At the end of an expensive court case argued by top lawyers and educational experts for both sides, the EOC won, and the Director of Education lost the case. The judge ruled that the SSPA was discriminatory and should be revised. These changes confirmed the fears of some school principals that without sex quotas, coeducational schools were becoming single-sex (all girls) school, vanquishing the intended benefits of coeducation. Some complained about inconveniences, such as the need to convert more toilets for girls in their coeducational schools as the sex ratio became imbalanced. Even among schools that were not affected by

At the launch of the EOC's kindergarten training kit, 1999.
Fanny is on the left.

the decisions, many educators continued to blame the EOC for enforcing a simplistic notion of equal opportunities, and that the court decision was purely legalistic without due consideration on the pedagogic nature of school education. It was only when I had the opportunity to meet some of these educators later and explained the updated research findings on the nature of sex differences in cognitive development and on educational psychology, that they toned down their complaints and gradually accepted the need for change.

The SSPA case illustrated how the complex contexts of ethical and legal decisions played out in the cultural perspective. The emphasis on tradition and social harmony, coupled with biases and outdated knowledge, could result in sex discrimination. Yet, a simple legal determination was insufficient to address the more fundamental basis of discrimination and change entrenched prejudice.

Managing the Expectations of Women's Groups

The most challenging critics of the EOC turned out to be the women's groups who had campaigned for the establishment of a women's commission alongside me. Initially, they had been misled by the government to believe that the EOC had satisfied their demand for the women's commission, which in effect was different. Under the SDO, both women and men were protected against discrimination on the ground of sex. The activists felt that EOC was not advocating for women when we attended to frivolous demands of men who had made use of the law to complain against discrimination against men, such as bars that offered free drinks to women on ladies' nights. The role of the EOC as prescribed by the law was less forthright in advocating women's rights, as the women activists had expected. As a statutory body independent of the government, the EOC was not part of the government. It was not in the position to offer special services to serve women's needs or to formulate government policies on women across different areas such as education, employment, welfare, health, housing, and security. Notwithstanding these constraints, I tried to expand our focus on pressing women's concerns within the scope of our educational activities. We organized workshops and conferences on violence against women to discuss rape, indecent assault, and domestic violence, which threatened women's safety, security, health, and well-being, and called for strategies in legislative measures, law enforcement, assistance measures, training, public education, and research.

Instead of continuing to defend EOC's limitations, I decided to take up a proactive approach to urge the government to set up a central mechanism on women's affairs distinct from the EOC. The United Nations Convention on Eliminating All Forms of Discrimination Against Women was extended to Hong Kong by Britain in 1996. Making use of the government's submission of the first CEDAW report to the United Nations in 1998, the EOC invited all the women's groups and other non-governmental organizations to a series of consultation meetings and submitted its own non-governmental organization report to the UN at the end of the year. The EOC position at the United Nations was awkward. Despite being the statutory body set up by the Hong Kong Government to implement the discrimination ordinances, it was not regarded as part of the government framework. Although the EOC was not party to the government's CEDAW report, its work in addressing sex discrimination and promoting equal opportunities was reported as the government's achievements in the implementation of CEDAW.

With UN CEDAW Committee Member Feng Cui at a 1999 meeting in New York.

On the other hand, our NGO status provided us the opportunity to voice our own views on the government's report. In our EOC's NGO report on CEDAW, I challenged the government's submission that setting up the EOC had fulfilled all the obligations of CEDAW by eliminating sex discrimination. I also rejected the government's claim that the ad hoc policy groups chaired by the Chief Secretary for Administration already served the purpose of a central mechanism on women's affairs. Instead, I recommended that a women's commission be established to implement and monitor Hong Kong's international obligations under CEDAW. The women's commission should formulate policies on women, review gender impact of government policies, address women's problems, compile gender statistics and analysis, provide direct funding into areas based on these policies and act as a clearing house on training programs for women.

In February 1999, I flew to New York as an NGO representative to attend the UN hearing on Hong Kong's first CEDAW report submitted under the China delegation. One of the CEDAW committee members was Ms. Feng Cui 馮淬, who I had met at the All-China Women's Federation. Feng had previously worked in the foreign ministry and was a secretary of the ACWF at that time. Proficient in English, she had assisted the ACWF in organizing the 4th UN World Conference on Women in Beijing in 1995 before she joined the secretariat and international liaison department of the ACWF in 1996. A dynamic character who was both patriotic and worldly-wise, Feng was knowledgeable about women's issues from a Chinese as well as international perspective. She and I have remained good friends up to this day. During the annual CEDAW hearings, Feng stayed with the other CEDAW Expert Committee members in New York for two months. She understood the operations of the CEDAW hearings and helped me to arrange a dinner gathering with some of the committee members, during which I could explain in detail the gaps between the EOC and a women's commission in Hong Kong. After the UN hearing, the recommendation for the Hong Kong government to set up a "national machinery" for women apart from the EOC was included in the CEDAW Expert Committee's Concluding Report on Hong Kong's submission. (I wouldn't be surprised if someone in the Hong Kong government might have raised an eyebrow to learn of their appointed EOC Chairperson singing a different tune to the government's report at the UN!)

Feng and I further collaborated on promoting international engagement of women in China and Hong Kong. When China had to host the APEC (Asia-Pacific Economic Cooperation) leaders' and ministers' meeting in 2001, she consulted me on the background of the APEC Women Leaders Network, which had met on the side of the annual APEC ministerial meetings since 1996. I had organized and led the Hong Kong delegation to these meetings when I was the EOC Chairperson. During the APEC ministerial meetings, the international delegations of the Women Leaders Network worked together to draft a proclamation to lobby the ministers to address women's concerns, which needed to be implemented in their own economies. The issues included the compilation of sex-disaggregated statistics, gender mainstreaming, and promoting women's representation in decision-making positions. These issues were later incorporated into the work of the Women's Commission in Hong Kong.

The Hong Kong government was initially resistant to the recommendation of the CEDAW Expert Committee's report. At a hearing in the Legislative Council on the CEDAW report, the Secretary of Home Affairs continued to reiterate that the ad hoc inter-departmental policy mechanism chaired by the Chief Secretary for Administration could serve as a central mechanism for women's affairs. Learning from the experience of the UN CEDAW report, I made use of other international instruments to push the call for a women's commission. After I returned to CUHK in the fall of 1999, I organized the annual Gender Role Workshop of the Gender Research Centre in 2000 with the theme of "Beijing Plus Five," the five-year follow-up on the 1995 UN Conference on Women in Beijing. The underlying agenda of the workshop was to re-focus the attention of the NGOs and to prompt the government on the need for a central mechanism on women's affairs stipulated in the Beijing Platform for Action (BPFA). At the workshop, I reminded the government representative that Hong Kong was party to the national delegation under the UK government at the time which had pledged to support the Beijing Platform for Action in 1995. With the pressure on the government continuing into early 2000, the Chief Secretary—who was planning to attend the UN meeting on Beijing Plus Five in July that year—made the announcement in her keynote address during the EOC conference on Beijing Plus Five held in May, that Hong Kong would be setting up a Women's Commission. The plan for the Women's Commission was included in the government's submission of the HKSAR report to the UN in July and listed as a policy objective of the Health and Welfare Bureau in October. In the 2001 Chief Executive's policy address, promoting women's well-being and interests was highlighted, finally marking a major milestone in the advancement of women's status in Hong Kong after decades of campaigns by women's groups.

Steering the Direction of the Women's Commission

To the disappointment of the advocates, the Women's Commission was set up under the Health and Welfare Bureau instead of the high-level locus under the office of the Chief Executive or the Chief Secretary for Administration. This reflected the government's stereotypic attitude that women's affairs were basically family-based and related to health and welfare issues. Subsequently, the government tried at different times to merge the WoC, the Elderly Commission, and the Youth Commission under a Family Commission, which

Members of the Women's Commission, 2001.

was firmly rejected by the then WoC chairpersons.

Notwithstanding its affiliation with the Health and Welfare Bureau, the effectiveness of the WoC as a central mechanism depended on the vision and drive of the chairperson and its members. The first cohort of members of the WoC steered the direction of the WoC. The founding chairperson of the WoC was Mrs. Sophie Leung 梁劉柔芬, a legislator representing the textile and garment industry. She admitted that she had little prior knowledge of women's issues but was open to the suggestions of the active members. As a legislator, she was effective in pressuring the government into action on our proposed initiatives. Apart from the Secretary for Health and Welfare, who was the Vice-Chairperson, and four ex-officio members (the Director of Social Welfare, the representative of the Home Affairs Bureau, the representative of the Education and Manpower Bureau, and the Chairperson of the EOC), there were seventeen non-official members, including four men. The EOC Chairperson resigned during the first term, citing potential conflict between the work of the EOC and the WoC. Her decision took place shortly after the Health and Welfare Bureau designated the WoC Chairperson to take over the role of leading the Hong Kong delegation to the APEC Women Leaders' Network from the EOC Chairperson, a role which I had originally assumed before the WoC came into being. I had no idea whether this conflict had anything to do with the resignation. It was a pity that the EOC withdrew from the WoC until 2005, when a new EOC Chairperson resumed collaboration with the WoC to promote gender equality.

I was one of several founding WoC members who had been actively engaged in the women's movement since the 1970s. We took the lead to set up the mission and strategic objectives of the WoC with the comprehensive aim of enabling women in Hong Kong to fully realise their due status, rights, and opportunities in all aspects of life. As distinct from the EOC, WoC took on a more long-term and fundamental strategy to address women's needs and development from both the individuals' and the structural perspectives. We identified three strategic objectives: empowerment, gender mainstreaming, and public education.

Empowerment

In Chinese, the translation of empowerment, 賦權 *fuquan,* connotes the emphasis on power for women, which we thought could be unpalatable to the traditional Chinese community. The goal of women's empowerment was to build up women's capacity by increasing their skills to enhance their self-reliance, face life challenges, and make decisions that affect their livelihood as agents of change. With only 32 percent of women in Hong Kong having received post-secondary education and 48 percent being in the labor force as late as 2020, there was a need to provide adequate and relevant education and training programs to women. Many of the existing vocational training programs did not cater to women's needs or interests in terms of class time, location, and academic prerequisites. During our brainstorming discussion on capacity building for women, we decided to create a new program to fill the gap. I recalled my previous experience as a counsellor for women returning to higher education while I was a graduate student at the University of Minnesota. Drawing from the American university credit unit system, where students could accumulate units to fulfil a program requirement with a flexible schedule for getting a certificate, diploma or degree, somewhat like the way that airline mileage schemes awarded benefits based on accumulated miles travelled, I suggested a Capacity Building Mileage Program for women. At that time, the Open University of Hong Kong (now Metropolitan University) offered a wide range of distance learning programs and courses with flexible pace and accessible learning modes, including radio broadcasts, face-to-face instruction, and e-learning. Other post-secondary institutions ran more structured programs. We approached the Open University to design courses to encourage women to pursue life-long learning and self-development even without educational prerequisites. To enhance accessibility, the Metro radio broadcast company was recruited as a partner, while women's groups and NGOs in different districts were invited to collaborate in the delivery and arrangement of courses. Participants who had attained sufficient credit units would be awarded a "Capacity Building Mileage Programme" certificate issued by the Li Ka Shing Institute of Professional and Continuing Education of the Open University. The pioneering barrier-free learning program was launched on March 8, 2004, and continued to flourish under the renamed Metropolitan University. Since 2005, Level Certificates have been awarded to participants in a formal graduation ceremony in recognition of their achievements. The levels of certificates start from Level 1 (twenty-five mileage points) and go up to Level 6 (200 mileage points). A Capacity Building Mileage Programme Student Association was founded in 2008 to sustain the positive impact of the program on participants, to further promote the culture of lifelong learning as well as maintain a peer support network. The program demonstrated that learning could open new horizons and become the pride and joy of women of different ages and backgrounds in Hong Kong.

Another goal of women's empowerment was to enhance their role in decision-making. Although there was a steady rise in the representation of women in the civil service, they remained in the minority in senior positions. Women rose from 4.9 percent in the directorate-level positions in 1981 to 24.6 percent in 2003. Among the network of about 400 government advisory and statutory bodies, in which the government appointed members from interest groups and community organizations to obtain advice through consultation, the percentage of non-official members in 2001 was less than 20 percent. The Women's Commission recommended that the appointment of diverse members in these advisory and statutory bodies could be the first step to enhance women's participation in decision-making, while the government could benefit from advice from different perspectives. A modest gender benchmark with a minimum of 25 percent of each sex was adopted by the government in 2004, which was reached in 2006. The target that was raised to 30 percent in 2010 was reached in 2020.

Promoting women's leadership in the corporate sector was a greater challenge, as the private sector operated on the "old boys' network" and independent from government policies. The WoC and women's groups could only advocate gender diversity through promotion and partnership with more enlightened multinational corporations. Even as late as 2009, only one woman (2.3 percent) held a top executive position among the forty-two blue chip listed companies in Hong Kong's Hang Seng Index, and a mere 9 percent of women held board independent non-executive directorships. The Hong Kong Stock Exchange (HKSE) was originally resistant to the push to set gender quotas for the boards of listed companies. Some local corporate tycoons brushed off the economic benefits of board diversity found in overseas research as irrelevant to the Hong Kong context. The HKSE reluctantly issued a consultation paper on board diversity in 2012, and initially rejected the imposition of a gender quota. In 2021, the HKSE finally accepted a board diversity policy for all listed companies, acknowledging that gender diversity was a good place to start because it was easily measured, objectively quantifiable and straightforward in terms of disclosure, compliance, and enforcement. It also acknowledged Hong Kong's current shortcoming in global comparison in this regard. Now publicly listed companies need to have at least one woman on its board of directors. I was pleased to note that a tycoon who had previously brushed off the value of board diversity had started a diversity and inclusion initiative in his corporation.

Gender Mainstreaming

In the twentieth century, the women's movement brought attention to areas of discrimination and violence against women. To promote women as agents of their own lives, building women's capacity to cope with life challenges helps to empower women. However, focusing on women's problems alone tends to marginalize women and implies women's deficits are the basis for gender inequality. An international report estimated that it would take another two centuries or more to shift the gender imbalance, if parallel measures were not taken to create an enabling environment and address the underlying structure of gender relationships that contributed to gender inequality.

The focus of a society's gender lens has traditionally been based on men's perspectives, which shaped the underlying power structure in the social system. Women's experiences, needs, and concerns had been sidelined in legislation, policies, and practices. Laws were written with reference to a person as "he," which was assumed to include the invisible "she." Public toilets were designed without consideration of the gender differences in usage patterns, which led to constant long queues outside female toilets. To create an enabling environment for gender equality, we need to begin with gender-based analyses of social phenomena and sensitive deconstruction of the divergent gender experiences.

The Beijing Platform for Action adopted by the UN Fourth Congress on Women in 1995 established gender mainstreaming as a key global strategy to address the twelve areas of concern affecting gender equality. The term "gender mainstreaming" refers to the approach of integrating a gender perspective at all stages and levels of policies, programs, and practices as the means to achieve the goal of gender equality. Gender-sensitive decision-making processes seek to ensure that women and men have equitable access to, and benefit from, society's resources and opportunities. Gender mainstreaming has become widely adopted in many countries as a government policy. Instruments and manuals have been developed by the United Nations and other international bodies to guide the processes of gender analyses, planning, implementation, monitoring, and assessment.

Even though the HKSAR Government accepted the recommendation of the WoC to adopt the global policy, we realized that with the adoption of the novel and abstract concept alone, bureaucrats would not be able to carry forward the policy. Even for the open-minded Secretary for Health and Welfare who was serving as the WoC deputy chairperson at that time, he had a hard time understanding why there should be occasional differential treatments of women and men when we were promoting gender equality. It took me a while to explain to him the differences between the concepts of equality in treatment and equality in outcome. Members of the WoC decided to draft a gender mainstreaming checklist as an analytic tool to facilitate the process. The government agreed to apply the Gender Mainstreaming Checklist into various policy areas on an incremental basis. We tried out the checklist on several policy areas with three government departments in 2002 before refining and revising the draft checklist. We managed to arrange a meeting with the Chief Executive for a few years to lobby him on the recommendations of the WoC before he finalized his annual policy address. In his 2005–2006 policy address, the Chief Executive stated: "Before introducing new policies and measures, we will insist on consideration of the different needs and perspectives of men and women and promote equality of the sexes and their opportunities to do their best." We rolled out the scheme modestly on thirteen policy areas in 2005. To complement the checklist, we arranged gender sensitivity training programs for civil servants with the support of the Gender Research Centre, targeting initially those units with more direct association with women's policies and services, including social workers, police, education officers, information officers responsible for press statements, and administrative officers responsible for drafting policies. To sustain the capacity and engagement of the government units, the first batch of seventy designated gender focal points were recruited, with the coordination of the Women's Division of the Health and Welfare Bureau, which was serving as the secretariat to the WoC.

Gender mainstreaming, as well as the other two key strategies of empowerment and public education set up by the founding members, had taken root in the work of the WoC. The Gender Mainstreaming Checklist was further refined and revised in 2009, and in 2015 became a requirement for all government bureaus and departments when formulating major government policies and initiatives. In the 2016 Chief Executive Policy Address, it was announced that the government would extend the checklist to non-governmental organizations in the social welfare sector in a voluntary pilot scheme. Currently, the Home and Youth Affairs Bureau which houses the WoC coordinates the government's efforts in gender mainstreaming. All bureaus and departments have designated a gender focal point, mostly at a directorate level. To further raise the awareness of gender mainstreaming among private sectors, in 2016 the government and the WoC set up the Gender Focal Point Network for all listed companies, which were encouraged to nominate a representative (at director level or equivalent) to be the gender focal point for the company.

Public Education and Community Engagement

Social norms and expectations are entrenched in the cultural gender paradigm. Sexist stereotypes and beliefs perpetuate prejudice and discrimination, which in turn result in gender inequality. To advance women's status in an enabling environment, continuous efforts in communication, education, and engagement involving the whole community would be required to modify the cultural paradigm.

Enhancement of gender awareness and elimination of gender stereotyping should start early in life and be sustained across the community in order to be effective and enduring. We espoused similar approaches in publicity and public education adopted by the EOC, such as collaborating with RTHK to produce television drama series and radio programs to raise general awareness and understanding about women's affairs. To cultivate gender sensitivity from an early age, we reached out to primary and secondary schools through essay competitions in which students expressed ideas on women's roles, challenges, and barriers. As expected, the schools were more receptive to the soft approach of promoting mutual respect and harmony between sexes. We further engaged the local communities as partners through roving exhibitions across districts to enhance gender awareness and showcase women's contributions and support them to organize their own projects under a funding scheme for women's development. Noting that gender scholars and women's groups had often criticized mass media for perpetuating gender stereotypes, we decided to engage media practitioners to discuss how gender-sensitive portrayal of women could be balanced with freedom of the press.

Focus on Priority Areas

While the three strategic objectives set up in the first term were intended to build a sustainable foundation for long-term cultural changes, they might not be perceived as being responsive to the immediate and urgent concerns voiced by many women's groups. In its second term, the WoC expanded its focus on some of these issues. By engaging women's groups and NGOs in a planning forum, the first set of priorities was determined for the second term: women's safety, nurturing a caring family, and gender awareness.

In April 2004, a triple murder occurred involving a family living in the new town of Tin Shui Wai in the remote New Territories. A father killed his wife and twin daughters before fatally injuring himself. The tragedy aroused public concern about the availability and effectiveness of resources to protect families at risk. Even though the mother had contacted social workers previously and the police the same day, it did not avert the tragedy from taking place, prompting questions as to why the system had failed. After the Tin Shui Wai tragedy, which unfortunately was only when huge public attention was attracted, the community called on the government to take stronger actions to address domestic violence. The tragedy afforded WoC the opportune context to focus on domestic violence as one of its priority projects. The project illustrated the unique role that the WoC could play as a central mechanism for coordinating multi-sectoral action on a multi-faceted issue that had traumatic impact not only on the individual, but also the family and the whole community.

When a woman is abused, her entire family suffers, including her children, who may also be abused. Research has also shown that children growing up in an abusive home are much more likely to become abusers themselves, transmitting patterns of domestic violence from one generation to the next. The involved costs to society range from the economy (due to lost productivity), services in healthcare, welfare and other social support for the affected individuals and families, and resources in law enforcement. In 2005, the UK government estimated that domestic violence cost the country around £23 billion a year, of which significant financial savings could have been made if domestic violence had been tackled early on to prevent the increase in its severity and/or frequency. According to the World Health Organization (WHO), domestic violence is both a human right as well as a public health issue affecting the whole community. The WHO's coordinated community intervention model coincided with the WoC's three-pronged strategy of providing an enabling environment, empowering individuals, and public education.

I took the lead and co-convened the WoC Working Group on Safety together with Margaret Wong 王鳳儀, who was the Executive Director of Harmony House at that time, to consult all stakeholders and propose strategies and measures to safeguard women's safety. We built a holistic framework to combat domestic violence by building partnerships with stakeholders and involving the whole community.

To identify stakeholders' concerns, we held sharing sessions with representatives from over fifty women's groups, NGOs, service providers, government departments, professional bodies, and academic units, as well as survivors and survivor groups. To identify gaps in the system and operational challenges, we met with all units participating in the HKSAR government's interdepartmental Working Group on Battered Spouses, including the Social Welfare Department, the Health, Welfare and Food Bureau, NGOs, the Housing Department, the Department of Justice, the Hospital Authority, the Education Bureau, and the Legal Aid Department. Recognizing the central role of the criminal justice system, we also reached out to the Police Force and the Judiciary. Meeting the frontline officers helped us understand some of the operational problems. We discovered one of the reasons for the lapses in early intervention was due to the general attitude that domestic violence was a private family affair and was not regarded as a criminal offense. Neighbors tended to mind their own business and avoided prodding into others' private affairs (各家自掃門前雪，莫管他家瓦上霜 *Gejia zisao menqianxue, moguan tajia washangshuang*) in accordance with traditional Chinese values. Housing officers were reluctant to intervene even when neighbors brought the disturbance to their attention. Frontline police officers who were called to intervene would usually merely pacify the family disturbance if no injuries had been incurred. Since different officers could be responding to the call for help at various times, they would not have identified the repeated incidences of domestic violence. In this case, we sat down with the Police Force to identify ways the police officers could quickly check previous incidents. During the process, we discovered how police officers could keep a redesigned *aide-mémoir* card/a checklist inside their caps to serve as reminder.

Based on the multi-sectorial inputs, we outlined strategies for victim's empowerment, prevention of violence, timely and effective intervention, community education and support. In the first report, *Women's Safety in Hong Kong: Eliminating Domestic Violence*, published in 2006 shortly before the end of our second term, the WoC listed a series of specific recommendations for action, including on law reform, to cover former spouses and cohabitees, as well as the power of arrest to cover threatened violence other than actual bodily harm; on service provisions, including strengthening court referrals to batterers intervention programs; on publicity and promotion of early intervention by all stakeholders; on training of healthcare workers and first responders, as well as on the sharing of our database, professional knowledge, documentation, and research. We further urged the government to apply the WoC Gender Mainstreaming Checklist to all aspects of its work on domestic violence and promote gender-related training to their officers.

In the third term of office, after the first cohort of members completed our two terms, the WoC continued to follow up on the progress of the recommendations and monitor the implementation of the new measures. The three-year update was published in 2009. This project demonstrated the value of a coordinated and proactive approach to tackle a multidimensional social problem. It took the passion, drive, and tenacity of the members involved to pierce through the bureaucracy and rally public engagement to achieve concrete action.

Addressing Discrimination against Sexual Minorities

My work on gender equality had primarily been focused on women's issues. Gender equality concerns covered not only women and men, but people of different sexual orientations. People from sexual minorities had suffered discrimination in many societies, and advocacy for their rights had been embroiled in controversial tensions.

When the Sex Discrimination Ordinance went through the legislative process in 1995, advocates called for the inclusion of sexual minorities as one of the grounds of discrimination, but without success. Subsequently, advocates continued their lobbying on the EOC and the legislature. However, there was insufficient broad-based community support for legislation, not to mention vocal opposition from some sectors, to prompt the government into action.

Community attitudes toward sexual minorities, as in attitudes toward equal opportunities, demand cultural changes. The swing in the legal status of homosexuality from being classified as a crime to being an inherent human right took place just over half a century ago. Under the influence of Christianity, which views homosexuality as immoral or sinful, laws had been introduced since the Middle Ages in Europe to criminalize homosexual acts. With the wave of colonialism, criminal codes which criminalized homosexuality were adopted in many colonial jurisdictions under British rule, including Hong Kong. During the 1960s, there was a move in Western countries to legalize homosexuality but with a higher age of consent than for heterosexual relationships as a safeguard to prevent young men from becoming homosexual. In the UK, partial decriminalization of homosexuality began in 1967. However, this change towards homosexuality was not universal. By 2023, homosexuality was still criminalized in sixty-two of 193 UN member states.

Even among mental health professionals, the shift in the views on homosexuality had been slow but abrupt. In the 1952 first edition of the American Psychiatric Association Diagnostic and Statistical Manual (DSM-1), used worldwide for psychiatric diagnosis, homosexuality was listed as a sociopathic personality disturbance. By 1974, homosexuality had been delisted from being a mental disorder in the revised version of DSM-II. Ongoing scientific research supported biological theories for explaining the causes of homosexuality, which included the brain structure, prenatal hormones on the developing fetus' brain and thyroid, as well as multi-gene contributions. Evidence for social influences on sexual orientation was weak. There is now scientific consensus that previous attempts by clinicians to change individuals who disclosed same-sex attractions or exhibited gender nonconformity to conform with social norms through what was grouped under conversion therapy is ineffective. Mental health professionals became concerned that advancement of conversion therapy could cause more social harm on people of sexual minorities. Since the turn of this century, the practice has been banned in more than twenty-six countries and regarded as fraud or a form of child abuse when performed on minors.

The call for legalization of homosexuality began in the 1980s in Hong Kong, following in the footsteps of the UK. However, there was strong opposition from the Christian church groups, schools, and parents, arguing that legalization would encourage young children to become homosexuals. Under the principles of human rights, the Hong Kong legislature finally agreed in 1991 to decriminalize private, adult, non-commercial, and consensual homosexual relations. By switching the term "legalization" to "decriminalization" in public discourse, the government bill downplayed the implication of promoting homosexuality. At the same time, a higher age of consent at twenty-one for gay relationships than heterosexual relationships (at sixteen) was established. All along, lesbianism had been left outside the scope of these laws. The unequal age of consent for homosexuality was later struck down as unconstitutional under the Bill of Rights Ordinance by the HKSAR court in 2005, and the provisions were finally removed from the Crimes Ordinance in 2014. Although there were several court cases that gave equal civic rights and benefits to couples in same-sex marriages legally registered outside Hong Kong, and the right for a transgendered woman to get married, the push for legalizing same-sex marriages was still strongly resisted by the government, legislature, and social conservatists.

With more people of sexual minorities coming out (of the closet), public opinion on homosexuality began to change gradually. In response to the push for inclusion of sexual orientation in the anti-discrimination ordinances, in 1995 the colonial government commissioned an opinion survey to gauge public views on the measures it should adopt in addressing discrimination on the ground of sexual orientation. At that time, public perception on various forms of sexual minorities was ambivalent and there was a low level of acceptance on homosexuality. In the 1996 public consultation on various governmental measures to combat discrimination, an overwhelming 80 percent of the submissions were strongly opposed to legislation in respect of sexual orientation. By 2005, a new government survey found more equivocal opinions among the public, with over 34 percent against, 29 percent support, and another 34 percent staying neutral on legislation. Given the strong divisions in society, the government opted for an educational and promotional approach and provided more support for the sexual minority community.

The push for legislation on sexual orientation by the sexual minority's community strengthened after a few successful court cases, including the right for a transgender woman to marry, and the housing and inheritance rights of same-sex couples to be on a par with those of opposite-sex couples. In 2013, the HKSAR government decided to set up an advisory group to advise on matters relating to concerns of discrimination faced by sexual minorities and the strategies and measures to address these matters. Given my previous experience in the EOC and WoC, and having advised the Home Affairs Bureau on its 2005 survey design, the government approached me to chair the advisory group.

Initially, I was hesitant to take up this task, as I had not participated actively in this issue in the past and I was not familiar with the stakeholders. I finally agreed to take up the challenge as I believed I could steer the group in a balanced approach. The thirteen members of the group consisted of social and religious conservatists at one end, and individuals from the LGBTI (Lesbian, Gay, Bisexual, Transgender, and Intersex) community at the other end, in addition to three legislators situated at different ends of the spectrum. The composition guaranteed tension. The advisory group met fourteen times from June 2013 to December 2015.

The Advisory Group meetings were contentious from the beginning. My first task was to try to build a collaborative working relationship. The primary consensus we achieved from the onset was to focus our scope of work only on discrimination on the ground of sexual orientation and gender identity, not on other rights for the sexual minorities. We also agreed that discrimination was wrong, and that strategies and measures should be identified to eliminate discrimination while addressing the needs and concerns of the whole community. The strategies and measures were the point of departure.

To find common ground, we started with a fact-finding exercise to provide the backdrop to the issues. The advisory group first took stock of major developments in Hong Kong on issues of concern to sexual minorities over the past thirty years and reviewed the developments in other jurisdictions. To focus on specific areas of discrimination experienced, we commissioned an in-depth qualitative study of over 200 sexual minority participants (including lesbian, gay, bisexual, transgender, post-gay, and intersex participants) from diverse socio-economic backgrounds to share their experiences of discrimination in different domains of their lives. We also arranged to meet with stakeholder groups and hear their concerns. It turned out that a few conservative church groups were the most vocal and bellicose in the hearings, pressing for repeated sessions to express their objections.

The subject matter itself evoked strong emotions and diehard opinions. Updated scientific knowledge was useful in countering unfounded claims. A few conservative members were reasonable and accepted my response to the challenge on the Western ban on conversion therapy raised by some post-gay representatives. By showing how the mental health profession had advanced through scientific research, therapy could help to address the dysphoria experienced by the patients rather than to change their sexual orientation. It was possible that the alleged effectiveness of the conversion therapy on some of the LGBTI patients claimed by a local psychiatrist could be attributed to the therapist's attributes or attention rather than the form and content of the treatment itself.

The interplay among the members affected the meeting dynamics. While the LGBTI members eagerly pushed their lists of suggestions for advancing the protection measures to the limit, the legislator members acted more arrogantly, often dropping in for a short time to say their piece in absolute terms and then leaving the meeting in a hurry to attend their other meetings in the legislative chamber next door. On several occasions, a transgender member broke down into tears under such overbearing haughtiness. I often had to steer the discussion back to the subject matter with a pragmatic focus. As our term of office approached the end, there was an urgency on both sides to put forth their views in the final recommendations. We had to resort to the procedural rule of limiting the speaking time of each member so that everyone had a chance to express their final views.

Eventually, the advisory group managed to compromise on its final report of recommendations, which proposed more training and resources for frontline workers to improve sensitivity, a review to identify gaps in support services, enhanced publicity campaigns, a voluntary charter on non-discrimination to be drawn up by the government, and further public consultation by the government on legislative and non-legislative measures. Even though two LGBTI members who insisted on a recommendation for legislation voiced their dissent, all the other members supported the compromised approach as a step forward.

Unlike the EOC, in which members converged on a common vision for collaboration, and the WoC, in which the founding members' shared passion propelled strategic action, the anchor for this advisory group was a balancing act to find common ground to take a step forward. In the world of opposing views and dissension, antagonism deters progress. We had to learn to compromise and find what was realistic to move ahead. Cultural changes on divided and emotionally charged values did not have to take generations. Psychological research has shown that contact and communication as individual human beings promotes understanding and eliminates prejudice. Sensitivity to the historical and local context, mutual respect, and perseverance will help to pave the way for a world without discrimination.

Breaking new ground literally means excavating and tilling the earth for cultivation. In breaking new ground, I was not really initiating any new venture. Many predecessors had laid the groundwork for advancing women's rights. Notwithstanding being called a trailblazer by some of my allies and supporters, I considered my role as more akin to tilling the soil and sowing the seeds to advance gender equity and equal opportunities to the next level, leaving trails along the path.

Personally, taking a leadership role in these ventures broke new ground in my own life course. Plucking up the courage to leave my comfort zone of professional and academic life and plunging into the politicized public arena, I was able to actualize my passion and vision beyond my traditionally low-key level. Advancing the profile of equal opportunities mechanisms locally and internationally also built up my competence and confidence in taking up further challenges in life. These seminal experiences have added significant dimensions to the meaning of my life.

SERVING
THE
COMMUNITY

Receiving the Silver Bauhinia Star Medal
from Chief Executive C. Y. Leung, 2016.

6

Whether in the job setting, the residential neighborhood, the professional community, the wider society, or the whole nation, everyone in the same community, whether geographical or relational, is in the same boat. In the long run, we thrive or languish together in our shared destiny. It is well-established in psychology and social sciences that social connectedness is basic to the well-being of the individual as well as of the community. Socially well-connected people and communities are happier, healthier, and more resilient in facing life challenges. Whatever position we hold, we can all participate in the steering of the boat to contribute to the collective goals and benefits. These connections provide members of the group a sense of community and belonging beyond their individual identities. The more fortunate members have the responsibility to assist and enable the vulnerable and disadvantaged members to build up the human assets of the community through emotional, informational, and instrumental support. This social value forms the foundation of philanthropy.

The Rewards of Philanthropy

Traditionally, serving the public good was considered a form of philanthropy, a word which comes from the Ancient

Greek word meaning "love of humanity." During the early colonial days, only British residents and later, some Eurasian elites in Hong Kong, were engaged in public services. However, Chinese community leaders began to contribute to charity organizations such as the Tung Wah Group of Hospitals, founded in 1870, to provide medical services to the local Chinese residents and take care of refugees. These Chinese merchant elites who organized and operated the Tung Wah Hospital rose to power to play a crucial political role mediating between the British colonial administration and the Chinese community during the nineteenth century. Public services and philanthropic efforts were recognized by the colonial government through its honors and awards system based on the British honorary award system, split into classes ("orders") and graded to distinguish different degrees of achievement or service, including the KBE (Knight of the Order of the British Empire), CBE (Commander of the Order of the British Empire), OBE (Officer of the Order of the British Empire), MBE (Member of the Order of the British Empire) and Medal of Honour. The honors and awards system in the HKSAR after 1997 was modelled after similar classes, including the GBM (Grand Bauhinia Medal), GBS (Gold Bauhinia Star), SBS (Silver Bauhinia Star), BBS (Bronze Bauhinia Star), and Medal of Honour. These honors were awarded at the Government House twice a year by the Governor before 1997 and the Chief Executive after 1997. The other honorary appointment of recognition for public service is that of Justice of the Peace, a legacy of colonial rule. The title of Justice of the Peace always intrigued my mainland friends, as the Chinese translation depicts a "gentleman." In the UK, from where the title derived, women were not allowed to become JPs until 1919. Unlike the other honors and awards, this honorary role entails official duties. After the establishment of the judicial system of legally qualified magistrates in Hong Kong, the functions of the JPs are mainly to visit custodial institutions, psychiatric hospitals, remand homes, places of refuge, and to administer statutory declarations. During the visits to prisons and detention centers, which are visited by different JPs twice a month, JPs are accompanied by the superintendent and staff to inspect all the facilities. The accompanying staff will announce: "Visit by JPs; please raise your hand if you have any complaints." If there are complaints, the JPs will interview the complainant and

Shaking the hand of Britain's Prince of Wales, presiding
at the OBE ceremony in Hong Kong, 1997.

record the allegations in the visit report to be followed up by the department
and then reviewed by the JPs. During the thirty-some years of my JP visits, I
found the conditions of the institutions to be generally well maintained, and
complaints were few.

The honors and awards could serve as extrinsic incentives to entice the rich
and talented to contribute to society. On the other hand, vanity cannot sustain
human good nature. The OBE and SBS that I received in 1997 and 2016 were
mere icing on the cake to me. Serving the community provided me with the
intrinsic gratification of philanthropy, public service, and meaning in life.

Philanthropy was often perceived as charity by famous people who gave
large sums of money as a donation or set up a foundation to provide help for
the needy. While the early days of the Tung Wah Group focused of medical and
educational services, the welfare needs of the poor in Hong Kong were served
by overseas emergency relief agencies and religious organizations. The older
generation still remember lining up for milk powder and other food supplies

from church groups in the 1950s. Some of these international organizations retreated from Hong Kong as the economy grew in the 1960s, leaving a gap in financial support for the small local welfare agencies. In 1968, a group of local dignitaries and community leaders set up a community fund, The Community Chest, to raise money on behalf of all member agencies to eliminate competition in their fundraising efforts and provide them with the resources to focus on service delivery. The Community Chest's signature fundraising event, Walk for Millions, which takes place at normally restricted areas such as cross-harbor tunnels and bridges, attracts widespread community participation from contributors who donate money to join the walks. Beginning from the first walk in 1971, which attracted close to 5,000 participants, these charity walks are typically joined by as many as 15,000 participants, exemplifying the concerted efforts of Hong Kong people's generosity and spirit of caring. The number of member agencies benefiting from the funds grew from forty-three at the beginning to over 165 in 2024, covering service areas in children and youth, the elderly, family and child welfare, medical and health, rehabilitation and aftercare, and community development.

Currently, the largest charity donor in Hong Kong is the Hong Kong Jockey Club, a non-profit organization which generates its surplus revenue primarily from betting and lotteries. Although the 1977 Gambling Ordinance prohibited organized gambling in Hong Kong, the Hong Kong Jockey Club, which was founded in 1884 as an exclusive club comprising members from the expatriate elites to promote horse racing, holds the monopoly on horse racing wagers, lotteries and football betting. Since the 1950s, the Jockey Club has devoted its annual operating surplus to charity and community projects. Its charity role exonerated its gambling operations and promoted its wider community acceptance. In 1993, The Hong Kong Jockey Club Charities Trust was formed to establish itself as a major social partner in fostering a caring and inclusive community. Donating about 90 percent of the club's annual surplus to the trust has made it one of the world's top ten charity donors. In 2022–2023, the Jockey Club paid HK$28.6 billion to the government in duty, profits tax and Lotteries Fund contributions, and approved donations of HK$7.3 billion to benefit 247 charity and community projects. The trust has taken a more proactive role in identifying priority areas and initiating projects that meet community needs not covered by the government. In 2023, the Jockey Club further established an Institute of Philanthropy to promote philanthropic thought leadership at local, regional and global levels.

In contrast to the traditional notion of charity, philanthropy is more than donating money for an immediate cause. It includes giving time, effort, talent, and funds to help make life better for other people, a particular cause, or the whole society over an extended period. This broader concept of philanthropy can engage anyone in the community, not just the elites or fortunate few. Most philanthropists are ordinary citizens who are generous in volunteering their time in addition to donating money without seeking power or fame. People from all sectors of Hong Kong have been generous in donating money for disaster relief across the world or for supporting some 10,000 charities of their choice with one-off or monthly donations. Many others have contributed their free time to volunteer for a wide range of social causes. Despite its materialistic image as a trading port in the early days, and then a business and financial hub, Hong Kong has not lacked volunteerism in building a caring community. Throughout my decades of community engagement, I was grateful to have come across many like-minded comrades who shared similar passion and compassion to serve the community.

As a child, I could not avoid looking at the big plaque hanging in the ancestral hall of my family home in Number 8, which had the following inscription: "The family that accumulates goodness is sure to have superabundant happiness". At that time, I did not understand what it meant, but I now know that it came from the *I-Ching*, or the *Book of Changes* 易經. My family followed the traditional practice of philanthropy in contributing to charity and funding education in Hong Kong through a foundation named after my grandfather. My father and one of my uncles served on the board of the Tung Wah Group of Hospitals. When I was young, I thought cynically that it was the typical path for merchant elites to gain social status. I cannot tell how much this family motto of accumulating goodness has been ingrained in me through repeated exposure, but it has always resonated with my lifelong experience of serving the community through government committees and civil society. Through working with people from diverse backgrounds, I built up my connection to the community and to humanity. I learned and grew through these engagements, which in turn enriched my life. My gratification came from witnessing the impact of these efforts on the well-being of the community.

A Sense of Community

In the field of community psychology, the concept "sense of community" refers to the members' feeling of belongingness and identification, the sentiment that they matter to one another and to the group, and a shared faith that their needs will be met through their commitment to be together. The active engagement of the members of a community promotes a sense of community, which is a key characteristic and prerequisite of a successful community.

The development of new towns in the rural areas of the New Territories in Hong Kong provided a living testimony to the importance of the sense of community. Back in the rural villages where my father came from, most people shared the same surname, which built their fraternity ties. After the mainlanders moving to Hong Kong, clan associations based on common surnames provided friendship and mutual support and offered social assistance to newcomers. My father hired several workers because they had the same surname and came from the same rural areas, though not necessarily from the same village. We all addressed them with respect as uncles. With the increase in refugees after World War II, the colonial government set up local community networks in the urban areas called Kaifong Welfare Societies as mutual aid organizations to serve the educational, medical and welfare needs of the residents in the neighborhood. *Kaifong* is the Cantonese pronunciation of the Chinese term 街坊 *jiefang*, which means people who live in the same neighborhood. The role of the kaifong societies as an intermediary between the local population and the colonial government declined after the government set up district offices in 1969, and the introduction of mutual aid committees in high-rise buildings in 1973, especially with the expansion of the public housing scheme. In

1982, Governor MacLehose established the district board system under the District Administration Scheme to advise the local government on the need for and coordination of services and facilities at the district level. The original goal of the District Administration Scheme of the colonial government was to maximize political stability by depoliticizing grassroot opposition with the "administration" of politics in government-sponsored channels.

Shatin, where the Chinese University is located, was among the early generation of new towns in the New Territories developed in the 1970s. In 1982, I was invited by the then District Officer, Donald Tsang, who later became the second Chief Executive of the Hong Kong SAR government, to join the Shatin District Board as an appointed member. Donald was conscious that there was only one female elected member on the board of over twenty unofficial board members and scouted around for another female candidate to improve the gender ratio. My appointment increased the number to two, which doubled the female representation but did not significantly improve the gender balance of the district board system. In all eighteen district boards in Hong Kong, there were only nine females among the 132 unofficial members in 1984. Donald was a more progressive district officer. He told me he got my name from different sources, including from the Vice-Chancellor of my university. I figured it was due to my active community involvement in the War on Rape campaign and in mental health issues, as well as being one of the few female university faculty members who had been more outspoken on social issues. At first, district affairs seemed unrelated to my professional and academic background. On the other hand, viewed from a broader perspective, psychology was embedded in our lives and the everyday livelihood of residents in the community. I felt that I could have something to offer as a psychologist and as a woman, while learning more about the real world outside the ivory tower. I served on the Shatin Board member from 1983 to 1994.

Shortly after I joined, I led the District Board to tackle the protest by the Sun Chui Estate residents against the establishment of the first psychiatric halfway house in the public housing estate. A tragic incident in June 1982 shocked Hong Kong when a discharged mental patient who did not continue to take his medication went on a rampage, killing his mother and sister

The 1984 Shatin District Board members' official photo, with District Officer Donald Tsang (first row, seated fifth from the right).

in his home in a housing estate in urban Kowloon, then went on to stab two neighbours on his way downstairs before ending up in the Anne Anne Kindergarten on the ground floor where he stabbed thirty-four young children, of which four were killed. The incident reflected the inadequacy of psychiatric rehabilitation in the community. The government decided to expedite its policy of building twenty psychiatric halfway houses in public housing estates, with the first one located in Sun Chui Estate in Shatin, targeted for operation in 1983. When the residents heard of this plan, the frightening memory of the Anne Anne Kindergarten incident was evoked, and panic spread among the young mothers in the housing estate. The residents rallied to protest against the halfway house, despite the fact that these community rehabilitation services would better serve the needs of discharged patients, many of whom would have been living in isolation in various housing estates in any case. Two of the elected members on the District Board took the lead to demand the government to scrap the halfway houses from the Sun Chui and other Shatin estates.

Given the stigma of psychiatric illness, the typical "not-in-my-backyard" attitude towards any unfavorable facilities in the neighborhood was expected.

Speaking at the Shatin District Board Mental Health promotion campaign opening in 1985.

However, responsible community leaders should first make a rational analysis of the proposal and communicate the pros and cons with their stakeholders instead of pandering to mass sentiments. I still remember the District Board meeting during which the government representative presented the plan to build the halfway house. As expected, the two elected members spoke out at length to oppose the government plan of locating halfway houses in public housing estates. A few other members echoed the fear of the residents. I was the only one who stood up to argue for support of the plan. I cited figures that showed the rate of violence among psychiatric patients was low and that their probability of committing suicide was far higher than the rare incident of homicide. There were higher rates of violence in the community from domestic abuse than from psychiatric patients. The enhancement of community psychiatric rehabilitation would provide better care for those who otherwise would be left living in the housing estates without support, and thus minimize relapse and disturbance. The debate was protracted and was not going to end before lunch. I was scheduled to teach a class on community psychology at the university in the afternoon. Mindful that if I were not around to champion the cause, the District Board would have voted against the plan. I decided to contact my students who were enrolled in the small class and invited them to come join the District Board meeting as observers. The students happily accepted the opportunity to witness in real time community planning in action. When the debate resumed in the afternoon, I confronted the two opposing members, who were a social worker and a teacher. I challenged them that as professionals who should understand facts rather than myths of mental illness, they should not discriminate against psychiatric patients. They then shifted to blame the government for not having promoted public education to prepare the residents. At this point, I swayed the other members to agree that as responsible community leaders, the Shatin District Board should take the lead to bridge the gap between residents and the government and promote public understanding on mental health. At the end of the day, the District Board voted to support the government's plan and set up a special task force to promote public understanding. Activities were organized in the next two years to engage district representatives, schools, religious organizations, and youth groups to promulgate understanding of mental health and support community psychiatric rehabilitation services. The Sun Chui Halfway House was finally opened in 1986.

My role in leading the District Board's campaign to promote community mental health following the incident expanded into a more broad-based coverage on the sense of community under the Community Development Committee, of which I served as the Chairperson from 1985 to 1994. The role of building up social connectedness in the community was particularly important in new town development. At the international level, Nobel laureates in economics, including Amartya Sen and Joseph Stiglitz, have reminded the world of the importance of community well-being beyond indices like the GDP as indicators of economic performance and social progress. Since the beginning of the twenty-first century, governments of developed economies have started to recognize the importance of quality of life, environmental sustainability, social equality and the wider notion of well-being as indicators of societal progress.

Compared to other first-generation new towns, the success of Shatin's transformation from a rural settlement of 30,000 population in the 1970s into a model new town of half a million can be attributed not only to the well-planned infrastructure and housing mix, but also to the deliberate efforts of community building to create a sense of community. For over ten years, our committee supported the formation of youth groups and women's groups, organized activities to promote social connections, engaged residents in mental health and fight-crime campaigns, and advised the local government on areas of needs for cultural, recreational and sports activities.

We prided ourselves on having nudged the government into cleaning up the pollution in Shing Mun River, which produced a pungent odor along the riverbank. In the 1980s, large amounts of untreated industrial, commercial, livestock and domestic wastewater were dumped into the river, contaminating the sediment. The clean-up beginning in the early 1990s saw the return of fish and other marine life to the river. Further treatment and dredging of the contaminated sediment commencing in 2001 turned the river into a popular recreational area for cycling and running, and a tourist attraction for the annual Dragon Boat Festival race. Festival lighting is lit up on the two bridges crossing the two rivers during Christmas, Chinese New Year and Mid-Autumn Festival, livening up the Shatin town center. Residents are proud of their collective identity as Shatin buddies, a homonym of the citrus fruit pomelo, originating from a village called Shatin in Guangxi province.

When the Shatin New Town development expanded across the Shing Mun River Estuary into Ma On Shan in the mid-1980s, we made sure that the same effort in building a sense of community would be included in the metamorphosis of the small village around the closed iron ore mine into a modern satellite town with a target population of 250,000. The town of Ma On Shan is located on the west side of Ma On Mountain, which can be translated into "horse saddle mountain" given the shape of the twin peaks. The bucolic setting was transformed when the new town was built with its own town center, government facilities, and high-rise private and public housing, which formed a concrete block screening half of the mountain view from across the Tolo Harbour. A large influx of young families started to move into the housing blocks beginning in 1987. Based on our experience with the Shatin town development, we engaged from the beginning the new town residents in all activities of the Shatin District, which built up their belongingness as members of the community.

In the early 1990s, the Home Affairs Bureau was contemplating splitting Ma On Shan from the administrative district of Shatin. The district of Shatin was gradually approaching the planning target of 750,000 and the government thought it would be convenient to split the new town Ma On Shan from Shatin and merge it with Sai Kung, a rural district on the east side of Ma On Shan mountain. The rural villages in both areas were not related traditionally and there was only a single-lane country road connecting the two communities. This forged marriage of convenience was objected to by the Shatin District Board as well as by the Ma On Shan representatives. Other than the restricted transportation link between Ma On Shan and Sai Kung, we showed the government the sense of community surveys we had conducted over the years, which indicated a strong identification of the Ma On Shan residents with the Shatin District. To break up this affiliation for bureaucratic planning convenience would put the efforts of community building at stake. Given the community sentiment, the Home Affairs Bureau eventually gave up and decided to merge Sai Kung with another newly developed town of Tseung Kwan O, both on the east coast of the New Territories and Kowloon peninsula. The more recent development of Tseung Kwan O allowed time for the new residents to cultivate their sense of connectivity with Sai Kung.

Working in Diversity

Throughout the years, I have served on many governmental and non-governmental committees with diverse membership in a wide range of subject matters, including AIDS, public broadcasting, civic education, community relations in anti-corruption, complaints against police, fight crime campaigns on juvenile delinquency, the performing arts, scientifically assisted human reproduction, social work training and manpower planning, and many others. In some committees, most of the unofficial members were professionals with relevant expertise on the subject matter. In other committees, the membership was more diverse to engage stakeholders from a cross-section of the community.

We were able to contribute our knowledge and experience to inform policies and planning. The colonial government had wisely engaged many professionals to serve as volunteers on advisory committees and statutory bodies, capitalizing on their talent to provide input into their policies. At the same time, involving community leaders facilitated communication with stakeholders and the gauging of public sentiment. On important matters involving wider public interest, a green paper on the tentative proposal would be put out for public consultation, whereupon feedback collected would be considered in fine tuning the policy in a white paper. These tools of participatory democracy originating in the UK were adopted by the colonial government before electoral democracy was introduced in Hong Kong in the 1990s. Government policies benefited from the input of these professionals and community leaders. The members' suggestions and public opinions were not always accepted by the officials, but their participation in the policy-making process gave them a sense of mastery that they had a role to play.

Interacting with members from diverse background in these committees exposed me to a wide spectrum of views, values, and characters, much more than what I would find in academia. These experiences built up my appreciation of and skills in managing diversity and inclusion. How to disagree without being disagreeable? How to stand my ground with adequate preparation and factual backup? They also trained my competence in governance and parliamentary procedures in running meetings, which were unfamiliar to most of my academic colleagues as they got into administrative positions at the university.

In many of these committees, there were few female members, and I got used to being one of the few. I never felt that my gender was a disadvantage, even when I was the only female councillor in the Regional Council (RC). The RC was the counterpart of the Urban Council. It was responsible for municipal services in the New Territories until 1999, when the HKSAR government decided to dissolve both the Urban and Regional Councils to streamline the municipal services and centralize the political structure from a three-tier system to a two-tier system, comprising only the Legislative Council and eighteen enhanced District Councils which replaced the original district boards. In 1991,

Official photo of Regional Council members, 1993, with Chairman
Cheung Yan-lung (first row, third from the right).

the Home Affairs Bureau approached me to serve on the Regional Council
as the first woman councilor since its establishment in 1986. The Deputy
Secretary of the Bureau, who had previously been a District Officer in Shatin,
was probably impressed by my constructive role in the Shatin District Board.
During my five-year tenure, about one-third of the RC members, including
the Chairman, were traditional rural leaders from different villages of the New
Territories, who formed a hierarchical status structure of men. Their indigenous
villager identity was defined by the colonial decree in the 1898 Convention
for the Extension of Hong Kong Territory as descendants through the male
line of persons residing in established villages in the New Territories before
that time. They enjoyed special rights to preserve their customs and privileges
related to their land. The main rural political organization, Heung Yee Kuk 鄉
議局, comprising heads of the rural committees which represented different
villages and market towns, was formed in 1926 to protect indigenous residents'
interests and welfare. The first two chairmen appointed to the Regional Council
were both chairmen of the Heung Yee Kuk, which reflected the political status
accorded to the indigenous rural leaders.

As protectors of customs and traditional values, the rural leaders held onto
age-old biases against women, who were deprived of equal rights and privileges
in terms of property and political representation. Heung Yee Kuk had opposed

granting female villagers equal inheritance rights in 1994 on the ground that these changes would interfere with rural traditions, although the bill was eventually passed by the Legislative Council. Women gained their statutory right to be elected as rural representatives after these rural elections were brought under the jurisdiction of the Village Representative Election Ordinance in 2003. In the election that year, seventeen women were elected among the total of 1,291 elected rural representatives, which was increased to twenty-eight women out of 1,320 elected representatives in the 2007 election. Women still constitute less than 5 percent of the total number of rural representatives now. The Heung Yee Kuk was exclusively operated by men until more women were elected as rural representatives and village heads. About 10 percent of Heung Yee Kuk elected councilors are now taken up by women.

Back then, rural men were stereotypically reputed to hold insolent attitudes towards women. I observed how some of them had disregarded other women as if they were non-existent and often did not address them by name, but just referred to them as "that woman." However, most of them were courteous towards me. The female staff of the Regional council were overjoyed to find me as their guardian angel. Despite my feminist activism, I did not choose this forum to be a battleground on sexism. I just ignored the chauvinistic male attitudes of some of the men during the meetings and simply stood my ground in presenting my views as a fellow councilor on the business of the council. I remained non-judgmental towards the Chairman's habit of bringing two of his three wives along on the overseas field visits. We just nonchalantly introduced both his wives to the confused European hosts as, "this is Mrs. Cheung, and this is Mrs. Cheung." If there was any sign of awkwardness from the hosts, I would privately explain the legal status of polygamy under old Hong Kong laws.

Compared to the rural leaders and grassroots politicians in our delegation, I was adept in Western etiquette and communication with our overseas counterparts. I enjoyed the cultural programs such as opera and classical music concerts, which bored some of the men who would slip out of these performances arranged by our hosts during our visits. It could have been worse if they began to chat or snore during the performance. Once during a meeting

The 1993 Regional Council visit to a Berlin art exhibition.

with city council members in Berlin, I surprised and impressed our delegates, including myself, when I launched my greeting remarks in German, which came out naturally twenty-five years after I had learned the language in the university. By being authentic, I deviated from the stereotype of women held by the old-fashioned rural leaders, who began to address me as "Dr. Cheung" or just "Doctor." In relating to me as a scholar, my gender identity was sidelined. I had earned my respect and esteem in the council. Gender was just one of our multiple identities that did not need to be highlighted all the time.

Serving on different committees of the Regional Council exposed me to municipal services in the new towns and rural regions in the New Territories, including liquor licensing, environmental hygiene, and cultural and recreational facilities and services, which were fundamental to quality of life in the community. I pointed out the problem of gender ratio in public toilets where there were always long queues for women, and pushed for the increase of compartments in women's toilets from that of an equal ratio with the men's. I gained support more for the pragmatic reminder of the long queues than for the ideology of sex discrimination. During the planning of the Hong Kong Heritage Museum to be built in Shatin, I kept reminding the curator that the history of women in Hong Kong, and particularly women in the New

Territories, would be an important theme for an exhibition in the museum. Finally, when the museum opened its door in 2000 after I had stepped down from the RC, the curator came back to me and said he had not forgotten my suggestion. Colleagues at the Gender Research Centre were exalted and proud to contribute to the planning and preparation of the first exhibition on Hong Kong women by providing research background and artefacts on women during the early era of the twentieth century. In 2002, the Heritage Museum presented an exhibition on "Hong Kong Women Identity—A Historical Survey," featuring artefacts, photos, interactive games, and audiovisual programs. The exhibition examined the lives and roles of women in Hong Kong in the twentieth century, from the older generations to their modern counterparts, focusing on three aspects of women's lives: work, family, and leisure. The exhibition also described the challenges that women encountered and the ways that they sought help. For the first time, contemporary women in Hong Kong were showcased in a thematic exhibition. Women's groups were enthusiastic and organized members' visits to the exhibition. Our only regret was that the museum could not store the exhibits after its six-month exhibition. As the exhibition took place before digitization became available, no copy of the exhibits was kept. Nevertheless, we were pleased to note that the Heritage Museum had continued to feature women as themes of several subsequent exhibitions, including women artists in Hong Kong as well as images of women in cultural relics.

Pride in Hong Kong's Reunification with China

The 1984 Sino-British Joint Declaration and Basic Law of the Hong Kong Special Administrative Region of the People's Republic of China passed in 1990 by the National People's Congress set the conditions under which Hong Kong was reunified with China under the principle of "one country, two systems" for a period of fifty years. The previous capitalist system and way of life would remain unchanged for fifty years under a high degree of autonomy. While the public were worried that their way of life might be depleted and were fixated on the "fifty years unchanged" (五十年不變 *Wushinian bubian*) clause in the Basic Law during its consultation period, I could not help remembering my visit to Shanghai during the mid-1980s before its soaring development since China's economic reforms. Many of the iconic buildings and the road around the Bund looked like nothing had changed in the past fifty years. At that time, I imagined what Hong Kong would have looked like if there were literally no change for fifty years. Nowadays, the urban transformation of major cities in China illustrates the power of progress and innovation. Despite doomsday predictions by Western media over the reunification, Hong Kong has survived periods of external and internal threats and continues to flourish due to its dynamism. It is up to the Hong Kong SAR government and its people to contribute to its continuing progress and prosperity while maintaining the stability of its system.

During the transition period toward reunification with mainland China, the Hong Kong-Macau Affairs Office of the People's Republic of China's State Council and the New China Agency in Hong Kong, which represented the People's Republic of China in colonial Hong Kong in the absence of an official representative in the territory, became more active in engaging community leaders in Hong Kong. I was appointed as a Hong Kong Special Delegate to the All-China Women's Federation in 1994 when I joined thirty-some local women leaders to attend the plenary sessions of the National Congress of Women which was held in the Great Hall of the People every five years. This gave me a glimpse of the operation of national congresses, albeit focused only on women's affairs. The fleet of buses taking around 2,000 delegates to the plenary sessions and the security check entering the Great Hall was meticulously choreographed. The seat arrangements of the delegates from different provinces ensured that no provincial delegation would feel slighted. All members of the same delegation had to stay in the assigned guest house during the period of the congress and attend the divisional meetings. We got to know the diverse group of Hong Kong women leaders well, including professionals, entrepreneurs, and the wives of tycoons. Their multiple talents in singing and dancing came in handy during subsequent social visits.

Receiving the Hong Kong Affairs Advisor certificate from Xinhua
News Agency Director Zhou Nan, 1995.

After Chris Patten, the last governor of Hong Kong, introduced in 1992 his electoral reforms to vastly extend the franchise in the last election to be managed by the colonial government, the Sino-British talks on the transition of Hong Kong stalemated. Between 1992 and 1995, China appointed four batches of Hong Kong Affairs Advisors, consisting of political leaders, business leaders, academics, professionals, and retired civil servants, to provide input on the future of Hong Kong as part of its United Front. Some pro-Beijing politicians and business leaders who had previously been sidelined from the elite circle or even shunned by the colonial government had begun to gain more recognition and influence during the transition. I was appointed in the fourth batch of advisors in a formal ceremony in the Great Hall of the People in Beijing, greeted by President Jiang Zemin and Premier Li Peng. As usual, there were few women in the total group of Hong Kong Affairs Advisors, and my husband often had to stand among other women as spouses in the group photo.

In the run-up to 1997, I participated in many discussion forums on the future of Hong Kong, which focused on its political, economic, legal and social development after the reunification. To me, the transition could be likened to the

At the rainy handover ceremony of the colonial government
at the Tamar site, 1997.

analogy of Hong Kong as a foster child returning to the birth mother after being brought up in a Westernized cultural context and expressly spoiled in the run-up to reunification, with different expectations and norms. The re-integration required a gradual passage of rebuilding a national identity with aligned values. Unfortunately, this soft enculturation process which needed extended time in socialization was largely neglected in the early years after the reunification. Simply promoting the national anthem without a comprehensive program at all levels to build up a national identity grounded in history and cultural values was inadequate. The gap of twenty-five years was precious time lost in the development of the post-reunification generation. The top-down efforts of introducing national education to students after the social unrest in 2019 became more of a strenuous uphill struggle. The spoiled brat image of Hong Kong lingered on.

The handover of Hong Kong from the United Kingdom to the People's Republic of China at midnight on July 1, 1997 was a proud and most memorable historical moment for me as a Chinese who grew up in Hong Kong.

It marked the beginning of a new era and a new identity, from being a British subject in the colony of Hong Kong to being a Chinese national citizen in the Special Administrative Region of Hong Kong. Prince Charles, the Prince of Wales, flew into Hong Kong to represent Queen Elizabeth II in the handover ceremony on the evening of June 30. He officiated the farewell ceremony together with Governor Patten in a purpose-built open-air arena next to the HMS Tamar, the Royal Navy's executive shore establishment. Under torrential rain, we watched the parade of a combined force of Royal Navy and British Army units as the British Hong Kong flag and the Union Jack were lowered for the last time. Even with the distribution of large souvenir umbrellas, all the VIPs were drenched. To keep ourselves dry, my husband and I moved over from our premium seating to empty seats at the top of the stand to avoid the water dripping from the umbrellas around us. It was a bittersweet moment when I reflected on the transition of the territory I had served in the first half of my life.

The State Banquet and the Handover Ceremony were held in the new extension of the Hong Kong Convention and Exhibition Centre, which was completed just in time for the ceremony. There is an episode unbeknownst to the public for which I can claim credit in having saved the government from international embarrassment. Given the importance of this site, it was unbelievable to me when I noticed on my way to work at the Equal Opportunities Commission office at that time a new road sign in which the English and the Chinese names of the roads directing traffic to the new extension were mismatched. I could imagine the headlines in the critical newspapers featuring the inept directions to the handover venue. I called up the relevant government department head to alert him of this error. He was surprised. The switched road sign was patched up one day later. I wondered when the mistake would have been detected had I not called. More importantly, why was there no quality check on the road sign to the most important venue of Hong Kong history?

The solemn and dignified Handover Ceremony began at 11:30 pm on June 30. My husband, who was a Regional Council member at the time, and I were grateful to be among the 4,000 invited guests, which included senior representatives from China and Britain, ministers from more than forty countries and representatives from international organizations as well as local community leaders. We were so proud to watch the tall and husky Chinese military guards of honor march in step to raise the Chinese national and the HKSAR flags at the stroke of midnight, after the Union Jack and the Hong Kong colonial flags were lowered minutes earlier.

After the departure of the Prince of Wales and the last Governor, the Inauguration Ceremony began at 1:30 a.m. on July 1, during which President Jiang Zemin formally declared the establishment of the Hong Kong Special Administrative Region of the People's Republic of China and presided over the swearing-in of the Chief Executive, principal officials, senior judges and members of the Executive Committee and the Provisional Legislative Council of the HKSAR government. There was no sign of fatigue among the officials and the guests through the early hours of the night, or during the celebration events throughout the next two days.

Both a Smooth and Disruptive Transition

The reunification was marked by joy and excitement above the political undercurrents. An interim Provisional Legislative Council operated temporarily from 1997 to 1998 to replace the pre-handover Legislative Council, which was returned from the 1995 elections pushed through by the last governor, and was deemed by the Chinese government to have violated the Sino-British Joint Declaration and the Basic Law. Otherwise, there was a smooth transition in life in Hong Kong. Western media were eager to predict the death of Hong Kong in 1997 after its return to Chinese sovereignty. This doomsday narrative persisted despite Hong Kong's continued prosperity and stability until 2019.

During its first twenty-five years, the central government refrained from involvement in local affairs, upholding the "One Country, Two Systems" policy. However, the political ecology of Hong Kong had become more prominent as a legacy of the colonial retreat, the impact of which was also found in other post-colonial countries. Responding to more vocal expectations from politicians, the HKSAR government was intent on promoting greater democracy and citizen participation, with the mainland government's implicit acceptance, until social unrests erupted in 2019. One of the side effects of politicization was the shift in the government's practice of appointment to committees from relying on mainly experts and business elites to emphasizing a balance of power across the political spectrum, whereupon professionals' expert opinions were divested in the power play. The substantive functions of many committees were often subjugated to nominal considerations of form and representation. The bureaucrats tended to ignore the political hot air, throwing out the mild expert advice with the bathwater. Many professionals lost interest in participating in this political grand-standing, where uninformed participants representing their political party took over center stage.

With the acceleration of democratization in Hong Kong politics after the reunification, the original role in local community affairs of the District Boards, which were expanded into District Councils after the elimination of the municipal councils, turned highly politicized. Many of the previously appointed members, including myself, had originally regarded serving in the district boards and other committees as a form of community service. Political opportunism sprouted after the termination of the appointment system in 2013, and the remuneration packages of councilors were drastically increased. The District Councils became more like the breeding ground for aspiring politicians to gain popular support for election into the Legislative Council. The politicization split the community, culminating in the radicalization of the District Council elections in 2019. Rhetoric and populism rode the tide, exploiting the electorate whose political literacy had not been cultivated during the jump-start on democracy by the colonial government before reunification.

The 2019 elections in November took place amidst the social unrest. Tension was high given the threat of potential violence outside and inside the polling stations. I was serving as one of the three members of the Election Affairs Commission (EAC) overseeing the elections at the time. The EAC was established in 1997 under the EAC Ordinance as an independent, impartial and apolitical body to ensure that the public elections in Hong Kong were conducted in an open, honest and fair manner. The EAC was composed of a chairman who had always been a high court judge, and two other members who were

EAC members opening the ballot box at the 2019 District Board election.

senior professionals without any political party affiliation appointed by the Chief Executive of Hong Kong. As a judge who was trained to act under the principles of independence, impartiality, and integrity inside the courtroom, the chairman was unpracticed in the politics of the day. His attention was focused on ensuring that election procedures conformed to the ordinance. Having been exposed to the politicized developments of democratization, I was more conscious of the potential risks of violence, disruption and sabotage during the riots.

Large-scale protests against the Hong Kong government started after the introduction of a bill to amend the Fugitive Offenders Ordinance in regard to extradition. The bill was initiated in February 2019 to try to bring justice to a case of murder in Taiwan, where a nineteen-year-old Hong Kong resident had killed his pregnant girlfriend and escaped back to Hong Kong. The current extradition law in Hong Kong did not provide a legal mechanism for transfers of fugitives within Greater China under Chinese sovereignty, including Taiwan, Macau and the Mainland. Widespread protests were fanned by the alleged claim by journalists, legal professionals and foreign governments that the bill would enable Mainland China to arrest political dissidents in Hong Kong. When the second reading of the bill came before the Legislative Council in June, the demonstrations escalated into mass protests and violent riots, which lasted for over six months during which public roads were often blocked, the Legislative Council building was stormed and ransacked, MTR stations were burned and sabotaged, shops deemed to be sympathetic to the Beijing government were vandalized, and universities, including CUHK and the Hong Kong Polytechnic University, were sieged and wrecked by protesters. Mainlanders who spoke Putonghua, as well as locals who did not share their views, were attacked by the protesters. Despite the subsequent withdrawal of the proposed bill, the protests prevailed and escalated. Ordinary citizens not supportive of the protesters were fearful of their safety when they went out. Cars could be stopped by roadblocks erected by the protesters and the passengers could be asked for donations or had their mobile phones inspected to see if there were social media messages unfavorable to the protests. The size of the protests outnumbered the police force. Police stations were attacked and besieged; officers and their families were doxxed and their children bullied in school. Meanwhile, the confessed killer remained at large, after serving nineteen months in jail in Hong Kong for withdrawing money from his deceased girlfriend's credit card, the only crime for which he could be prosecuted in Hong Kong. Even though he later volunteered to turn himself in to the Taiwan law enforcement agency to face trial and serve the sentence, he was not granted a visa by the Taiwan authorities.

Despite the risks of violence and chaos, the EAC decided to go ahead with the scheduled elections, as postponement would further fan conspiracy theories giving cause to escalating violence. The 2019 District Council conducted in November took place just over a week after the occupation of CUHK, whereas the Hong Kong Polytechnic University was still under siege. It was the only election in Hong Kong history during which we needed heightened security measures and personal protection. One of the polling stations was besieged by protesters before vote counting and the returning officer had to retreat into a locked room until security was restored. The polling and vote counting throughout the night survived the intense tension. With record numbers of registered voters, especially among young people, and a record 71 percent turnout rate, the outcome of the elections returned many radical candidates who had no prior experience in serving the community other than the active participation in the social protests.

Following the 2019 social unrest, the National Security Law in Hong Kong was passed by the National People's Congress in 2020, which restored order and peace in the territory, and electoral changes were made to restrict candidate eligibility to those who pledged allegiance to the Basic Law and the national and HKSAR government. The SAR government further reverted to the appointment system and drastically reduced the number of elected members to the District Council, with the intention of reviving the functions of the original district boards to look after the well-being and living environment of the residents in the districts. While the international community blasted the electoral changes as a big step backwards for the progress of democracy, this was the unfortunate consequence when the radicalization of democracy overrode the aim of serving the needs of the people in the community and the peaceful development of society. To many local residents who underwent the turmoil of the social unrest, safety and security were more important human rights than electoral rights.

Violence destroys the core values of democracy, which is premised on fairness of the election process and peaceful transfer of power. Ironically, the acclaimed model of democracy in the United States came under attack by mob violence after the 2020 presidential election. On January 6, 2021, supporters of the then American President Donald Trump, who was defeated in his presidential election, stormed the Capitol Building during a joint session of the U.S. Congress for the certification of the results of the election. The Senate Chamber was occupied, and offices of the evacuated lawmakers were vandalized. In this satiric replay of the storming of the Hong Kong Legislative Council in 2019, extensive physical damage was caused to the Capitol Building. Afterwards, 1,424 people were charged with federal crimes relating to the event, of which close to 900 were sentenced (but later pardoned by President Trump in his second term). Despite its criminal nature, there was polarized public perception and partisan narrative by the political parties on the event itself and its aftermath in American politics, raising international concern about the U.S.'s position as the model democracy. Political analysts warned that pernicious political polarization in America and partisanship espousing policies that benefitted just one party or a small elite instead of the whole society would escalate political violence and deride the fundamental institution of democracy itself. A lesson on the promotion of democracy and its ultimate object.

Building up Governance in Civil Society

Civil society may be referred to as the "Third Sector" or "non-government organizations", apart from the government and commercial sectors. People in society sharing common values come together to contribute to benevolent causes, address civic and humanitarian needs, and promote social progress. There is a vibrant and dynamic civil society in Hong Kong, comprising over 16,600 NGOs according to a 2004 report by the Central Policy Unit of the HKSAR government. These NGOs contribute to the provisions of social services and community development in Hong Kong.

Whereas governmental bodies are established under formal rules, regulations, or legislation, NGOs vary in terms of the maturity of their corporate governance. Many NGOs come into existence out of the collective efforts of a few volunteers sharing a common purpose. Their operations are propelled by passion without the constraints of formality. Without a legal form dedicated to NGOs, most NGOs in Hong Kong are registered with the government as a society under the Societies Office of the Police Force, or more formally as a company limited by guarantees with an incorporated structure and limited personal liability under the Company Ordinance. There is no government restriction on NGO governance in terms of size or composition of its governing board. Fledging NGOs might rely on the advice of honorary legal advisors to help them navigate the incorporation procedure, including drafting the memorandum of the association outlining the details of the company, and articles of the association specifying internal management, procedures, and regulations. For non-profit organizations, the directors do not receive any remuneration, and the revenue will remain in the organizations to further their causes. Under section 88 of the Inland Revenue Ordinance, charitable organizations may apply for tax-exempt status. Beyond the legal structure, company directors bear the responsibility for supervising the proper operation and governance of the NGOs.

Serving on governmental committees taught me about terms of reference, the roles and duties of members, and parliamentary rules of conducting meetings. The government executive and administrative officers were well trained in preparing for and recording the proceedings of the meetings to ensure that rules, procedures, and operations were structured and maintained. Legal advice might be sought from the government lawyers at the Department of Justice when substantive and procedural matters were at stake. These experiences helped me build up the governance of the NGOs in which I served.

Occasional scandals and fraudulent cases exposed the weak regulation of some charity groups and poor governance of its directors in Hong Kong. Before email solicitation became prevalent, I would receive letters appealing for donation to support the cause of deprived children across the world, with greeting cards enclosed allegedly drawn by the children. Even though the name of the organization bore a generic philanthropic label, I was not familiar with this charity group. On closer check of the organizational structure of the group, I discovered that the chairman and directors of the board, as well as executives of the organization, were apparently members of the same family. I could not find its annual accounts and how much the donations it received were put into direct benefits to its targets. I wondered how many other such charities were in operation, preying on the generosity and good will of the public.

A more high-profile case involved a Christian charity organization set up for the rehabilitation of drug addicts. In 2009, the association was alleged to have used government subsidies to invest in overseas real estate and set up a travel company that operated vice establishments in mainland China. At that time, after an investigation by the Independent Commission Against Corruption, no corruption or malpractice was identified. In 2024, four directors of the association were arrested on suspicion of conspiracy to defraud HK$50 million from donors, and warrants were issued for three directors, including the founder, who had absconded overseas after the investigation began. A police investigation found that less than 10 percent of the donations raised went to the boarding school run by the association for young people recovering from drug addiction. The rest of the donations went into its overseas branches with transactions via other accounts, including the private accounts of some of its directors. The fraudulent case left the school operations in limbo and the continuing education of the students uncertain. It also raised questions about the grossly inadequate governance of charity groups with large donations, even though there was a board structure with respectable directors and public reports of its activities.

According to the Hong Kong Council of Social Services, the social welfare NGO sector provided up to 90 percent of the social services delivered in Hong Kong, mostly focused on children, youth, the elderly, families, and persons with disabilities as target groups. Women, sexual minorities, and ethnic minorities were latecomers. While the colonial government relied on the philanthropy of elites and corporations for donations and then neighborhood resident or kaifong associations to support welfare services during the early days, government provisions for social welfare expanded under Governor MacLehose in the 1970s. In accordance with the colonial government's principle of small government, subventions were allocated to NGOs to operate welfare services. The social services which had previously operated mostly from donations became more stable and standardized. NGOs could take the initiative to experiment with pilot projects in service delivery before the government determined their value for sustained financial support. In 2023–2024, 177 NGOs received government subventions to run services for family and child welfare, social security, services for the elderly, rehabilitation and medical social services, services for offenders, community development, and young people. The quality and financing of the services under these subvention schemes were subject to more direct supervision and oversight by the government. These NGOs were required to strengthen their organizational and governance structure with annual meetings of its members, election of officials, and reports of audited accounts.

The New Life Psychiatric Rehabilitation Association

The New Life Psychiatric Rehabilitation Association is one of the largest welfare service NGOs in Hong Kong, receiving 79 percent of its total operating income of HK$554 million in the form of subvention from the Social Welfare Department in 2023. It is the NGO which I served for the longest time, beginning with its subcommittee on a female halfway house in Kwun Tong in 1976 when I was working at the United Christian Hospital.

New Life was founded in 1959 by Dr. Stella Liu 劉曼華 at Castle Peak Psychiatric Hospital with a group of discharged patients under the original name New Life Mutual Aid Club. Before the Tuen Mun new town was developed in the northwest part of the New Territories, Castle Peak, or Green Hill, was a remote rural area where the first modern psychiatric hospital was built in 1961. The Chinese name, Green Hill (青山 *Qingshan*), became identified with "lunatic asylum," and people with psychiatric disorders were referred to as people having come from Green Hill, reflecting the stigmatization of mental illness. After participating in the group psychotherapy that Stella pioneered in the 1960s, some of her patients wished to continue their groups beyond hospital care. Together with these participants, Stella formed a club with fifty-five basic members, from which committee members were elected to run the mutual aid club. Concerned that some of the patients ready to be discharged from Castle Peak Hospital did not have a home to which they could return, Stella managed—with the help of friends in the civil service—to acquire a piece of farmland next to the hospital where the discharged patients could grow vegetables and feed pigs in a secluded and bucolic setting close to their familiar hospital location. The club services expanded into halfway houses for men and women where people in recovery could stay for a short time before they were ready to return to their family or the community, and a shelter workshop for vocational training before they could take up regular employment. Even without government funding, dedicated volunteers provided the much-needed aftercare services for psychiatric rehabilitation. With the expansion of service development, the club became incorporated as a formal association in 1966.

At the New Life Farm & Greenhouse opening ceremony, 1979.

At New Life's 30th anniversary, with Raymond Wu (third from the right),
S.C. Ho (fourth from the right) and Founder Stella Liu
(fourth from the left), 1995.

In 1978, I became the chair of the female halfway house subcommittee and joined the Executive Committee. The initial members of the Executive Committee were mostly psychiatrists, with Dr. Raymond Wu 鄔維庸, a cardiologist, serving as the first chairman after the incorporation of the association. Apart from his leadership role in the Hong Kong Medical Association in the 1980s, most of Raymond's commitment had focused on community well-being, including psychiatric rehabilitation and social capacity development in Hong Kong. Raymond played a pivotal role in building up New Life from a small mutual aid club staffed by volunteers to the leading mental health service NGO in Hong Kong. Under the long tenure of his leadership, the staff structure expanded from a few dozen staff members headed by a diffident general secretary to a team of 900 diversified professional and supporting staff commanded by a confident and entrepreneurial Chief Executive Officer, Ms. Deborah Wan 溫麗友. Raymond solicited donations from a range of charities such as the Rotary Club and the Hong Kong Jockey Club to support new initiatives in service delivery. He set up an Institute of Psychiatric Rehabilitation to provide specialized training for mental health professionals and public mental health education as an effort to contribute to the development of the expertise and advocacy in the field. Many of the pilot service models of New Life were later adopted into the standard provisions subvented by the government. Coming of age, a new purpose-built headquarters was completed in 1996, consolidating the central administration team in a permanent location. The premises also housed residential and vocational training facilities together with the Institute of Psychiatric Rehabilitation in its annex.

In 1990s, Raymond noted that mental health service in mainland China tended to focus on medication rather than community integration. He promoted New Life's practice of community psychiatric rehabilitation services with the mainland counterparts and built up a series of exchange programs with the China Disabled Persons' Federation (CDPF), which was headed by former Chinese paramount leader Deng Xiaoping's 鄧小平 son, who became a paraplegic after being injured by the Red Guards during the Cultural Revolution. A memorial fund was set up in Raymond's name after his death in 2006 to support the exchange programs and collaboration with mainland

行政總裁溫麗友小姐榮休晚宴
Celebration Party in honor of
Miss Deborah Wan

At Deborah Wan's (fourth from from right) 2009 retirement dinner.

China. With the firm foundation built up by Raymond and Deborah, New Life became the largest NGO providing psychiatric rehabilitation services.

Raymond served as New Life's chairperson for forty years. With membership in the Executive Committee remaining stable or stationary for decades, and most of the members coming from the same profession, there was a lack of diversity and new ideas. When Raymond passed away unexpectedly in 2006, the management team headed by Deborah had a strained working relationship with the then Vice-Chairman who succeeded Raymond as chairman. It highlighted the delicate balance in boundary setting between the roles of management and the executive committee or its chairman.

The founding President of the Association, Mr. Sai-chu Ho 何世柱, skillfully intervened and I was elected Chairman from 2008 to 2018, when I was asked by Mr. Ho to succeed him as President. The President's primary role was to chair the general meetings of the association, oversee the election of the executive committee members and supervise the governance of the association. As President, Mr. Ho had been an anchor of stability and a staunch champion. A prominent business figure and a philanthropist with remarkable contributions

Fanny (first row second from left) with Dr. Harry Fang
(standing in the back row, on the left)
at the 1996 Rehabilitation International World Congress.

to the construction industry, employer-employee relations, education, social well-being, and the promotion of Chinese art and culture, Mr. Ho had a long career of public service for which he was awarded the Grand Bauhinia Medal (GBM), the highest honor of the Hong Kong SAR. Even in his eighties, he continued tirelessly to serve the government's Labour Advisory Board and attend international conventions with the government delegation, sharing his valuable experiences with cohorts of government officials. His dedication to the New Life Psychiatric Rehabilitation Association was unfailing, despite his other commitments. When he stepped down as President, he happily accepted our invitation to remain as Patron of the Association so that he could continue to be affiliated with our work and attend our annual functions. His sincere and genuine support was an inspiration.

Having initiated and led different NGOs of varying sizes, I learned to appreciate the importance of corporate governance as these organizations grew. The history of New Life provided a glimpse of the lessons to be learned in corporate governance of NGOs as well as of the evolution of mental health services in Hong Kong.

During the early stages of New Life, funding was limited and there were few professional staff. Committee members, who were mostly mental health professionals, were more hands-on in the operation of the services. Major advances in rehabilitation services in Hong Kong began in the 1970s under the advocacy of Dr. Harry Fan 方心讓, an orthopaedic surgeon who became known as the "father of rehabilitation" in Asia. Dr. Fan had advocated for the rights of persons with disabilities all his life and was influential in steering the colonial government in formulating a coordinated and comprehensive rehabilitation policy for Hong Kong when he served as a member of the Legislative Council and the Executive Council of the colonial government from the 1970s to 1980s. He was knighted in the Queen's Birthday Honours in 1996 and received the GBM from the Hong Kong SAR government in 2001. After his retirement, he continued to champion the cause of integrating persons with disability in the community, leading delegations to attend conferences of Rehabilitation International, an international disability rights organization with member organizations in every region of the world, to which he was elected Vice-President and Chairman of its Asian Regional Assembly in 1972.

Through his advocacy, the government tabled a Green Paper entitled *The Further Development of Rehabilitation Services in Hong Kong* in the Legislative Council in 1976, which was circulated for public consultation before the White Paper finalizing the policy, *Integrating the Disabled into the Community: A United Effort*, was published in 1977. The White Paper outlined the government's plan to address the needs of people with disabilities, including the establishment of a statutory Rehabilitation Development Coordinating Committee, the appointment of a Commissioner for Rehabilitation, and the adoption of a ten-year program plan with funding allocations. The program plan recognized the necessity of comprehensive rehabilitation services to enable persons with disabilities to develop their physical, mental and social capabilities to the fullest extent that their disabilities permitted. Designated funding was allocated to governmental and nongovernmental organizations to deliver the services. A second White Paper on rehabilitation, entitled *Equal Opportunities and Full Participation: A Better Future for All*, was published in 1995, to extend the concept of community integration with inclusion and equal opportunities. Women and persons with disabilities shared many similar experiences of discrimination in society. The coalition of these advocacy groups led to the government's enactment of the Sex Discrimination Ordinance and the Disability Discrimination Ordinance in 1995, and the establishment of the Equal Opportunities Commission to implement both laws in 1996.

As soon as I became the EOC Chairperson, I was invited by Dr. Fang to join the Hong Kong delegation to attend the World Congress of the Rehabilitation International in New Zealand in 1996, where I learned much more about the range of needs of persons with all forms of disabilities besides those with mental disabilities. What impressed me most about Dr. Fang's unadorned style and common touch was his insistence in flying in economy class for the long haul flight so that he could stay close to the other delegates, despite his status and seniority. The only special treat he gave himself was buying the whole row of economy seats so that he could lie flat across the seats or on the floor of the cabin.

With the active participation of Dr. Raymond Wu and Deborah Wan in the advocacy for mental rehabilitation policy and services, New Life benefited from the government's rehabilitation program plan resources. A more competitive salary structure comparable to the civil service scale was available to build up the professional team. Although lacking the fringe benefits of civil service, the mission and core values of New Life helped to attract and retain dedicated staff. Each year, we were proud to present long service awards to our devoted colleagues.

Beyond the standard services provided under the government subvention scheme, Raymond and Deborah initiated new ventures in services. To provide service users opportunities for training in a real work setting beyond the protected environment of a sheltered workshop, and to help them gain necessary skills and confidence for open employment and community integration, New Life launched its first social enterprise in 1994. As a simulated business, a vegetable stall was set up in a wet market in Tuen Mun, close to the New Life Farm where the halfway house residents and shelter workshop trainees helped to grow organic vegetables and herbs. These initial experiences in the simulated business approach expanded the traditional form of welfare services in

At the 2010 Mindset Place opening with Sania Yau (first from the right).

psychiatric rehabilitation into a combined platform of training and employment which promoted financial sustainability, community integration and social impact. New Life had become one of the pioneers in social enterprises in Hong Kong. By 2024, it was running twenty-two social enterprises covering a wide sector including catering, retail, ecotourism, direct sales, cleaning services, and property management to create diversified work opportunities for persons in recovery.

The next CEO who succeeded Deborah upon her retirement in 2009 was Ms. Sania Yau 游秀慧, who had returned from a brief sojourn in Canada before 1997, and had been a supervisor for staff training and development at New Life for thirteen years. With a management style that was more egalitarian, she fostered a cultural shift in her professional team and the service orientation of the association. I nominated Sania for a fellowship of the International Women's Forum, where she was mentored in leadership skills and international networking. My working relationship with Sania was seamless, as I trusted her capability and management style. While the Executive Committee's role was to set the strategic directions and review the performance of the CEO, it was more important for me as the Executive Committee chairperson to empower

At the Dayday 330 opening ceremony in 2024. Annie Tam
(fourth from the right), Ho Sai-chu (fifth from the right)
and Fanny (third from the left).

her to take up challenges, keep abreast of her progress, and provide advice when assistance was needed.

Sania put her heart into advancing mental health services. I fully supported her initiative to pioneer the recovery model in mental health, which emphasized the rights and dignity of people to control all aspects of their lives regardless of their symptoms or stage of recovery. This service model required attitude changes in the service providers to value service users as holistic persons who could take charge of their recovery, and not as psychiatric patients who passively received services decided by the experts. Service users who were ready would be involved in the planning of their recovery process. To destigmatize mental illness and promote better understanding of mental health for all, social-inclusive programs and activities were organized to engage the public. Sania embraced my emphasis on evidence-based practice and conducted research to review and improve our services.

In the transformation of its services, New Life launched a new branding of its identity under the theme of "New Life 330" in 2011 to complement the original name of the association, which highlighted psychiatric rehabilitation when it was incorporated. The Cantonese pronunciation of the numbers "330 *saam saam ling*" is homophonic to "body" (身 *san*), "mind" (心 *sam*), and "spirit" (靈 *ling*), referring to the holistic health notion of physical, psychological and transcendental well-being.

While the public was more conscious of physical fitness, which could be built up through physical activities, quality sleep and balanced diet, its integration with psychological and spiritual well-being had been neglected due to the adoption of the Western model of disease-centered medicine, which used to segregate physical and mental health in healthcare systems. Attention to holistic health, which shared cultural roots in many traditions of indigenous healing such as Chinese herbal medicine or Indian Ayurveda, broke through the scientific barricade of Western medicine in recent decades, when research evidence demonstrated how physical health affected mental health or vice versa.

The concept of psychological well-being, which had traditionally been associated with the stigma of mental illness, had remained on the periphery of healthcare. The World Health Organization (WHO) defined mental health as the state of psychological well-being that enabled people to cope with life stresses, realize their abilities, learn well, work well, and contribute to their community. The subject of psychology was often perceived by many people as a mystery. When people I first met learned that I was a psychologist, the first thing they would ask was whether I could read their mind, as if I was a crystal gazer or psychic. I had to tell them psychologists studied how the mind worked as revealed by their thoughts, emotions, motivations, and behaviors. Similar to building up physical fitness and immunity, psychological well-being and resilience could be enhanced through activities such as relaxation exercises to reduce stress, mindfulness exercises to become more aware of one's thoughts, feelings, and body sensations happening in the present moment, and cognitive restructuring exercises to replace negative and unproductive thoughts.

The WHO regarded mental health as an integral component of health and well-being that underpinned our individual and collective abilities to make decisions, build relationships and shape the world we live in. The role of social determinants of health risks underscored the salience of social connections in the form of social support, social networks, and the absence of perceived social isolation as protective factors. In positive psychology, happiness and quality of life were defined by relationships, engagement, and meaning, in addition to achievement and positive emotions. Social connectedness involved a give-and-take process beyond the focus on the individual self, highlighting the relevance of philanthropy and the sense of community that contributed to spiritual well-being.

The concept of transcendental or spiritual well-being might seem abstract and elusive. The contemporary concept of spirituality involved more than the traditional notion of religion or mystic experience, but a broader range of personal quests for meaning. Psychological research extracted three distinct aspects of the meaning in life—comprehension (a sense that one's life and the world are understandable and coherent), purpose (a sense that one has valuable goals towards which one is working) and mattering (a sense that one's existence is of significance in the world). Having meaning in life was shown to be related to physical and psychological well-being and was considered a fundamental cornerstone of happiness. Meaning would increase when people's concerns expand beyond their personal interests to include concern for other people, other groups, or all of life and the universe around them by showing gratitude, learning to forgive, and giving back. By taking time to reflect on our core values and purpose, we could become connected to things greater than ourselves. As such, meaning in life would entail self-transcendence.

By promoting the universal importance of holistic well-being, the New Life 330 campaigns helped to narrow the social divide between the public and people in recovery of mental illness. Collaborating with my psychology colleagues at CUHK, New Life developed simple evidence-based tools and activities for helping people to enhance their well-being in daily life through outreaching community-wide holistic health campaigns. The 330 movement attracted corporate and business partners in the development of corporate social integration programs, and propelled New Life onto a higher platform in leading innovations and influencing both government and other service providers in the field of mental health services and education. Beyond the provision of psychiatric rehabilitation in the 1960s, holistic 330 health became integrated into primary health care and everyday lifestyle. The range of services at New Life further expanded, and the staff size grew to over 1,200 employees.

Despite its success, the corporate and governance structure of New Life lagged behind its rapid expansion. Its frailty came to the fore upon the sudden death of Sania in a tragic traffic accident in 2017. Like her predecessor, Sania capably and wholeheartedly steered the operations without sparing the time to groom the team for succession. The high-level position of the CEO was created during the association's expansion, but there was a lack of second-tier senior management who could deputize and bridge the gap between the CEO and the frontline supervisory staff in middle management. Although the Executive Committee had recommended moving in this direction, it was not a top priority amidst the demanding daily operations. Sania's sudden departure threw the executive function into limbo. As Chair of the Executive Committee, I joined the management meetings to calm the grief of the colleagues and reassure them of the support of the Executive Committee to carry on Sania's legacy. However, recruitment of Sania's replacement took time. Without a clear deputy in place, the three unprepared service supervisors from middle management took up the interim role of the CEO by rotation under my weekly off-site supervision. Given my busy work as the Pro-Vice-Chancellor at CUHK at that time, this loose supervision was far from ideal.

A silver lining fortuitously appeared on the horizon when my former student, Annie Tam 譚贛蘭, who had just retired as Permanent Secretary for Labour and Welfare, contacted me. She was interested in offering lectures on public policies for the university, which would be an asset for our colleagues and students. Annie was an undergraduate student in Social Work at CUHK who had taken a couple of psychology courses from me. I remembered her as a bright and dynamic student whose brilliance had continued to shine in her government career. Given her wide portfolio as a senior government official, she was familiar with and supportive of the work of New Life. Realizing that she was not yet ready to stop working after leaving her position, I invited her to help New Life in addition to lecturing at the university. Annie joined the Executive Committee of New Life, which entrusted her with the interim supervisory role to guide the work of the acting CEOs before a new CEO was recruited. With the restricted pool of candidates in the field, external recruitment was not an easy task. External candidates also needed time to familiarize themselves with the range of professional services, the diverse staff, and the corporate culture. It took another round of turnover before one of the service supervisors was deemed ready to take up the leadership position. The importance of grooming the second-tier management for succession planning was clearly demonstrated. Good management was not just about star leadership, but also strong team building and mentoring.

I was reminded of the forty-year tenure of Dr. Raymond Wu as Chairman of the Executive Committee. Even though he was a capable leader, his unexpected death highlighted the importance of planned turnover in the governance structure. NGOs were typically run by dedicated volunteers who were committed to the social cause throughout their lives. On the other hand, as committee members aged, we needed to inject new blood for succession planning and innovation. With expansion of its services, New Life also needed more directors from diverse backgrounds beyond mental health professionals. I had served on the Executive Committee since 1978 and became Vice-Chairman in 1981 until I resigned in 1996 to become the EOC Chairperson. Upon my return, I served as the Chairperson of the Executive Committee from 2008 to 2018. That was long enough to move on and rejuvenate the steering and oversight committee. I had been working towards strengthening the governance structure along these lines when Annie arrived. Annie's dynamism revitalized New Life during its transition from the loss of Sania. Her extensive network built up from her government portfolio expanded the horizon of the Executive Committee and facilitated the operations of the management. Her contributions impressed other committee members. Despite her short tenure in New Life, she was unanimously elected as the new Chairman when I stepped down to take up the role of President in 2018.

Notwithstanding the temporary respite, the issue of succession planning in both the Executive Committee and in senior management remained a perpetual concern for New Life, as well as for many NGOs in Hong Kong. This issue had usually been put on the back burner while more urgent operational tasks remained the focus. Serving the clients and the community was always the priority. On the other hand, the path towards perpetuity requires building a strong foundation on governance and developing holistic succession plans.

How to recruit volunteers who share the selfless compassion to serve, balance their passion with boundary setting, build up the succession ladder and manage smooth transition are important lessons for civil society to continue to thrive and serve the community.

BRINGING
A CHINESE
VOICE
TO
PSYCHOLOGY

The 1985 Minnesota Multiphasic Personality
Inventory Beijing training class photo. With
Song Weizhen (first row, fourth from the
right), James Butcher (first row, sixth from
the right) and Fanny between them.

7

I did not start my career in psychology with any ambition of bringing a Chinese voice to mainstream psychology. Having been trained in Western psychology, I just wanted to apply what I had learned to serve my own society when I returned to Hong Kong. Colonial education in Hong Kong did not provide us with a foundation in understanding Chinese culture. In our English-medium school, the only Chinese subjects were Chinese literature and Chinese history. Chinese history was an unpopular elective in secondary school as it was not deemed to have instrumental value.

The Chinese history syllabus stopped at the fall of the Qing dynasty in 1911, very remote from our daily life. There was only a brief reference to the Treaty of Nanking following China's defeat in the first Opium War, which gave Hong Kong to Britain without indicating its unequal nature, as the first in a series of treaties imposed on Qing China. These treaties had been termed as "unequal" because they were not negotiated by nations treating each other as equals, but had encroached upon China's sovereign rights. There was no analysis of the background of the illicit import of opium into China by Britain designed to balance the British trade deficit, resulting in widespread opium addiction in China. When the Chinese government tried to enforce its prohibition of opium, including burning the opium stocks confiscated from the British merchants, the

British government sent a naval fleet to bombard the southern ports in China to force the Chinese government to pay reparations and allow the opium trade. The weak Qing-dynasty army—which was no match for the Royal Navy—was defeated, resulting in the first unequal treaty between China and Western powers related to the opium trade. It was easy to understand why the colonial government did not want to cover the background of the Treaty of Nanking and the subsequent unequal treaties in school.

With our curtailed Chinese history curriculum, we knew nothing about the warlord era that divided China into different regions occupied by different military factions during the early period of the Chinese Republic. We did not learn about the civil war fought between the Kuomintang-led government of the Republic of China and the forces of the Chinese Communist Party, which lasted from 1927 until 1949, leading to the establishment of the People's Republic of China. Many students taking the science stream opted out of this Chinese history subject altogether. The chronological account of the dynasties over the centuries taught in class demanded rote memorization and did not stimulate interest or national sentiment, even though I did well in the examinations. As part of a lost generation, I had no clue about contemporary Chinese history after the establishment of the Republic at the end of the imperial dynasties. My quest to understand China only evolved from my exchanges with fellow Chinese students in college and graduate school. Being away from home made us think more about who we were and where we came from.

Interest in Learning about China

At UC Berkeley, a few graduate students from Hong Kong and Taiwan started a Chinese newsletter in the Chinese Student Association to report on Chinese cultural topics, events back home, as well as social issues in the San Francisco Chinatown. (Before the U.S. and China resumed diplomatic relations, there were no foreign students from mainland China.) I began to realize how rudimentary my Chinese knowledge was, having left Hong Kong before I finished secondary school. I enrolled in a Chinese literature course in the hope of keeping up my language ability. I discovered that half of the class were undergraduates from Hong Kong who were there to get an easy grade. When called upon by the teacher to read out passages from the selected readings, we were ashamed that the non-Chinese students were more proficient and accurate with their Mandarin pronunciation than our Hong Kong group. Not having learned Mandarin in secondary schools, we all created our own twists in Cantonese pronunciation as if they were Mandarin enunciation. Although I fretted during every class that I would be called upon to recite passages, I enjoyed the new discoveries of short stories by Lu Xun 魯迅 like *Diary of a Madman* (狂人日記 *Kuangrenriji*) and a Communist article on population control by Ma Yinchu 馬寅初. Lu Xun's characterization of the Chinese common folks stimulated my interest to write up a character analysis of Ah Q from the *True Story of Ah Q* (阿Q正傳 *Ah Q zhengchuan*) in my term paper for my personality psychology course. Lack of exposure to contemporary Chinese literature revealed to me how ignorant I had been about modern China. It also demonstrated the absence of national identity among my generation (and probably many generations up to now).

With the cultural awakening sparked by the Chinese newsletter and discussion groups at the Chinese Student Association, some Hong Kong students became attracted by the romanticized version of the Cultural Revolution, which was launched by Chairman Mao Zedong in 1966 with the stated aim to purge the bourgeois elements of capitalism and to preserve Chinese socialism. Schools were closed and educated youths were sent to work in the countryside to learn from the farmers with the purpose of minimizing the differences between industrial workers and farmers, between urban and rural areas, and between manual labor and brain work. The idealism of equality and true democracy was so alluring that a couple of quixotic students decided to quit school to join the rural reeducation program in China. Their utopic myth was soon proven wrong by the harsh reality. They left China in disillusionment. It took them a while before they could pick up the pieces in their lives to resume their studies.

At the University of Minnesota where I pursued my graduate studies, students from the Hong Kong Club started a China Study Group and printed a newsletter on contemporary events about China. In the early 1970s before the historical visit by U.S. President Nixon to China, there were no diplomatic relations between China and Western countries. Publicly available information on modern China was scarce. We managed to organize a documentary film show on China by Edgar Snow, the American journalist and China correspondent known for his close friendship with the Communist leaders and for his famous 1937 book, *Red Star over China.* To our surprise, the film show sold out to a full house of university students on campus. When the groundbreaking *Exhibition of Archaeological Finds of the People's Republic of China* was presented in the St. Louis Art Museum, we were exhilarated and chartered two tour buses to travel to Missouri to visit the exhibition. News about the territorial dispute between China and Japan erupting on the Diaoyutai Islands located in the waters of the East China Sea prompted us to investigate the history of the islands. We found historical records showing that since the fourteenth century, the islands had been used as the Ming dynasty imperial envoys' navigational reference points, a military post of Chinese naval forces, and as a Taiwanese fishermen's operational base. The Japanese claimed that the islands were incorporated into its territory following their occupation in 1895, although it refuted the claim that the territory belonged to the Island of Taiwan ceded to Japan by the Qing dynasty following the first Sino-Japanese war. The disputes aroused patriotic sentiments among overseas Chinese students all over the U.S., who formed alliances to protest Japan's claim on the islands. Some of them joined the protests at the Japanese consulate in Chicago in January 1971, shivering in the freezing blizzard in their Hong Kong winter outfits, which were totally unfit for the Mid-Western subzero temperature.

At that time, I had no knowledge about pro-independence politics in Taiwan. When I helped to prepare the program of the international students' festival organized by the International Students Office, I put down the performance of a Taiwanese students' puppet show as "Chinese puppet show" as a matter of fact. I could not understand why the performance group vehemently objected and insisted that it should be "Taiwanese puppet show." We later learned that apart from the pro-independent Taiwanese students, some other students from Taiwan were starting to sense repercussions from their government. The university's student newspaper, *Minnesota Daily*, reported that about four to ten students from Taiwan were acting for their government as spies on other Taiwanese students. Allegedly, the Taiwan students would be threatened or harassed if they tried to learn about mainland affairs or befriended people knowledgeable about the mainland and thus would be labelled as sympathizers of the enemy or the bandits. It was claimed that the Taiwanese government's surveillance on its students tightened as the U.S. moved closer toward normalized relations with the mainland, and particularly after President Nixon's visit to China in 1972.

Most of us from Hong Kong had little prior knowledge about the mainland other than the demonized images of the communists or leftists we gained from the colony's media, especially after the 1967 anti-colonial riots in Hong Kong which were supported by pro-China labor unions. Under Western sanctions, mainland China had been closed off from the rest of the world. When we were young, children were warned not to walk close to the mainland Chinese emporium stores without specific reasons. Our nationalistic awakening was evoked only when we had the opportunity to gather more information about modern China after being away from Hong Kong, and when the United States was making its overture toward the mainland in the early 1970s. We were jubilant in learning that the United Nations' General Assembly passed a resolution in October 1971 to recognize the People's Republic of China as the sole legal representative of China, and when it was seated in November 1971. We were glued to the television to watch Nixon's visit to China in 1972 when he met with Premier Zhou Enlai 周恩來 and Chairman Mao Zedong 毛澤東 in Beijing. During our reunions, some of our cohort's UM alumni still shared with great passion memories and memorabilia they had kept from the Hong Kong Club days.

Exploring Chinese Mental Health

After my return to Hong Kong in 1975, China was slowly opening to the outside world. Upon the death of Chairman Mao in 1976 and the downfall of the Gang of Four later that year, the decade-long Cultural Revolution came to an end. Universities were gradually reopened, and academic disciplines were resumed. I was keen to visit and see China first hand. My first opportunity came when the Sociology Department at CUHK organized a field trip in 1978 to study the people's commune (人民公社 *remin gongshe*) in Taishan, a county in Guangdong province in southern China. At that time, the psychology minor program was housed under the Sociology Department. I volunteered to join the field trip to study mental health services in the commune.

The hotels in rural towns were very rudimentary in the late 1970s. There was no air conditioning, but at least there was a fan and a mosquito net hanging over the bed. The lights were dim and hot water was only turned on in the evening. I brought my own plastic tube to connect to the faucet for my shower. I had to get used to the squatting toilets without falling into the pit. Nevertheless, the room was clean.

For a whole week, I followed my sociology colleagues to visit the rural communes in the village. We accompanied the barefoot doctor on his home visits, toured the public hospitals, inspected the rural public hygiene facilities and the tertiary septic tanks behind public toilets, and sat in meetings when the villagers discussed their shares in collective production and labor. The commune leaders were forthcoming to speak to us as the first group of outside scholars coming to visit their village. However, I was not getting anywhere with my topic on mental health care in the early stage of our trip.

During one of the daily rides on the minibus we took from the hotel to the commune, the woman cadre assigned to escort us during the field trip asked me about my interest in visiting mental hospitals. She was sympathetic about my disappointment and confirmed that it was not an easy topic for studies as it was difficult to find patients. I was surprised with her categorical explanation that there was no mental illness in new China. There must be some mental patients in hospitals, I pushed on. She then insisted that those few cases would be remnants of the old society. Realizing the futility in pursuing this line of inquiry, I decided to switch to another term for mental illness that had been used in popular Chinese books on mental health. What about neurasthenia, I asked. Her answer was even more surprising. She lit up and revealed there were plenty. She confessed that even she herself suffered from neurasthenia. She often had difficulty sleeping and poor appetite when there was work pressure.

Indigenization of Neurasthenia

I pondered the cadre's puzzling turnaround attitude. Apparently, under the Marxist theory of dialectical materialism, mental disorders were regarded as a social ill resulting from the conflict of social forces. With Communism replacing the corrupt feudalistic society, these social ills should have been eliminated in New China. On the other hand, in Chinese folk medicine, neurasthenia, which literally meant weak nerves, was often attributed to overwork. It connoted diligence, seriousness, and responsibility, which were regarded as virtuous qualities, thus removing the social stigma of madness.

Neurasthenia was an outdated diagnosis removed from the current Western psychiatric nomenclature due to its ill-defined collection of symptoms characterized by lassitude, fatigue, headache, and irritability. The imported term had been incorporated into the nomenclature of Chinese folk medicine, assuming a new identity. Popular Chinese folk medicine books were written on neurasthenia, attributing causes to lifestyle, psychological factors, and health problems. Recommendations on treatment emphasized self-help approaches through changing health habits, reviewing negative attitudes, tonic care, and relaxation. Neurasthenia remained in both the formal and informal taxonomy of Chinese psychiatrists, who used the term interchangeably with "neurosis" to communicate with patients and their family members to minimize the shame of mental illness, although it was not a formal diagnostic category.

As a broad and all-inclusive term, neurasthenia could be used to refer to a symptom or syndrome, a disorder, or a causal explanation. Traditional Chinese medicine adopted a holistic health paradigm which enabled the co-existence of psychological and physical factors in the expression of neurasthenia. The vagueness of the label became a useful camouflage to avoid social stigma not only for depression and anxiety, but a wide range of psychiatric conditions. In my early clinical practice, if I told patients or their families about their psychiatric diagnoses, they would be reluctant to see a psychiatrist for fear of the stigma. By resorting to the neurasthenia label, especially with less educated clients, I could gently nudge them to accept the referral. My probe of the cultural shaping of this originally

Western psychiatric diagnosis into a concept of Chinese illness experience sparked my interest in understanding Chinese psychopathology from a local context.

Do Chinese Somatize Their Psychological Problems?

I began to investigate how Chinese people expressed their mental problems and sought help. To understand Chinese psychopathology, which was not covered in my training, I read up scholarly literature in cultural psychiatry. Transcultural psychiatry first became a sub-branch of the discipline of psychiatry in the late 1950s. It questioned the universal applicability of Western psychiatric diagnostic categories and highlighted the cultural context of mental disorders and psychiatric services. Researchers and practitioners in non-Western countries became interested in culture-bound syndromes, which were identified with "exotic" conditions of mental and somatic symptoms found outside Euro-American societies. Shenkui 腎虧, which was attributed to excessive sexual activities, and neurasthenia were two common culture-bound syndromes associated with Chinese culture. In Chinese folk medicine, neurasthenia and other mental problems were described in terms of imbalance of the internal organs associated with excessive cold or heat according to the Yin and Yang system, which was totally foreign to Western medicine.

In the 1980s, Prof. Wen-shing Tseng 曾文星 at the University of Hawai'i initiated a series of conferences on Chinese culture and mental health at the East-West Center in Honolulu, from which I learned more about various manifestation of mental health problems in Chinese societies. A common observation by cultural psychiatrists was that Chinese patients tended to "somatize" their psychological problems. The 1977 seminal paper by Prof. Arthur Kleinman, a sinologist and professor of psychiatry and of social anthropology at Harvard University, on depression and somatization was credited for having heralded the "new cross-cultural psychiatry." Prof. Kleinman had conducted research in Taiwan from 1969 to 1978, and later in mainland China. He observed that Chinese patients presented their psychological distress as bodily and organic symptoms for which they would seek help from medical practitioners. In his early writings, Kleinman observed that Chinese patients were more prone (than middle-class Americans) to attribute their psychological states to physical illness. Other cultural psychiatrists jumped on the bandwagon and offered post-hoc interpretations to explain this tendency. Some scholars labelled somatization as a culture-bound syndrome and alleged that Chinese people were prone to deny their psychological distress. In one of these papers, the author even suggested that the reason for Chinese somatization was that the Chinese language was deficient in expressive emotional terms, which could not be further from the truth given the richness of Chinese literature and poetry expressing diverse emotions throughout the centuries.

Despite my limited clinical experience in Hong Kong at that time, this distorted interpretation of somatization did not make sense to me. So, I initiated a series of empirical studies to see if Chinese patients in fact denied their emotional problems and how they sought help for their psychological problems. With the collaboration of Dr. Bernard Lau Wai Kai 劉偉楷, a psychiatrist in private practice, and Dr. Edith Waldman, a general practitioner whom I knew from the War on Rape campaign, we interviewed patients attending Edith's clinic. Using a checklist consisting of different psychological symptoms, we found that these patients in general practice, who could have been diagnosed with depression, would present to the doctor only their somatic symptoms, including sleep disturbances, general malaise, aches and pains, dizziness, and menopausal symptoms, which prompted them to seek help from the doctor. When directly asked using the symptom checklist for depression, these patients admitted having various psychological features, including dysphoric mood, self-reproach, and a loss of interest in social activities and in sex. The discrepancy between the pattern of presenting physical complaints and admitted psychological symptoms suggested that patients were aware of their emotional disturbance even though they tended to express these disturbances in somatic terms in their help-seeking processes. They did not hide their psychological problems deliberately. In another large-scale community survey, we analyzed the responses of a random sample of around 4,000 people in Hong Kong to a mental health measure and found that they admitted just as many psychological symptoms, if not more so, than other psychophysiological and physiological symptoms. The earlier suggestion that Chinese people tended to deny their feelings could not be established from the observation on this cross-section of the population in urban Hong Kong. From these empirical studies,

Visiting Harvard Fairbank Center in 1999, with Arthur and Joan Kleinman
(standing and seated right) and Ezra Vogel (standing left).

Meeting Edith Waldmann in London, 2009.

we might infer that for the Chinese people, medical doctors were supposed to treat their physical symptoms only and should not be bothered with their emotional state. Meanwhile, busy doctors in Hong Kong hospitals and private practice generally saw their patients for a few minutes and did not have time to talk to their patients beyond listening to their presenting complaints and then writing out the prescriptions.

To further explain the alleged somatization tendency, we conducted other studies which showed that patients as well as students would reserve their personal and emotional problems for their friends and family, who were willing to listen to them. In the course of psychiatric illness, Chinese patients travelled a detoured route of self-help and help-seeking before arriving at the psychiatric consultation. Doctor shopping was common as they sought help from multiple general practitioners for their somatic symptoms without being relieved from their suffering until their psychiatric problems were identified and eventually got referred to psychiatry. The longest delay in our sample of patients was thirty years before the psychiatric problem was identified and a psychiatric referral was made!

These studies suggested an alternative explanation of the somatization tendency in terms of the health-seeking patterns in Chinese society: i.e. patients would approach primary care doctors for their physical symptoms but their friends or family for their psychological needs. After rounds of doctor shopping, the psychological problems were finally identified, and the patients got referred to specialists in psychiatry. General practice could be seen as a traffic roundabout in which patients would go around and around if they were not directed to the right exit or referral. The role of general practitioners, or family doctors as they are now called, in detecting psychiatric problems and directing the movement of patients is cardinal. Their role is now fully recognized in the stepped care model of primary mental healthcare delivery.

Other international studies started to show that somatization was not unique to the Chinese. It was prevalent not only in non-Western countries but was also found in Western societies. The relevant term used in the current Western diagnostic classification system could be chronic fatigue syndrome. My attempt to debunk the myth of the Chinese somatization tendency led me to a deeper understanding of cultural differences in epistemology. The original concept of somatization was construed in the dichotomization of the mind and body, which could be seen as an artifact of Western metaphysics attributed to the French philosopher Rene Descartes' theory of mind-body dualism. The dualistic mindset is still prevalent in the Western worldview, which pitches good versus evil, democracy versus autocracy, or "I win versus you lose," and the like. Under the Western dichotomous conceptual framework of highly specialized biomedical diseases, the mind and the body became separate systems.

On the other hand, in the traditional Chinese medical paradigm, health and illness were conceptualized in terms of the interactive balance between the body and the mind for both psychological and physical disorders. Chinese people adopted multiple causal attributions and coping strategies in dealing with their problems depending on the situation. These cultural characteristics suggested the importance of an interactive paradigm, in which psychological processes, somatic factors, as well as the situational and social contexts all contributed to an understanding of Chinese psychopathology. Similarly in the Chinese worldview, pluralism, multilateralism, and dialecticism could coexist in harmony. It was only in the late 1970s that a biopsychosocial model that integrated the multiple contexts of the body, the mind, and the social environment was introduced in the Western mental health paradigm.

As a true scholar, Prof. Kleinman was very gracious and subsequently refined his conceptualization of somatization as an idiom of social distress, an illness narrative, and a call for help, contextualized in the strategies of adaptive coping and help-seeking in different cultures. Arthur and Joan Kleinman, also a sinologist, had become good friends of mine. We visited each other in Hong Kong and in the United States. Unfortunately, in the early 2000s, Joan began to struggle with a rare form of early Alzheimer's disease at the young age of fifty-nine. Even as her eyesight was deteriorating, she accompanied Arthur in his global travels. To maintain her independence, Arthur meticulously guided her down the staircase with verbal instructions to our dining table at the college restaurant when they visited me at CUHK. Arthur lovingly took care of Joan until she died in 2011. In his 2020 touching book, *The Soul of Care: The Moral Education of a Husband and a Doctor*, he recounted how even his medical career did not prepare him for the challenges of being a caregiver.

Translating Psychological Tests for the Chinese People

In the early twentieth century, standardized psychological tests were developed in Europe and the United States to assess cognitive abilities and personality for educational and occupational purposes. These tests were exported to other countries where psychology was a fledging profession. Without the resources and expertise to develop their own scientific measures, psychologists and educationists working on the ground began to translate and adapt imported tests for domestic use to support their professional practice.

In China, the imperial examination 科舉 *ke ju* system of selecting talent for government positions—which originated in the Shang and Zhou dynasties (1,700 to 256 BCE) and formalized during the Han dynasty (202 BCE) until its termination at the end of the Qing dynasty in 1905—had been credited as the forerunner in systematic psychological testing. Like many ancient Chinese inventions, these old traditions were overtaken by new scientific developments in Europe and America. Modern psychological testing in cognitive abilities was introduced to China by a British scholar in 1915, which sparked interest in local scholars to translate Western tests and develop their own tests for educational assessment. The development of psychological testing was disrupted by the Sino-Japanese war in 1937 until after the Cultural Revolution in the late 1970s.

Prof. Zhang Houcang 張厚粲, the granddaughter of the famous late Qing imperial minister Zhang Zhidong 張之洞, was hailed as the "Mother" of modern Chinese testing and assessment. Prof. Zhang's legendary career of over seventy years began in 1948 when she graduated in psychology from Beijing Fu Jen University, which later merged with Beijing Normal University, where she stayed on to teach until she passed away at age ninety-five in 2022. During the Cultural Revolution, when higher education and psychological research were suspended, she was imprisoned for several years and subjected to "re-education." She courageously persevered and survived without bitterness despite the attack on psychology as a pseudoscience at that time. After psychology was resumed, Prof. Zhang established the testing research group at the Psychology Department in Beijing Normal University in 1980 to conduct a systematic analysis of the test items of the public examinations, which led to the adoption of standard scores and the scientific foundation of public examinations using modern psychometric methods. She initiated the translation of the major cognitive and intelligence tests in China and led the establishment of the Psychological Measurement Division under the Chinese Psychological Society in the 1980s. In 2016, the International Union of Psychological Sciences honored her with the "Achievement Against the Odds Award" as "a researcher who succeeded in conducting psychological research under extremely difficult circumstances." Even in her late eighties, she was still actively participating in international psychological conferences, where I often ran across her managing her own travels independently without a large entourage of subordinates like other famous professors. She was much more deserving of my respect than I was of her compliments for my work on Chinese personality assessment, which she often mentioned to her students.

My own career in personality assessment was not planned. It evolved out of a simple practical need in clinical practice into a lifelong journey to develop culturally relevant personality assessment for the Chinese people. My journey converged with the stages of development in cross-cultural psychology during my times. Let me start by providing a simple summary of the various stages of cross-cultural psychology and psychological testing.

Stages of Cross-cultural Psychology

In the early stage of cross-cultural psychology, it was common to transport Western models and tests to non-Western cultures as if they were universally applicable. In cross-cultural psychology, this is called the "Etic" Stage. "Etic" is derived from the word "phonetic" (objective sound of the word) in linguistics. The etic approach assumed that the established Western models and Western tests could be used for everyone in the world without considering their cultural relevance or local validation. Early translations of Western tests by local practitioners were often casual and inadequate. Using a reputable Western test gave the guise of scientific practice. There was little regard as to whether the translated test was equivalent to and could be used in the same way as the original test. Some psychologists had criticized this "transport and test" approach as the "Imposed Etic" Stage.

As a reaction to the imposed etic approach, psychologists in different parts of the non-Western world, especially in Asia and Latin America, started the indigenization movements in psychology in the 1970s. Part of the motivation arose from the resistance to colonialism and Westernization, which was considered a form of intellectual imperialism. Local psychologists questioned the "universality bias" which could be captured in the Chinese metaphor of "cutting the toe to fit the imported shoes" (削足就履 *xiaozu jiulu*), a metaphor that my former colleague in social psychology at CUHK, Michael Bond, often quoted to describe how local phenomena could be fitted into these imported concepts.

The indigenization movement was referred to as the "Emic" Stage in cross-cultural psychology. The word "emic" is derived from "phonemic" (subjective meaning of the word) in linguistics. The emic or indigenous approach adopts in-depth analyses of psychology in a specific cultural context to address local phenomena and experiences originating within the culture. Indigenous psychologists would derive culture-specific psychological constructs from their own cultures and develop indigenous measures.

The indigenous movement in Chinese psychology may be attributed to Prof. Yang Kuo-shu 楊國樞 from Taiwan. Prof. Yang visited the Psychology Section at CUHK from 1979 to 1981. While in Hong Kong, Prof. Yang raised the discussion on the rationale for, and approaches to, the indigenization of the social and behavioral sciences. He formally presented this idea at the 1981 Conference on the Sinicization of the Social and Behavioral Sciences. Together with anthropologist Li Yih-yuan 李亦園 and sociologist Wen Chong-yi 文崇一 in Taiwan, and anthropologist Chiao Chien 喬健 and sociologist Ambrose King Yeo-chi 金耀基 at CUHK, Prof. Yang started the movement of Sinicization and later indigenization of social sciences in Taiwan and Hong Kong.

One major problem of the early indigenous psychology movement was what could be called "reversed ethnocentrism." Local researchers emphasized the uniqueness of the indigenous phenomena in their own culture without adopting a comparative approach. In cross-cultural comparative studies,

On an outing with Yang Kuo-Shu and family in Hong Kong, 1978.

Western psychologists challenged that many of the so-called emic constructs could have been subsumed under existing universal models and did not add new insights to psychological knowledge. Besides, most of the indigenous research studies were published in the local language and were inaccessible to international scholars. This isolation limited the opportunity for international communication, or more widespread dissemination and discussion of indigenous psychology. As such, indigenous psychology remained in a small circle under cross-cultural psychology.

With globalization toward the end of the twentieth century, multiculturalism was becoming a way of modern life. Western psychology began to recognize the need to understand not only people in other countries, but also the multi-ethnic population and immigrants within their own countries. Moving into the "Internationalization" Stage, cross-cultural psychologists called for integrating the etic and emic approaches to reach a more balanced view on the universal and culture-specific aspects of psychology.

Now let me turn to the cross-cultural stages of my own research in psychology and how they connected Chinese psychology with the West.

The Etic Stage of My Career

One of the reasons I chose the University of Minnesota for my graduate studies was the fame of the Minnesota Multiphasic Personality Inventory (MMPI). The MMPI was the most widely used measure of personality and psychopathology especially in clinical and forensic assessment and was covered in all introductory psychology textbooks.

People have always been interested in learning about personality throughout Western civilization as well as in Chinese culture. Ancient Greeks classified four fundamental personality types or temperaments based on the body's chemical fluid system called "humors." The ancient art of face reading and palm reading was commonly used in traditional Chinese fortune telling to describe personality. Like astrology, these practices did not stand up to the tests of modern science. World War II was ascribed as the origins of the scientific assessment of personality in Western countries when large groups of soldiers were screened for mental fitness before being sent to the frontline. Self-report measures of personality were developed for which people would respond to questionnaire items selected to represent samples of their personality characteristics. These responses were then scored and compared to the normal distribution of scores collected in large samples. Research studies were conducted to confirm the accuracy and usefulness of the test results when applied to different life situations. The scientific foundation of test development and validation supported the trustworthiness in these measures.

Curiosity about themselves has driven many people to answer the ten or twenty items in the dozens of free personality quizzes in magazines or the Internet to find out what their music taste, color preference, or even choice of pizza toppings showed about their personality types. Although most people would take their ascribed personality types from these free quizzes with a grain of salt, few would bother to question the credibility of these quizzes. Personality testing has become widely used in organizational settings. Some popular tests such as the Enneagram of Personality and the Myer-Briggs Type Indicators (MBTI) had acquired cult-like devotion and become multimillion dollar businesses despite being discredited by many skeptical psychological experts for the lack of scientific basis in personality assessment. In a 2018 book, *The Personality Brokers: The Strange History of Myers-Briggs and the Birth of Personality Testing,* the author Merve Emre traced how a novelist and homemaker mother-daughter team designed the MBTI on their kitchen table in the 1920s, which then took on a life of its own into the boardrooms across the world and became the most popular personality test in organizational settings. Few people would examine the scientific basis required of psychological assessment before taking a psychological test.

UM was renowned for its research in personality and individual differences, as well as in quantitative and psychometric methods. We learned the importance of establishing reliability and validity for developing psychological measurement and how to distinguish between scientifically sound and questionable assessment tools. The MMPI was developed in the 1940s at the university and later revised with further research by several generations of UM faculty and graduates. Testing was administered through 567 true or false items to cover a wide sample of behaviors reflecting normal personality and psychiatric syndromes. The items were chosen based on the statistical analysis that showed their ability to distinguish between the normal population and psychiatric patients. Another set of scales was included to check whether the test takers were truthful and careful with their answers. Its worthiness rested on the hundreds of research studies conducted on its useful applications in different settings and with different groups. It has been used to screen suitability for high-risk professions such as airline pilots to ensure that they would deliver passengers safely to their destinations, or to establish the psychopathology of defendants in court to ascertain whether they were fit to stand trial or they were legally responsible for their crimes.

Although I learned to use the original MMPI during my graduate studies, I told my classmates upon my graduation that I did not expect to be using the MMPI again in Hong Kong, as it was such a long English test with over 500 items. Few Chinese test takers would be able to comprehend the English items well enough to sit through the long test. The contents of some items might be unfamiliar to the Chinese people. Little did I know that local psychologists regarded the MMPI as the most scientific clinical assessment tool and had been using it with their individual translations as they administered the tests to their clients.

Given my knowledge of the psychometric properties that were required of a psychological test, I was concerned about the inconsistency and quality of the individual translations. There was no assurance that the individually translated versions were equivalent to the original MMPI and could claim to be scientifically sound. That could not be a standardized application of psychological assessment. I looked for a proper Chinese version of the MMPI and found a few early Chinese translations in Taiwan, but some of the items were poorly or erroneously translated. There was no standardization of the test scores or research on the validity of these translated versions in determining psychopathology. As a UM graduate, I believed I had better knowledge of the test. I embarked on developing a proper Chinese translation myself, which launched my lifelong association with the test and with the Institute of Psychology at the Chinese Academy of Sciences.

When the institute resumed psychology in 1980, the leaders wanted to use the best scientific tool for personality assessment and decided to translate the MMPI for China. The researcher assigned to the project, Prof. Song Weizhen 宋維真, was initially at a loss. She could not speak English and she was trained in Pavlovian psychology in the Soviet Union, where she studied associative learning in dogs. At first, she could only find a German translation of the MMPI in Beijing. She did not know about my work on the MMPI in Hong Kong, which was later introduced to her by Prof. Raymond D. Fowler, who was invited to visit the institute with an American Psychological Association delegation in 1980. Prof. Fowler and I were part of the network of international researchers attending conferences on translated versions of the MMPI organized by Prof. James Butcher, the principal MMPI researcher at that time. Prof. Song was elated with the discovery of my translated version and studies in Hong Kong. Even with limited research facilities before the availability of office desktop computers back in the late 1970s, I had collected MMPI samples of psychiatric patients and college students, using hand scoring stencils. These studies provided the preliminary support for the use of the Chinese MMPI.

Prof. Song was a serious scholar. She wanted to ensure that the Chinese MMPI was developed properly. She set up a national committee of MMPI researchers and practitioners to prepare for its translation in China. She attended Prof. Butcher's MMPI workshop in Hawaii in 1982, not knowing

Discussing the Chinese Minnesota Multiphasic Personality Inventory
with Song Weizhen, 1985.

any English. I tried my best to help her to understand what was going on. In 1985, she invited me and Prof. Butcher to Beijing to the first MMPI training workshop for the Chinese researchers. Prof. Butcher had been very generous and had returned to China three more times with me to provide free training to different groups of mainland psychologists on research and applications of the MMPI.

In 1985, training facilities at the Institute of Psychology were very basic. When I arrived one day after Prof. Butcher (Jim) at the classroom, I was horrified to find that they had let go of the interpreter for Jim, assuming that I could take over the job. My Putonghua was not any better than my Berkeley days. I was unfamiliar with the Chinese translation of psychological terms. With the help of a few participants who were from Guangdong, my Cantonese-Mandarin rendition was back translated into proper Putonghua and the correct technical terms were provided. I could see the faces of the other participants lighting up as they were getting the point from the back translation. It took me another decade before both my Putonghua and my Chinese glossary of psychological terms had improved to a competent level that I could independently present a full lecture in Putonghua.

In appreciation for our training, the forty-some participants of the workshop chipped in to invite us to a Peking duck dinner. When we arrived at the famous duck restaurant, we were embarrassed to discover that it was only the two of us with the hosts from the institute. It was too expensive for all the participants to join the dinner. Chinese professionals were still poorly paid in the 1980s, but Chinese hospitality was paramount.

It was Jim's first visit to China, and he indicated interest in visiting Xi'an during the weekend in between our training days. The institute arranged for me to accompany him on the trip, as I had not been to Xi'an either. It was an unforgettable experience, not because of the scenery, however.

The adventure started with our arrival at the old Beijing airport. Prof. Song presented our tickets at the check-in counter, whereupon we were told that our flight was delayed. We had to wait for an hour before we could check in to get our boarding pass, whereupon Prof. Song and her staff saw us off at the departure gate. When we got into the central waiting area for all the flights, Jim checked his flight number on the board and found that the flight was further delayed for another two hours. Since there was nothing else to do in this crowded waiting room, I checked out a few magazines from the wooden bookshelf, for which I had to exchange my boarding pass as a deposit. Soon after I started to read the magazines, an airline attendant came rushing toward us with my boarding pass and said that we were late for our plane. She dragged the two of us past the lines waiting for the transfer bus and put us on the departing plane, which took off as soon as we sat down. I was glad that I had borrowed the magazines with my boarding pass. Otherwise, we would have missed the flight.

Jim was a veteran of the Korean War in the U.S. Air Force. During the flight, he kept looking out the window and remarked with great unease that this was an old Soviet plane. Given that China and the Soviet Union had split up for twenty years, where would China get the spare parts for the plane? I could sense his anxiety as he was holding on to his armrest tightly. The two-hour flight was uneventful, fortunately.

Conducting Minnesota Multiphasic Personality Inventory training with James
Butcher in Beijing, 1985.

James Butcher and Jing Qizheng of the Institute of Psychology at a Peking duck
dinner, 2006.

When we exited the luggage area, I was greeted by a tour guide holding a placard with my name. He was going to take me to my hotel. What about Prof. Butcher? The guide said he was just responsible for my arrangements. As a foreign guest of the institute, Jim was supposed to be picked up by the officials of the Xi'an branch of the Chinese Academy of Sciences, whereas being a Chinese compatriot from Hong Kong, I did not share the same protocol. As such, Prof. Song made my arrangements through a travel agent. After scouting out the arrival hall in the Xi'an airport three times, those academy officials for Jim were still nowhere to be found. I told the tour guide to take both of us to my hotel and he found a room for Jim. Although the tour guide was able to arrange the sightseeing for us, it was essential to find the contact for Jim because he needed to get the return plane ticket from them. That was the time before return tickets could be bought directly from the starting location. Jim was obviously worried that he would be stranded in Xi'an.

As it was over the weekend, there was nobody at the Institute of Psychology in Beijing that we could contact. It was long before the quantum leap to the modern era of mobile phones when everyone in China was holding at least a 5G cell phone. Even land lines were very limited in China at that time, and I did not have a phone contact for Prof. Song. I finally got through to the local branch of the academy, where a doorman answered the phone. In desperation, I became uncharacteristically assertive and discourteous. In fear that I would lose my only link, I directed the doorman to hold the line while he went around the building to grab our contact, who happened to be having dinner in the cafeteria. I told our contact to come over that evening with Jim's ticket. He felt aggrieved when I asked him why he did not show up at the airport. He said he had been waiting there for two hours at the revised arrival time and could not find us. It finally transpired that my flight was different from Jim's, which was delayed by two hours behind my departure time. That explained why Jim thought our flight was further delayed at the Beijing airport, whereas I was told by the flight attendant that we were late for our flight. It baffled me how both of us could have been shuttled into the same flight.

Jim was relieved to get his return ticket to Beijing. But the saga did not end there. After settling Jim's ticket, I took a closer look at my own ticket from the travel agent for our next morning's flight. I was alarmed to find that the flight date on my ticket was one day after Jim's. By then, it was too late to find my tour guide to change the ticket. My hotel was fully booked for the next day. I studied the handwritten ticket and considered forging the date, but decided against it for fear that the ticket would be forfeited altogether. Finally, I opted to bite the bullet and repeat the same way we came from Beijing. If we were put on the same flight with different tickets, it might happen again.

Upon arriving at the Xi'an airport the next morning, I asked Jim to present both our tickets with his on top at the check-in counter and request for two adjoining seats. With a foreigner speaking English only, we were hoping we could confuse the local ground staff. However, she was meticulous and caught the different dates on our tickets. I insisted something must be wrong because we came together, and we should be leaving together. Finally, with the privilege of accompanying a foreigner, I could cut through the waiting list and got my seat on the same flight to return to Beijing with Jim in time to resume our training workshop.

This saga has taught me the lesson of not relying on travel agents and always checking my plane tickets and travel arrangements ahead of time. It is amazing how much the aviation industry has advanced in China since 1985. Online booking of return tickets is now just a click away on the mobile phone. Advanced technology, including digitalization and facial recognition is standard operation in modern Chinese airports. Such mistakes with the Xi'an trip are probably historical relics.

From 1981 to 2000, I collaborated with Prof. Song and her team at the institute to standardize and validate the Chinese MMPI and later the MMPI-2, with large-scale representative samples and rigorous methods. Prof. Song was resourceful and efficient in gathering large representative samples from different parts of China, sometimes too quickly before I had time to double check all the test materials. By the time I discovered a mistake in an item for the pilot test, she had already collected a sample of 3,000 participants. Never mind, she said, she could easily get another 3,000 for the correct test form. Those were the days before we paid our research participants, who were willing to volunteer for the scientific cause for the country, or at least were compliant to requests from their units. By the time we refined the translation of the Chinese version of the MMPI and standardized the scores with a national Chinese norm, the English version of the MMPI was revised into a new version by Prof. Butcher and his team. We repeated the same scientific process of translation and standardization for the MMPI-2. It had to take the resourcefulness of the Institute of Psychology and the resolution of Prof. Song to achieve one of the best translated versions of the MMPI in the world.

Could we assume that the Chinese MMPI was as good as the original MMPI? We further conducted research to demonstrate that the translated test was equivalent in psychometric properties and in functions to the original MMPI-2. We studied the test profiles of different psychiatric patients to confirm the diagnostic validity of the Chinese version. Based on the national standardization study, we developed the Chinese norm for local application. We added a special Infrequency Scale specific to the Chinese people to check if the test participants were feigning pathology by giving more weird answers than the genuine patients. I gave the Chinese Infrequency Scale the nickname of the "Peking Duck Scale." It was developed one evening when Jim was treated to a Peking duck dinner in Beijing. The institute hosts had learned that duck was Jim's favorite dish and ordered two big Peking ducks. Being an American, Jim was not aware of Chinese proprieties that as a guest, he should not empty his plate so quickly. As soon as he finished what was put before him, the hosts kept piling more pieces on his plate. He probably consumed more than half of the two ducks on our table that evening! As a result, he suffered from indigestion when we got back to the hotel. As he could not sleep, I suggested we kept working and started going through the data on extreme percentages of item endorsement from the standardization study to select the items for the Chinese Infrequency Scale.

The Chinese version of the MMPI and later the MMPI-2 were distributed by The Chinese University of Hong Kong Press with permission of the University of Minnesota Press to Chinese-speaking test users in different parts of the world. It was reputed to be a role model in test translation for international testing. That was the "imposed etic stage" of my research on personality assessment. We took the best available Western tools and supported their use with local research evidence.

The Chinese MMPI provided psychologists in Hong Kong a scientific measure to assess psychopathology that could stand up in court in forensic cases. In the early 1990s, I was called as an expert witness at the Coroner's Court on a tragic case involving a young female patient whom I saw in the late 1980s at the psychiatry clinic of our medical school. This patient was first admitted for panic attack when she was criticized at work. At that time, the psychiatrist's diagnosis was anxiety disorder. She took the Chinese MMPI and the results showed a spike in her clinical scale of schizophrenia, reflecting her potential for psychotic dissociation even though there was not any overt symptom at the time. Over a year of psychotherapy, she hinted at a childhood history of severe abuse by her stepfather. Given her heightened emotional reactions associated with these memories, I decided that she was not ready to delve into the trauma. Instead, my goal was to build up her personal strength at the time to cope with her normal daily functioning. Her conditions stabilized over the next year, and she met a boyfriend who was very caring to her. He accompanied her on her psychiatric consultations, and later became her husband. I was happy that she had found the family support she needed. After I completed my psychotherapy sessions with her, I encouraged her to continue to consult her psychiatrist when her conditions became unstable.

Three years later, my former patient was found by the police in a catatonic stupor at home next to the bathtub where her husband was drowned. She was given the diagnosis of schizophrenia at the forensic psychiatric hospital. I was called to the witness stand at the Coroner's Court to explain the results of the MMPI she took five years ago that foretold her predisposition to a psychotic episode. The judge asked detailed questions on the scientific foundation of the assessment tool and the score interpretation. After my testimony, I came across my former patient in the corridor of the court room. She greeted me and told me that she had made the stupid mistake of joining a "personal growth" training course, during which she had to confront her early life trauma in a group setting. I thought trainees admitted to these programs should have been screened for psychological suitability, but apparently, my former patient was not. These popular psychological training programs imported from the West claimed to bring about a fundamental shift in what is possible in peoples' lives and transform ordinary lives into success stories. A local newspaper interviewing the casualty cases from these training courses questioned whether the training was "life-mending" or "mind-bending." In Hong Kong, many such courses were run by teachers who might not have had appropriate psychological qualifications. I was indignant that the effect of the unprofessional training on my former patient was life shattering.

Now and then, we received requests from American clinicians who expressed delight and relief for having "discovered" the Chinese version of the MMPI for their forensic assessment of ethnic-Chinese immigrants who were not proficient in English. After observing that the test results they obtained when using the English version of the MMPI did not always fit their clinical observations, they finally took the initiative to inquire if there was a Chinese version. I was struck by the apparent lack of familiarity with culturally relevant measures among those practitioners working with ethnic minorities. It showed there was a definite need for enhancing training and research in the cross-cultural perspectives of personality assessment in Western psychology programs.

Developing the Indigenous Chinese Personality Assessment Inventory

When reviewing our research on the Chinese MMPI, I noticed there were cultural differences in which even normal Chinese people scored higher than Americans on several clinical scales, which might lead to misinterpretation of psychopathology. I identified the items on those scales that contributed to the higher clinical scores and compared the item endorsement and social desirability ratings. Many of those clinical items were rated as acceptable or even desirable by normal Chinese participants, such as one item that reported one's preference to just sit around and do nothing. To the energetic Americans, this dull behavior could be symptomatic of depression. To the phlegmatic Chinese, this could mean a form of relaxation from their hectic lifestyle. This suggested that those items were not actually measuring the clinical symptoms.

I started to ponder the cultural differences in the assessment tools and wondered why we had to go through the tortuous process of test translation and make various adaptations on the translated measures to render them useful in the Chinese setting. With the Chinese people constituting one-fifth of the world population, we should develop our own personality test for them. The leaders of the Institute of Psychology concurred. Prof. Song and I embarked on the development of the Chinese Personality Assessment Inventory (CPAI) in 1989. Prof. Song's assistant, Zhang Jianxin 張建新, who later became my graduate student, joined the institute's team. I also recruited Leung Kwok 梁覺, a dynamic cross-cultural social psychologist in my department to join the team.

We started by exploring how ordinary Chinese people described and defined personality, instead of relying on dictionaries, which would be too narrow in scope. To derive the folk concept of Chinese personality, we adopted multiple sources to extract personality terms used in contemporary Chinese novels, magazines, and radio talk shows, as well as in psychology research. We asked students to collect street polls by asking passers-by to describe themselves. We surveyed different professionals, including asking teachers to describe their students and vice versa, supervisors to describe their subordinates, doctors to describe their patients, and so on. Over 1,000 different personality terms were written on index cards, which were sorted and grouped into clusters from which our expert team selected the personality dimensions. Items were then written for the scales to be included in the CPAI. Learning from the state-of-the-art personality tests, we included normal personality scales and clinical scales for different assessment functions, as well as validity scales to ascertain the veracity of the test responses.

Based on our experience of standardizing the Chinese MMPI, we conducted several rounds of preliminary testing to screen over 900 items before selecting the final items and refining the scales. The scoring of the final version of the CPAI was standardized using large-scale national samples in China and Hong Kong. The CPAI was the first indigenously derived comprehensive personality measure that was developed and standardized for the Chinese people according to the scientific requirements of test development.

Has CPAI identified culture-specific constructs that could not be subsumed under the universal models of personality? The dominant personality

The Chinese Personality Assessment Inventory mainland China team (from
right) Zhang Jianxin, Song Weizhen, Fanny and Xie Dong
on a visit to Hong Kong in 1989.

theory in psychology at that time was the Five Factor Model (FFM), which
claimed to represent the universal structure of personality. Were the CPAI
personality dimensions different from the FFM?

In selecting the personality attributes for the CPAI, we included concepts
that were considered important in Chinese culture, as well as those that had
been studied by Chinese psychologists in the indigenous psychology movement,
such as family orientation (親情 *qinqing*), veraciousness vs. slickness (老實-圓
滑 *laoshi–yuanhua*), traditionalism versus modernity (傳統-現代化 *chuantong–*
xiandaihua), self- versus social-orientation (自我-社會取向 *ziwo–shehuiquxiang*),
discipline (紀律性 *jiluxing*), face (面子 *mianzi*), harmony (和諧性 *hexiexing*),
and reciprocal relationship (人情 *renqing*). Prof. Song specifically chose the
Ah-Q mentality (defensiveness) from Lu Xun's story of Ah-Q, which parodied
the defensive mechanism used by Chinese people. She also wanted to include
thrift vs. extravagance (節儉-奢侈 *jiejian–shechi*), which reflected the virtuous
qualities during the less economically developed stage of modern China (in
the revision of the CPAI after 2000, when China's economy had markedly
improved, this scale was less useful).

We used factor analysis to group the personality scales and extracted four factors. At first, we thought the results from the mainland China sample might be different from those from the Hong Kong sample, whose subjects lived in the Westernized social context under British colonial rule. Apparently, our cultural heritage was deep-rooted and the factor structures of the two samples were consistent. We could combine the results into a single Chinese model.

We then compared these four CPAI factors with the five factors in the FFM. Three of our factors corresponded with those of the FFM, but the CPAI did not include an Openness factor like that of the FFM. In cross-cultural studies of the FFM, the Openness factor had been found to be less coherent in Asian cultures. On the other hand, some of the CPAI culture-specific scales grouped under a factor that our Chinese colleagues immediately recognized as the Confucian characteristics of "inner sage and outer kingliness" (內聖外王 neisheng waiwang) or "rounded outwardly and square inwardly" (外圓內方 waiyuan neifang). This factor was distinct from all the five factors of the FFM. When we tried to publish our findings in Western psychology journals, the reviewers were very critical of the Confucian term. It was probably too foreign and nuanced to the Western reviewers. After trying out different terms with my colleague, Michael Bond, I decided to use the label "Interpersonal Relatedness" (IR) for this factor, which was more accessible to Western psychologists even though it was not able to capture the complexity of this Confucian characteristic.

In mainstream psychology, there was still an ethnocentric mentality that rejected unfamiliar non-Western concepts. The FFM researchers who had a stronghold on mainstream personality journals found all kinds of criticisms to dispute the uniqueness of this CPAI factor or the value of the CPAI altogether. Academic publications are not always purely based on science alone. Biases and networking can affect the acceptance of novel research. Our initial attempts were not able to break through to the orthodox journals. Instead, our papers found more sympathetic reception in culturally oriented journals, in which we published most of our early research results in the 1990s.

One of the misgivings of the FFM researchers was the lack of the "universal" openness factor in our CPAI personality structure. At the time when we first explored the personality dimensions for the CPAI, openness was not a salient feature in Chinese person descriptions. As China underwent rapid transformation during the end of the twentieth century, innovation and entrepreneurship became more important as drivers of the economy. Could social changes affect the perception of personality? I decided to refine and update the CPAI after ten years. Prof. Song had retired by then and had migrated to Canada to live with her daughter after the death of her husband. Zhang Jianxin, who had obtained his PhD at CUHK, took up the leadership of the team at the Institute of Psychology. To explore the possibility of an openness factor in the CPAI, we developed six new scales related to folk concepts of openness, in the same way with which we developed the original scales of the CPAI. We re-standardized the scores of the CPAI-2, again using large-scale representative samples from different parts of China as well as in Hong Kong. During the data collection period, an unexpected encounter took place when I was attending a government committee meeting in Hong Kong. The government office attendant who was serving us tea approached me and said he would offer me two cups so that I would not send an interviewer to his home again to ask him to fill out another long questionnaire of over 500 items. Apparently, he was one of our test participants from the random sampling process!

With the six new scales on openness, we thought we could extract an Openness factor from the CPAI-2 like the FFM. To our surprise, it did not come out that way. Instead, four of the new scales converged with the previous Extraversion factor to form a Social Potency factor that depicted a combination of sociability and agency found in leadership qualities. The other two openness scales related to interpersonal tolerance and social sensitivity were subsumed under the other CPAI factors. In this sense, the Openness to Experience factor of the FFM was not as culturally relevant to the Chinese context. It was not as universal as it claimed.

When we conducted a joint factor analysis of the CPAI-2 with a FFM measure, the uniqueness of the CPAI Interpersonal Relatedness (IR) factor stood out again. In Western concepts of personality, emphasis has been put on the individual and the self. In Chinese culture, how we relate to others helps to define our personality.

To demonstrate the usefulness of the IR factor, our team and other researchers conducted studies which showed that this indigenous factor added predictive value beyond the universal personality factors on many psychological outcomes, including persuasion tactics, leadership, job performance, career choice, life satisfaction, and psychopathology. In personnel selection assessment for managers in foreign enterprises, which were burgeoning in China, the CPAI-2 IR factor helped to identify candidates who had difficulty adjusting to the local organizational culture. A few problematic expatriate managers were found to score very low on the harmony and *renqing* scales, which might explain their strained interpersonal relationships in the Chinese work setting.

To cover the assessment needs across different ages, we further developed an adolescent version of the CPAI using the same test development and standardization method. These measures provided useful tools for vocational development, career planning, and clinical assessment of the Chinese people. We compiled the bibliography of research on the CPAI on a website and offered free use of the scales for authorized research purposes.

Although I was not keen to turn the CPAI into a business enterprise, we made it available for licensed use for vocational and clinical assessment under the Assessment and Training Centre that I initiated in the Psychology Department at CUHK. What prompted me to move in this direction came from my experience of recruiting the senior staff at the Equal Opportunities Commission. The consultant from the headhunting firm adopted a FFM measure for the personality assessment of the shortlisted candidates. While I was aware of the shortcomings of the FFM in the Chinese cultural context, as the EOC Chairperson, I did not want to recommend the CPAI as the more appropriate measure for this recruitment to avoid conflict of interest. Upon my return to CUHK, I immediately set up the Assessment and Training Centre as an external arm for our psychology colleagues to bring their evidence-based psychology tools to serve the community.

Developing the CPAI indigenously may be considered the emic stage of my career. The CPAI encompassed both indigenous personality factors that were salient in Chinese culture and universal personality factors that were shared across cultures. This approach had become known as the "combined

With Fons van de Vijver (left) and a South African researcher in 2004 at the
Beijing International Congress of Psychology.

emic-etic approach." Our CPAI research attracted the attention of other
cultural psychologists. One of them was the late Fons van de Vijver, a Dutch
cross-cultural psychologist who had been active in helping psychologists in
Africa and the Middle East to develop their own personality measures using
the combined emic-etic approach. Fons and my colleague, Leung Kwok, had
collaborated in developing statistical methodology in cross-cultural psychology
advocating the combined emic-etic method. During the 2004 International
Congress of Psychology in Beijing, Fons introduced the principal South African
researcher, Deon Meiring, to me. They wanted to emulate the development of
the CPAI as a blueprint for their development of the South African Personality
Inventory (SAPI).

The SAPI is particularly noteworthy as an ambitious project for developing
eleven parallel official language versions for the various cultural groups within
South Africa, all using the combined emic-etic approach as in the CPAI.
After apartheid was abolished in South Africa, national legislation was passed
to ensure that psychological assessment should be culturally sensitive to the

different tribes and should not disadvantage any cultural group due to test bias. A large team of researchers participated in the development of the SAPI, starting with interviews with tribal representatives to gather the indigenous personality concepts. Scales had been developed for several language versions which identified social-relational dimensions of personality distinct from the FFM factors. Despite the untimely death of Fons and Deon, the noble goal of the SAPI to achieve culture-fair personality assessment was carried on by the other team members.

The combined emic-etic approach had become a role model in developing culturally relevant measures in cross-cultural assessment. It enhanced cultural sensitivity in applying assessment tools to diverse ethnic groups. It also showed respect for the local context without imposing an authoritative model originating from a foreign culture. I hope the detailed account of my journey in personality assessment will not only inform test users of the scientific process required in building a tool that could be trustworthy, but also encourage scientists of our generation to proudly stand on our own feet in carving out our research agenda.

Looking ahead, the field of objective personality assessment will be moving into a digital age involving analysis of big data, further expanding the range of items beyond what could be included in a self-report questionnaire. Recent studies have collected a wide array of everyday behaviors, activities, social relationships, and manifestations of problems for analysis through machine learning models to quickly predict suicidal risks. The potential of data mining is enormous and comes with responsibility. The 2018 scandal involving Cambridge Analytica illustrated the power of data mining of daily activities on social media and the malice that could be involved. Scientists from Cambridge Analytica used data mining to harvest the personal data of users on Facebook as well as an app to collect answers to a series of personality questions to determine the psychological profiles of allegedly up to eighty-seven million users of the social media, many without their consent. The profiles were then used for the purpose of influencing users with microtargeted political messages during political campaigns. Whether these tactics had influenced the outcome of the elections could not be proved scientifically. Yet, as researchers, we need to be reminded of the ethical principles along with the adoption of these technological advances in assessing personality.

While the development of objective personality tests in the twentieth century had ushered in scientific personality assessment, lengthy self-report personality inventories would eventually become obsolete with the advent of new technologies. Whatever the method of assessment, the original intention of assessment would still be one and the same. As the next generation of psychologists take up automated methods for personality assessment, they still need to remember the advances in the understanding of personality, the importance of including culturally relevant factors in their models for diverse populations, and respecting the sensitivities of different cultural groups to ensure that the assessment is fair, ethical, and beneficial.

From Indigenous to Cross-Cultural Assessment

The incremental validity of the CPAI and its empirical research grounding led it to be recognized by cultural psychologists as the most solid indigenously derived personality measure. Through my presentations at international psychology conferences, more international psychologists had become interested in our work. The CPAI-2 was translated into other languages, including English, Korean, Japanese, Dutch, Romanian, and Vietnamese and tried out with different cultural groups in a reversed etic approach, the first time a Chinese personality measure was translated into multiple languages. This gave us the opportunity to investigate the relevance of the CPAI emic constructs outside of the Chinese culture. Fred Leong, a Chinese-American psychologist, and I collaborated in a series of cross-cultural studies comparing Chinese, white American and Asian American samples. The IR factor was found to be more intact in Asian and Asian American samples but less coherent in individualistic cultures, such as the Dutch and white American samples.

Given the relevance of the CPAI-2 to other cultures, its name could be revised as Cross-cultural Personality Assessment Inventory instead of just

The 2002 Chinese Personality Assessment Inventory symposium at the International Congress of Applied Psychology (ICAP) Singapore, with (from right) C. Spielberger, F. Leong, E. Shen, S.F. Cheung and J. Kwong.

Chinese Personality Assessment Inventory. Fred jokingly suggested that the C in CPAI-2 could stand for my name, Cheung, as some psychologists had used their names for the measures they developed. I declined as it would be too immodest for me to do so.

International Psychology Networks

With the networks built up in these international exchanges and collaborations, I was invited to join the board of several psychological associations, including the International Association of Applied Psychology (IAAP) and the International Test Commission (ITC).

My connection with the IAAP began when the late Prof. Stanley Sue, a Chinese-American psychologist teaching at the University of California, Los Angeles at that time, contacted me in 1990 to take over his role as President of the Division of Clinical and Community Psychology of IAAP. Coming

The International Association of Applied Psychology award ceremony
in Paris 2014, with Secretary General Michael Knowles (right)
and President José M Peiró (left).

from a family of Chinese immigrant parents with little understanding of what psychology was, Stan and his two brothers all became renowned psychologists who brought attention to ethnic minority issues in American psychology. Their interest in understanding human behavior was ignited by their early experience of being ostracized by their white American elementary school classmates due to their Asian heritage. Stan was a trailblazer in the field of ethnic minority psychology and advocated for social justice and cultural competence in psychology. He was among the first to raise the problem of the unnecessary divide between the emic and etic approaches in cultural psychology. Stan had invited me to visit his ethnic minority research team at UCLA in the 1990s and thoughtfully offered to help me relocate to the U.S. in the run-up to 1997. Thanking him for his concern, I reassured him that it was perfectly safe for me to stay in Hong Kong after the reunification. Many of my American colleagues still expressed to me these concerns about freedom and safety in Hong Kong based on what they had read in the American media.

The IAAP was formed in 1920 to promote science and practice in applied psychology around the world. It provided a forum for interaction among

Visiting UCLA ethnic minority research team members Stan Sue
(standing right) and Nolan Zane (seated right).

psychologists from different parts of the world without the dominance of a single country. Non-Western members felt more embraced in this global community. However, until the end of the twentieth century, its leadership were still predominantly Caucasians from America, Europe and Australia. I was one of the few Asians who was actively involved at that time. After my term as Division President was over, I rejoined the board of directors as an elected member for another twelve years. Serving as the convenor of the Task Force on Outreach to Asia, I hosted gatherings for Asian members to welcome them to the international congresses and made them feel at home in the unfamiliar environment. Many of the young psychologists from Asia were attending, for the first time, such international congresses housed in huge convention centers with thousands of participants. Forming connections with other attendees facilitated their participation in the meetings as well as built mutual support for the fledgling research and practice in their countries thereafter. By the time I stepped down in 2018, there were more Asians serving in leadership positions in divisions and the board of directors.

My involvement with the International Test Commission (ITC) was more fortuitous. I was attending a talk at an international conference in Sweden in

2000 when Prof. Thomas Oakland, a renowned school psychologist from the University of Florida, came up to introduce himself. He had read my works in personality assessment and found them to be aligned with the mission of the ITC. He invited me to give a keynote address on cross-cultural assessment at the next ITC conference in 2004. I was invited to join the ITC Council in 2006, in which I served until 2016. I was elected as its president in 2014.

The ITC was initiated in Europe, where psychologists became concerned with the use of psychological assessment tools to make life-changing decisions by people who lacked sufficient training and experience, while many of the tools used lacked adequate psychometric quality and diagnostic value. There was a call for national psychological associations to set up national commissions on testing to develop and promote standards governing test development and use. In the 1970s, the ITC was formed as an international commission consisting of national commissions or psychological associations as its members to assist in the exchange of best practices on test development and use through publications and conferences. Wide consultation with stakeholders across the world enabled ITC to produce sets of guidelines on important issues in relations to test use, test development, translation and adaptation, quality control, test security and technology-based assessment that were relevant to the diverse populations. National associations were encouraged to disseminate these guidelines in their own languages to promote the standards of testing and assessment in their countries.

In 2010, I hosted the ITC International Conference in Hong Kong, the first time that this conference was outside of Europe and North America. This Asian location brought together more global participants and provided the opportunity for direct exchanges on assessment issues in the East and the West. Apart from the active interactions among over 400 international delegates on testing research and practice, the participants were amazed by the cultural experiences watching the martial art lion dance provided by the Hong Kong Tourism Board at the opening ceremony and being treated to the unending courses in the Chinese banquet at the end of the conference. Many of the Western guests had never seen the heads of chicken or fish in their diet. They were astounded by the blinking lights representing the eyes of the roast suckling pig. They were amused by my introduction to the culinary anthology of Chinese food, that the employee to which the chicken head was pointed at the company's year-end dinner would be the one to be fired, but the head and the tail of the fish would be served to the guest of honor in each table. A few delegates were game enough to try the fish head. With my explanation of the loving care behind the brewing of Chinese soups, including the hidden reference to men visiting their mistresses, they all finished their bowl of soup heartily. The support of my colleagues and students in the Psychology Department contributed to the efficient logistics of running the conference with a surplus in the budget. The success of the conference in Hong Kong impressed our international colleagues. Organizing an international conference with hundreds of participants without a professional conference organizer required a detailed design with operational procedures with timelines. For Hong Kong summers, we also had to prepare for contingencies on typhoons, when offices and schools would be closed and transportation would be curtailed. We were fortunate that the ITC conference narrowly missed the typhoon shutdown. With the torrential rain, the souvenir folded umbrella we prepared in the conference bag came into handy. After the conference, I compiled a manual for the planning and execution of an international conference for the ITC, which was later shared with a few other international organizations.

The stalwarts at the ITC were dedicated to promoting evidence-based research and practice in psychological testing and assessment. As one of the early leaders, Thomas Oakland built a supportive community and caringly mentored young scholars from the emerging economies in Africa, Asia and Latin America, where the field of psychological assessment was nascent and resources were limited. Some of these mentees had become leaders in the field in their own countries. In 2015, we were alarmed to learn of Tom's tragic murder at his home, committed by a former convict. The kind-hearted professor had been helping to rebuild the murderer's life as a good Samaritan. Sadly, his generous monetary support and good deeds were repaid by greed and violence. In 2016, ITC set up in his memory the Thomas Oakland Award for Distinguished Contributions to Testing and Assessment to recognize an individual who had made noteworthy and significant contributions to research

The 2004 International Test Commission council dinner in Hong Kong,
with Thomas Oakland (second row, second from the right).

or practice in educational or psychological assessment with a positive impact at
a national or an international level.

In the past, cross-cultural psychology used to be marginalized to the
fringes. During one of my presentations at an international conference, the
then director of the American Psychological Association's (APA) Office of
International Affairs, Merry Bullock, who was in the audience, was impressed
by the cultural sensitivities revealed in our studies and suggested that I should
bring this research to the attention of mainstream psychology. Undaunted by
the previous barriers I encountered with mainstream journals, I decided to
take up the challenge of not only bringing a Chinese voice to psychology, but
also advocating for the incorporation of the cultural perspective in mainstream
psychology. To broaden the perspective of my intended manuscript for
the *American Psychologist,* the flagship journal of the American Psychological
Association, I invited Fons van de Vijver and Fred Leong to be my co-authors.
Our 2011 paper, "Toward a New Approach to the Study of Personality
in Culture," promoted the integration of global and local perspectives in

The 2012 American Psychological Association award, with Merry Bullock.

psychology using a combined emic-etic approach rather than dichotomizing the emic vs. etic approaches.

The message was in line with the Zeitgeist in the development of psychology as a discipline. Since 2010, psychological knowledge had begun to be criticized for being unrepresentative of the world population. Studies were dubbed "WEIRD" because as much as 80 percent of the study participants came from Western, educated, industrialized, rich and democratic (WEIRD) societies who only constituted 12 percent of the world's population. Most of the majority world was unrepresented in our knowledge base. This WEIRD critique was extended beyond the participant pool of psychological research to also cover its theoretical models, methodological assumptions, and institutional structures as a WEIRD enterprise. Yet, this knowledge base was what we had been teaching in psychology as if it were universal.

As psychology evolved onto a more internationalized stage, so had my own career moved onto an international stage. My research on personality assessment originated with the practical intention of providing useful tools for assessing the personality of Chinese people. My cross-cultural research has led me down the theoretical path of examining the need for incorporating a cultural perspective in the study of personality, as well as the field of psychology itself. The awakening of psychology to the rest of the world later encouraged me to publish *The Cambridge Handbook of the International Psychology of Women* (mentioned in Chapter 4) to fill the cultural void in the scientific foundation of the field and present more culturally relevant evidence beyond Anglo-centric research literature. Reflecting on my career journey, I have worked in my small way to help to internationalize psychology.

Through my international engagements and more mainstream publications, my research was recognized more widely, and my contributions to personality assessment were honored in several international research awards, including the APA 2012 Award for Distinguished Contributions to the International Advancement of Psychology and the IAAP 2014 Award for Distinguished Scientific Contributions to International Advancement of Applied Psychology, the first time an Asian psychologist received these international awards. My contributions to the field of women psychology were also recognized in the 2020 International Council of Psychologists Denmark-Gunvald Award, named after two pioneer leaders in women scholarship, for "having sustained a history of research and service that directly benefited the health, promotion, and well-being of women in the world." A more important meaning of these awards to me was the acknowledgement of the contributions of non-Western psychology to the field of psychology, by which Asia had become visible on the international map of psychology.

Mainstreaming Culture in Psychology

With the rise of globalization, sensitizing the psychology discipline with a cultural perspective is a priority. Psychology programs in non-Western countries have largely adopted Western models of psychology and relied on Western textbooks. Sometimes, our students questioned the relevance of the examples they found in the textbooks. As teachers, we often had to add local examples and materials to the training, providing students with a broader cultural context. On the other hand, the cultural perspective had been inadequate in

Western psychology. There was a scarcity of psychology textbooks that covered non-Western research, or culturally diverse contents and perspectives. This prompted me to contribute to a few edited books on international perspectives in psychology. In my 2012 APA International Award article, I argued for the incorporation of cultural perspectives in mainstream psychology by borrowing the concept of gender mainstreaming. Like gender analysis, cultural analyses involving diverse cultural groups and social subgroups help to provide divergent cultural perspectives to enhance our psychological knowledge base and inform when culture-sensitive approaches should be adopted in psychological practice.

For half a century, cross-cultural psychologists have promoted culturally sensitive approaches in research and assessment. The ITC has published guidelines for testing and assessment with diverse populations for close to thirty years. Since 2012, even the traditionally Anglo-centric APA has published a new journal on international perspectives in psychology which "promotes the use of psychological science that is contextually informed and culturally inclusive." Psychology is slowly awakening to the need to address culture. As non-Western psychologists gained our confidence in bring our voices to Anglo-centric mainstream psychology, we were able to develop the field into a more truly universal as well as culturally relevant epistemology.

In addressing culture, we are dealing with complex human environments that include both universal and local contexts. Take the example of the globalization icon McDonald's, which grew from being a local fast-food restaurant in the U.S. to a global sensation in the fast-food industry with franchises in over 120 countries, exposing the children in the rest of the world to American hamburgers and French fries. McDonald's initial globalization strategy emphasized homogenization of their menu and ingredients, advertising proudly that the local outlets imported their potatoes from the U.S. to ensure the universal standards. Nowadays, we find McDonald's offering congee and red bean bubble tea in the menu in China, or McAloo Tikki Burger in the Indian menu to adapt to the local tastes. To be effective, globalization needs to involve localization, whereby global influences are internalized and localized in the process of "glocalization."

At the individual level, people are becoming multicultural through exposure to, identification with, and internalization of different cultures.

Growing up in colonial Hong Kong, getting my education in the United States, returning to work in Chinese societies, and collaborating with international colleagues have facilitated my navigation across different cultural contexts with multicultural competence. Multiculturalism helps us to function effectively in the modern world by being more empathetic and accepting of others, and by being more creative with diverse solutions.

GROWING WITH THE UNIVERSITY

Innovation initiative highlights in the retirement souvenir card from the Office of Research and Knowledge Transfer Services colleagues, 2020.

8

Having served on the faculty of The Chinese University of Hong Kong for over forty years under its first eight vice-chancellors and having lived in campus residences for most of that time, the university had become my second home. I regarded the university not as my employer, but more importantly as an intellectual, social, and ecological community which connected its current and past members, of which I was one.

CUHK was set up in 1963 by amalgamating the three foundation post-secondary colleges, New Asia College, Chung Chi College, and United College, which were set up in Hong Kong after 1949. I witnessed the evolution of the university, from its humble roots as the supplementary university to take in graduates from Chinese-language secondary schools who were not eligible for admission into the elitist University of Hong Kong, to become one of the top universities in Hong Kong with distinguished international standing. Starting with three faculties, Arts, Science, and Social Science with 1,395 students and about 100 teachers and staff members, it had grown into one of the top universities not only in Hong Kong and Asia, but also among the top 100 universities in the world. Over six decades, five more faculties were added to offer a broad range of major subjects. Student numbers had expanded to over 21,000 and the number of full-time teachers and staff

Outside the Psychology Section office in Chung Chi College
Teaching Block 8, 1979.

numbers exceeded 8,000. With the increase in student population, there are now nine colleges which provide a unique collegial environment for students and faculty members.

A great university is built on the footprints of not only its leaders, but also its numerous stakeholders including faculty, staff, students, alumni, donors, and supporters. A flourishing academic ecosystem cultivates cognitive flexibility, creativity and innovation while fostering the satisfactory experiences and the positive affect of its constituents. As its constituents, we play our roles in shaping its success or decline.

The rapid evolution of the role of universities with the advances of modern technology challenges us to reflect on where we came from and where we are going. The European model of universities evolved from the medieval elitist institutions of training scholars originating from the framework of church-based schools in the twelfth century to the current system of undergraduate and postgraduate teaching and research led by the United Kingdom and the U.S. With the rise of organizational performance assessment, university rankings took on a life of their own that dominated the orientation of the stakeholders of universities, especially the parents of potential students. Despite the initial resistance of many universities to participate in the simplified assessment of universities, the reputational and financial consequences of the rankings had tempted some university administrators to manipulate their responses to the surveys and promoted the commercial enterprise of ranking enhancement strategies in the markets of emerging universities.

Meanwhile, modern technology had presented alternatives modes of teaching and learning that were traditionally dominated by universities. When I first joined CUHK in 1977, education was more teacher-centered when we imparted one-size-fit-all knowledge to passive learners. The availability of digital resources due to the introduction of Internet and educational technology promoted more interactive learning. Massive open online learning platforms popularized by Coursera, which was cofounded in 2012 by Prof. Andrew Ng 吳恩達, a Hong Kong immigrant then teaching at Stanford University, now challenged the role of universities and the traditional university degrees. Micro-credentials that could be flexibly offered through online short courses tailored to specific skills for the job market became favored by employers. The amount of information that students could find on the Internet shifted the educational function of teaching to that of learning. The advent of generative artificial intelligence posed further challenge to the ways in which research and knowledge were produced and disseminated. Given these rapid developments, how could the university ecosystem adapt and reinvent itself? How should we educate our next generation of students to prepare for their future lives? The transformative vision for future education, or what is termed "Education 6.0," aims to prepare students to navigate and thrive in a rapidly changing world in the twenty-first century by fostering a collaborative relationship between humans and machines, while encouraging innovation and ethical decision-making. The growing dominance of big data and artificial intelligence highlights the necessity of grounding knowledge and skills in values and responsibility. Even the 2024 Nobel Laureate in Physics, Prof. Geoffrey Hinton, who built the technology system that paved the way for artificial intelligence, expressed regrets and cautioned about the risks of his invention, which might pose a danger to human existence when technology gains the capacity to eclipse human intelligence and take control. The 2021 book *In AI We Trust: Power, Illusion and Control of Predictive Algorithms* by Prof. Helga Nowotny, former President of the European Research Council and the recipient of the honorary degree of Doctor of Social Science from CUHK in 2023, challenged us to rethink what "intelligence" is and control in the co-evolutionary path of humans and the technologies created by them.

These questions did not occur to me when I started teaching at CUHK. As a junior faculty member, I simply followed the prescribed structure of the tertiary education system, taking on the normative teaching load of four courses a year, divided over two semesters of thirteen to fourteen weeks to fit the annual calendar. Nobody questioned the pedagogic design of two lectures plus a tutorial session per week for each course. The duration of the class sessions had to take into consideration the time that students could make their way across campus for their next class. Before the advent of PowerPoint and multimedia presentations, using handwritten transparencies with overhead projectors was already a great advance from writing on blackboards with chalk.

Back in 1977, female students made up less than one-third of the undergraduate student population at CUHK. At that time, many girls from working-class families in Hong Kong had to quit school to work in factories to support their families while the resources would be deployed to send their brothers to college. The introduction of free and mandatory secondary school education in 1978 allowed more girls to finish Form 5 of secondary school. During the late 1980s, CUHK introduced a Provisional Acceptance Scheme to attract students with superior results in the Hong Kong Certificate of Education Examination at the end of Form 5 by giving them provisional offers before the normative matriculation in Form 6. The number of female students gradually increased due to their good results in the public examination even though parity was not yet achieved. This increase evoked the gender bias of the patriarchal male leaders in the Faculty of Social Science who believed that female graduates would be less successful in their future careers and thus would disadvantage CUHK in its alumni impact. I could not help raising my objection to the faculty's undergraduate admission report, which stated the gender ratio had "deteriorated" from the previous year! During the faculty board meeting, I suggested that even if we did not acclaim that the gender ratio had improved, we could at least be more objective by simply noting that the gender ratio had changed. The admissions tutor conceded and changed this statement in the report. One year later, I was shocked to find the original statement repeated in that year's report. Apparently, the same Microsoft Word template for the original report had been used without checking, reflecting how entrenched was the bias. No ruffles had been raised during the previous twenty-five years, when two-thirds of the student population were males. The female proportion further increased in the 1990s after the number of university places had been increased with more universities established in Hong Kong. By 2024, the proportion of female students had increased to 56 percent for undergraduates although they were still in the minority in the research postgraduate programs. Shouldn't we pay more attention in developing the careers of our graduates, especially for the women who excelled in their studies but needed mentoring for their career advancement? Meanwhile, educators could make better use of their time to reflect on how to motivate young boys, as well as girls, to learn and study during the early stages of their education, instead of complaining about the feminization of higher education.

Engagement in College Life

At CUHK, all students and faculty members were assigned to one of the colleges, providing the lived experiences of campus life. The CUHK collegial system was unique in Hong Kong. The colleges provided general education and pastoral care for the students while academic studies were managed under the faculties. When I joined CUHK, the small psychology minor section was housed in Chung Chi College. I naturally went along with the same assignment, as did my other three colleagues in the section. I remained a member of the Chung Chi College from the beginning to the end of my tenure.

When Chung Chi College began in October 1951 as a post-secondary institution of higher education, there were only sixty-three students who were taught in borrowed and rented premises. It moved into the remote Ma Liu Shui valley down the Tolo Harbour coast near the Shatin rural town center in 1956 and was later joined by the two other foundation colleges when CUHK was established in 1963. During my first year at the university, the tooting diesel train of the Kowloon Canton Railway was stopping at the Ma Liu Shui Station in the valley of the campus once an hour. I could watch students sprinting from the hilltop after class to catch the approaching train in the valley to get into the city. In the evenings or weekends, students rowed boats across the Tolo Harbour to the shore on the other side to dig for clams on the beach at Ma On Shan for recreation. Teachers joined students on the annual hike to the peak of Ma On Shan. These idyllic experiences remained nostalgic memories of the alumni who formed a solid and affectionate identity as "CUHKers."

Our daily lives revolved around the college. Many faculty members got together at the college staff club for lunch and dinner. Some of them stayed behind after dinner to play Chinese Go games. In the early days, the staff club was run by a manageress who served us home-cooked set menus. It provided the hub for social interaction and intellectual exchange. We hung around to chat with colleagues from other departments over tea and coffee. With the growth in the staff size and the renovation of the staff club, the homey setting was turned into a restaurant run by a commercial caterer. The staff club had lost its role as a niche community and was reduced to a mere eatery for most members.

Student-Centered College Life

Our cohort of junior staff members stayed close to our students and were ardent about their personal developments. We explored ways to enhance their space of experiences and cultivate their horizons of aspirations. A sizeable proportion of our students came from low-income families and were the first generation to get a college education. Their life goals were largely shaped by their parents' expectations for them to attain a stable career. In employers' surveys of our graduates throughout the years, they were preferred by the employers due to their dependability and honesty, even though they were not as savvy and worldly as the graduates from the other more elitist university.

In the early 1980s, the activities students used to run in the hostels were mostly for fun when they were living away from home for the first time, like midnight snacks or "sweet soup gatherings." To broaden their social awareness as university students, we designed new programs like the "Tolo Nocturne," an evening talk series in the hostels in which guests from diverse backgrounds were invited to share with students their personal and unique experiences and viewpoints on social, cultural, and academic issues. Given the students' receptivity to the Tolo Nocturne, we added "Flying Beyond the Lotus Pond," which organized activities for both residential and non-residential students to learn about Hong Kong heritage, sustainable environment, and cultural life outside campus. The names of these programs were chosen to reflect the beautiful landscape of the college. The College Head at that time was the late Prof. Philip Fu 傅元國, who was open to new ideas and receptive to our initiatives. He actively participated in student activities and proudly showed off his role model for gender equality as the odd man who would be carrying his baby daughter in a baby carrier while walking in the busy Hong Kong downtown districts. With his enthusiastic support, we began discussion groups on gender roles and equality. I was gratified that some of the student programs we initiated during that time had become an established tradition in college student life.

The affinity between staff and students culminated during the celebrations of the annual College Founders' Day. Teachers cheered their students taking part in different competitions and participated in the round-campus run. We joined our own students at the open-air dinner tables during the Thousand People Feast in the Lingnan Stadium. We then moved to the Chapel to cheer our students in the inter-departmental singing contest. The evening did not end with the contest, following which we were expected to treat our students to midnight snacks at the open food stalls in the nearby markets.

The Bucolic Campus Environment

The college campus is distinctive in Hong Kong, nestled between the mountains and the waters, covered with trees and green lushness, away from the hustle and bustle of the urban city. My office in the Psychology Section was housed in the highest teaching block on the hillside in Chung Chi College, which has now become the Lee Wai Chun Building after the redevelopment of the teaching

Fanny (second from left standing) at Chung Chi College Founder's Day Thousand People Banquet with psychology students, 1982.

Chung Chi College Founders Day staff choir, Fanny is first from right, 1982.

blocks. We had to walk up five flights of stairs from the street level to get to the office. One of my students who had polio had to be carried by his classmates up the stairs to come to class. At that time, I wondered how I could manage those stairs when I got old. I was so relieved when the teaching blocks were redeveloped with elevators in the 1990s. This relief was swung back before my retirement when I had to tackle the inaccessible stairs to get to my Pro-Vice-Chancellor office in the University Administration Building, which did not have an elevator. It was ironical that inaccessibility at the central governing nucleus of the university not only posed as an obstacle for our aging administrators, but also for anyone suffering from disability conditions, as I witnessed personally after my leg fracture.

Before the redevelopment of the teaching building of the Psychology Section, there was a shortcut to get to our office on the hillside next to the Chung Chi College Chapel. Every time as I made my way through the steep weedy path, I had to look out for snakes which were often spotted in the Chung Chi campus. Once, our laboratory technician caught a snake with a wire-hooked pole and triumphantly showed off his trophy back in our office. It was the first time I had a close encounter with a live snake. To overcome my initial fear and show that I did not have ophidiophobia (snake phobia), I ventured to hold the snake, with its head around the hook of the pole. Going through my old photo album, which showed a picture of me holding the snake, I could see how frozen my smile was. The jubilant technician and the excited office clerk discussed how to dispose of the snake. Snake soup was a Cantonese delicacy, and naturally, it was the snake's destiny. In our small office on the hillside, we managed to concoct a delicious brew with the ingredients and cooking pot brought in by our clerk.

Snakes were not the only wildlife adventure on campus. Living alone in the Chung Chi staff quarters at the time, I always made sure that all the screened windows and balcony doors were closed tightly at night. It did not stop a bat from intruding into my bedroom one night when I was reading in bed. After a few banging sounds on my bedroom door, the bat slipped through the crack under the door and flew over my head circling the ceiling light. This was the first time in my life I'd come face to face with a bat, and of all places, above my own bed! I started to imagine vampire bats sucking blood from my neck if I

Holding the snake caught in Chung Chi College, 1985.

shared the same bedroom with it. With no clue as to how to get rid of the bat, I retreated into my adjacent study, stacking piles of books to block the crack of the bedroom door from the outside to make sure it would not follow me. It was a long tortuous night sleeping on the sofa before the next morning when I could call for help from the university maintenance office to save my flat from the invader.

In addition to the nocturnal animals, ghost stories—like the story of the phantom of a girl who purportedly died on the "braided lady road" behind the Chung Chi Library, appearing at night without a face but with long braids on both sides of her head—added to the eerie vibes of the nighttime wooded campus. However, during the daytime, the diverse plantations showcased the Chung Chi campus as a botanical garden. At our suggestion, staff and students from the Biology Department labelled the trees on campus to introduce the plants around us.

Unfortunately, the green campus was infested with mosquitos. Students took it for granted that they would have mosquito bites on their arms and legs going around campus, as they were in the countryside. For those of us working in air-conditioned offices and living in residences with screened windows, we were able to protect ourselves with minimal open exposure. It was a common assumption that when there were trees and grassland, there would be mosquitos.

When my husband joined me in the Chung Chi staff quarters shortly after our marriage, he got more than 130 bites all over his body while practicing his favorite weekend past-time in America, fixing our car, in the college residence carpark for about an hour. That was his first and last practice of his favorite craft in Hong Kong. I decided to tackle the mosquito problem on campus head on. Having met officers from the Food and Environmental Hygiene Department at the Shatin District Board, I discovered that the countryside assumption was a myth. According to the experts, mosquitos only bred in still water when trapped in potted plant saucers, garbage, and dead leaves in the gutters and so on. I proposed to the college to set up a College Environment Committee in 1988. We invited the environmental hygiene experts to tour the campus with us to identify the black spots and recommend preventive measures, including the type of mosquito oil to be poured into the gutters regularly. We organized an annual campus clean-up walk for students and staff to pick up soda pop cans and empty cups thrown over the hill slopes by pedestrians, drain the water from the plates under plant pots in the nurseries, and check for dead leaves clotting the gutters. We recorded the black spots for the campus maintenance staff to follow up. The group activity was meant to create a sense of ownership among staff and students for the environment. The college also hosted a lunch for the cleaning staff as a token of appreciation and to boost their commitment to vigilant efforts throughout the rest of the year. For the next ten years, the mosquito problem was greatly reduced, only to resurge again in recent years after the passionate community spirit dissipated. Without a shared vision, staff and students started to query why they had to take up the job of the cleaners while the maintenance staff went through the motion of spraying the gutters with mosquito oil without even looking at where the oil was going.

Those were the early days of college life when faculty members were enthusiastically engaged in extracurricular activities, before teaching and research performance became the major criteria for faculty evaluation. With objective goal posts stipulated for staff appraisal, there was less incentive for junior staff to serve the community with only intangible recognition for their engagement.

Building the Psychology Department

When I joined the Psychology Section under the Sociology Department at CUHK, I was one of the four lecturers (before the junior faculty members were given the title of Assistant Professor). Without a senior faculty member guiding us, we were left on our own to cover the whole range of basic courses in psychology. In those days, when we did not have access to myriad psychology teaching videos online, we had to design our own teaching materials. For my counselling psychology laboratory sessions, I wrote my own scripts of do's and don'ts in micro-counselling skills each week and videotaped our two teaching assistants role-playing the vignettes. These low-quality homemade productions were probably more effective than the professional videos imported from the U.S., as they were tailor-made for the local context.

My Canadian colleague in social psychology, Michael Bond, was the most dramatic teacher. To demonstrate the bystander effect in social psychology, he would have his teaching assistant pretend to faint in front of the class to see who would come forth to help. His funniest jokes were when he tried to say something in Cantonese to the students, which took them awhile to figure out what he was saying. He often came over to my office to ask for the pronunciation of a Chinese idiom which he could use to illustrate a psychological concept in the Chinese cultural context. Having been his office neighbor for thirty years, I often teased him for not having acquired Chinese proficiency during the length of time he had made Hong Kong his home while becoming an expert on Chinese psychology. Despite not being Chinese, Michael took the initiative to edit the first English volume on the psychology of the Chinese people published by an international publisher in 1986, to promote better understanding of the psychological and social processes that

American Psychological Association delegates visiting the Psychology Department,
with Michael Bond (seated front) and Leung Kwok
(back row, far right), 1994.

characterized Chinese people. This set the stage for our department to serve the function of bringing together psychology in Chinese societies and the West.

Psychology was a popular subject, but it was only offered as a minor subject until a major department was established. In the absence of a senior faculty member, I became the section head in 1979 to take on the task of preparing the proposal for our major program.

In the late 1970s, the university curriculum mostly followed the UK system. To ensure that our proposed major program would meet international standards, I reviewed similar programs in American and British universities. In particular, the British Psychological Association (BPS) had prescribed the required courses and training for curriculum to be accredited and the graduates of those programs to be eligible for graduate membership. I invited the then President of the BPS and Head of the Psychology Department at the University of York, Prof. Peter H. Venables, to come to Hong Kong in 1980 and review our proposal.

Peter H. and Bess Venables at home in York, 1983.

Peter was a remarkable scientist and a kind gentleman. His classical research on schizophrenia and psychophysiology began with a longitudinal study on the mental health outcomes of children from parents with schizophrenia in Mauritius. While at CUHK, Peter showed us how the diverse theoretical, experimental and applied domains in psychology could be interrelated. I still remember Peter's guileless and childlike nature despite his academic eminence. While in Hong Kong, he was excited to find his favorite snack, Kit-Kat, the wafer crisp chocolate bar which was popular in England. When he invited me to visit him in York during my sabbatical in the UK in 1983, he and his wife Ness hosted me in their country cottage where they kept a magnificent garden. Ness taught me the skills of cooking healthy delicious dinners. On our way back from Peter's office one day, he stopped by a store and picked up a pack of Kit-Kat. Like a little boy who had got his candy, with a twinkle in his eyes he whispered to me that Ness would not have let him eat it.

Despite what we thought to be a very strong proposal prepared with Peter's input, the university decided to defer the establishment of our major program until a senior psychologist was recruited to head the department in 1982. With

Prof. I. M. Liu (standing next to Fanny) and Psychology Department staff with
the first cohort of major students in 1982.

the arrival of Prof. I. M. Liu 劉英茂, a cognitive psychologist from Taiwan
who specialized in the study of Chinese language processing, in the helm, the
Psychology Department commenced with six faculty members. Prof. Liu was a
serious and reserved scholar, more interested in science than in administration.
Universities in Hong Kong often hired professors to administrative positions,
including those of deans and presidents, more for their scientific achievements
and with less regard for their administrative experience or skills. At least Prof.
Liu did not mind when we took the initiative to prepare and introduce the
master's and doctoral programs in Psychology and Clinical Psychology over the
next ten years.

After Prof. Liu's retirement in 1992, our former student in the minor
program, Leung Kwok, who had returned to teach in our department in
1985, became the new Chairman. Apart from his dynamic and efficient
administration, Kwok was an affable colleague and popular teacher who
had mentored the careers of many of our graduates. Kwok formed the Asian
Association of Social Psychology (AASP) in 1995 with three other leading social
psychologists from Japan and Korea, holding the first meeting at CUHK. The

AASP and its journal, the *Asian Journal of Social Psychology*, provided a focused platform for Asian social psychologists to share their cultural understanding of the region and to provide an international launching pad for young scholars from Asia.

When I returned from my appointment at the Equal Opportunities Commission in 1999, Kwok had decided to move to another university to take up a chair professorship in management. At first, I wanted to catch up on my research and did not want to take up any administrative position. One year later, complaints filed by the majority of the junior faculty members over the autocratic and unfair treatment of Kwok's successor led to a change in leadership. I became the chair of the department from 2000 until 2012 when I was appointed as the Pro-Vice-Chancellor. To engage all colleagues in the management of the department, I set up committees to formulate the policies and procedures for student admission, teaching load assignment, space and resource distribution, and other administrative matters, which would then be voted or endorsed by all faculty members at the departmental board meeting. While colleagues originally complained that the collective decision-making process in committees was too time consuming, they came around to appreciate the transparent governance and the rational principles derived through the deliberations. Their shared responsibilities created a sense of ownership for the well-being and advancement of the department. Above all, colleagues could feel safe in an open academic environment to pursue their work.

Having attained cooperation and harmony within the department, my role as chairperson could focus on the strategic development and external liaisons. Over the years, our department built up extensive international collaborations and became a leading Chinese voice in psychology in the twenty-first century. In 2024, our department was ranked the #1 Psychology Department in China by research.com, an international academic website, and five of our faculty members were listed among world's top 2 percent scientists (Chinese scholars in psychology).

A Research University

In the past sixty years, CUHK has evolved from an intimate collegiate university focused on nurturing students into a professorial university geared towards the transmission and creation of knowledge. The new emphasis was steered by the University and Polytechnic Grants Committee (UPGC, later renamed the University Grants Committee, UGC, in 1994), which advised the Hong Kong Government on the strategic development and resource requirements of higher education and indirectly influenced the development of funded institutions through its decisions on funding allocations. In the late 1980s, the government decided to massively increase the number of undergraduate students while differentiating the roles of the various universities into research-focused and teaching-based functions. The distinction soon dissipated when all institutions vied for the richer resources available to research.

The Changing Research Landscape

The UPGC established the Research Grants Council in 1991 to provide competitive funding support to research projects submitted by the universities. The new direction for universities provided much-needed support for research. Until 1990, we did not have any resources to conduct our research projects. I had to inspire the dedicated teaching assistants to help me with data collection and data entry beyond their tutoring duties. We brought stacks of punch cards to the computer center to submit our data analysis job. To look up references on past research, we had to visit the library and go through the journal index, and copy the relevant citations on index cards before finding the journal articles in the specific issues. Until we acquired the first generation of Apple II desktop computers for our office use in the mid-1980s, we had to type multiple versions of our manuscripts on manual typewriters. With access to the World Wide Web in 1991, Yahoo Search in 1995, and Google search in 1998, we entered the digital age when most of these jobs were just a click away. The launch of artificial intelligence tools like ChatGPT in 2022 further facilitated the automation of literature review and data analysis, prompting a recalibration of the role of researchers.

Somehow, the time saved through digitalization did not result in more active intellectual interactions among our colleagues in the university. With performance appraisal focusing on grants received and papers published, there was a trend among colleagues towards working in silos with their own projects, often hiding in the office in front of their computer screens instead of having lunch with others. To facilitate intellectual communication, many departments organized departmental research seminars to share colleagues' research. In the Psychology Department, we arranged a free lunch after these seminars to encourage colleagues to continue their discussions. With the turn of the century, many of our young colleagues preferred to pick up a sandwich from the coffee shop and eat it in their offices while preparing their lectures or manuscripts. Gone were the collegial days when one of us would knock on the others' doors to gather everyone to go out for lunch together.

Supporting research requires more than just funding and hardware. University policies and systems need to be aligned with research activities. When Japhet, my husband, first joined CUHK in 1986, he brought with him two commissioned grants that required him to return to the U.S. for research meetings twice a year. He found it unbelievable to be told by his department head that as a new staff member, he was not entitled to any leave until after a year of service. He finally had to give up his American grants. In his former American university, getting external research grants was considered an achievement to be facilitated and supported.

The university administrative system in Hong Kong used to be archaic, following static practices clung onto as the stronghold of the bureaucrats. When Japhet took up the responsibility of undergraduate program coordinator for the Faculty of Business in 1987, he was shocked to find business major students having to queue up overnight during the registration period to ensure that they could get a place in the popular business courses. Otherwise, those courses would be filled by other non-major senior students because the registration system was only based on seniority. The major students were worried that they could not fulfil all the required courses before graduation. Japhet questioned the registration administrators about the inefficient registration system, which had been computerized in modern universities elsewhere where registration ran smoothly with much larger student populations. He got the typical bureaucratic response that "this is the way it had always been done." Bypassing the inertia and objections from the bureaucrats, he designed his own pre-registration system specifically for the business administration undergraduate courses to ensure that major students could fulfil their course requirements. He later designed his own computerized registration for his own faculty. It took the university administration a couple more years to follow suit to modernize the whole registration system. How could universities in Hong Kong reach world-class level and gear up to compete internationally?

Faculty members often lamented about obstacles created by the administrators, who were insensitive to their needs and intransigent to changes unless they were ordered from the top. In a university, the primary role of administrative units should be to facilitate academic colleagues to excel in their work. No one leader alone can cover all the details, whereas involving the users can help to improve policies and systems. Catching up with the new research landscape gradually, CUHK set up a Research Committee to study research policy issues and appraise research projects for internal and external funding. The committee of senior professors provided diverse input to assist the university to address the emerging research needs. The Research Committee was a step forward from when all previous research decisions were made by a single Pro-Vice-Chancellor. I was appointed Deputy Chair of the committee from 2001 to 2013, serving with Prof. Joseph J. Y. Sung 沈祖堯, Chairman of the Department of Medicine and Therapeutics, at that time. In 2003, during the Severe Acute Respiratory Syndrome (SARS) outbreak which began in his hospital ward, Joseph and his team spearheaded the efforts to contain the spread of the epidemic, for which he was recognized as an "Asian Hero" by *Time* magazine. I still remember going over to talk to Joseph at the Prince of Wales Hospital before it was sealed off. The first comment he made to me was how I was wearing my N99 mask incorrectly. He was still busy multitasking his clinical duties while talking to me until he was suddenly overwhelmed with emotion, telling me that his former student had just died after getting infected from a patient she was trying to resuscitate in the intensive care ward.

Serving on the Research Committee exposed me to the range of excellent research across the university. Yet, the function of the committee had focused on serving the policies and procedures stipulated by the Hong Kong Research

Grants Council, leaving little time and effort to address the broader research culture and strategy of the university.

Cultivating the Research Culture

In 2013, I was invited by Prof. Joseph Sung, who became the seventh Vice-Chancellor/President of CUHK, to be the Pro-Vice-Chancellor (PVC)/Vice-President for Research, becoming the first woman to take up this senior position in the university's fifty-year history. In most universities, this research leadership position would typically be taken up by a faculty member from the STEM (Science, Technology, Engineering and Mathematics) or Medicine disciplines. This reflected the bias of most research universities in Asia towards the STEM areas, which failed to recognize the equal importance of research in non-STEM subjects. Having previously deputized Joseph in the university's Research Committee, I had earned his trust in my research leadership. My background in psychology helped me to promote intersections among the diverse disciplines in the eight faculties of our comprehensive university. As a multi-faceted discipline, psychology could bridge the divide between humanities and social science on the one hand, and natural science and medicine on the other hand. Still, there was a steep learning curve involved in broadening my understanding and appreciating the exciting advances in all the diverse disciplines.

I took on my new role as a facilitator of the university's research mission. How can we build up a vibrant and sustainable research ecosystem? Observing the publication trends of specific disciplines, I noted that recent research had become so highly specialized to the extent that the findings would seem so remote from addressing the complexities of our contemporary multifaceted reality. Nowadays, we seldom find well-rounded scholars resembling luminary Renaissance polymaths like Leonardo da Vinci, who excelled in multiple fields including painting, science, and engineering. While specialized approaches allowed for in-depth analysis of aspects within single disciplines in order to build the groundwork of the research area, the narrow mindsets of academics who dwelled in their solitary silos ran the risk of stagnation and rendered research findings to be perceived as irrelevant to people outside the specialized coterie. The publish-or-perish culture at CUHK often detracted junior scholars from venturing into innovative and groundbreaking investigations, scrambling to publish whatever they could get into print to boost the number of publications. When the unhealthy research pressure became toxic, questionable research ethics and scientific misconduct would surface. Even though many scholars detested the pressure, research-oriented universities found it a dilemma in managing unhealthy aspects of the practice while subscribing to the counting game of research rankings.

With greater attention paid to research misconduct by the scientific community, we anticipated receiving more allegations of plagiarism, duplicate publications, falsification of data, and other unethical research conduct. I quickly reviewed our existing research misconduct policy—which was written in the good old days, when such allegations were rare and seldom came to the surface. The definitions as well as the handling procedures were unclear. The disciplinary procedures were not aligned with the general disciplinary policies of the university. All these policies were probably designed in isolation. In the process of the review, I had to enlist our administrators from the human resources office, student affairs office, and the University Secretary to sit together with our research personnel to align and streamline the interrelated policies to ensure efficiency and procedural justice. Research was not confined only to our researchers and research administrative units. Our university's entire infrastructure must be in sync.

Whereas a research misconduct policy could set the standard for upholding research integrity, it mainly served as a gatekeeper. I took on the task to address the broader issue of cultivating a research culture that drew upon the curiosity of our researchers in seeking new frontiers of knowledge. While defining performance indicators in publications and grants for decisions in tenure and promotion could provide a form of incentive, bean counting by administrators could stifle creativity and result in perfunctory outputs delivered just for the sake of reaching the goalpost. How could we bring back the joy of discoveries and the meaning of research? For our young researchers, we ran workshops on grant applications in which seasoned researchers shared their experiences of success. We appealed to their passion for seeking cutting-edge research frontiers and how they could benefit humanity, which would have been one of the key reasons for their choice of an academic career. In appealing to our colleagues' intrinsic motivation, which was the principal driving force or their original aspiration, what I could draw on was less about duty and more about passion and interest.

Encouraging cross-disciplinary collaboration on thematic areas by enticing researchers to work outside their silos to form research consortiums took more strenuous effort. While we had many outstanding individual researchers, getting them to shed their blinders and work together was not an easy task. I often reminded my colleagues with the celestial analogy that we had many stars in our university, but to be more visible and impactful, we needed to form galaxies. At one brainstorming session to foster collaboration in a new research unit, I literally had to draw a matrix on the whiteboard to show how the individual researchers' own research interests from medicine, engineering, and behavioral science could be connected to provide a fuller picture of the brain. We often heard colleagues moan and groan about how time-consuming it was to sit together in meetings to discuss collaboration. I continued to host cross-disciplinary sessions on common themes. Gradually, the interactions inspired some colleagues on the exciting potentials of the broadened horizons of interdisciplinary projects.

For me, being able to forge these synergies was a rewarding experience. Connecting human talent and the dots in the lattice of their research topics exposed us to new horizons. In drawing up the university's Five-Year Strategic Research Plan for 2016–2020, I recruited a group of senior researchers to join a task force to identify the research foci which were of critical importance to the flourishing of humanity in the twenty-first century. The collegial input of our members, including our university's Distinguished Professor-at-Large and Turing Award winner, Prof. Andrew Chi Chih Yao 姚期智, on the forward development of research frontiers that addressed global challenges was an inspiration. Shedding our previous practice of just putting resources into legacy areas of research excellence associated with individual colleagues, the task force reviewed international trends in cutting-edge research as well as our own areas of research expertise to ascertain strategic areas in research frontiers that addressed global challenges. We ensured that these areas took advantage of the broad range of disciplines in our comprehensive university, which facilitated cross-disciplinary perspectives and collaboration. We came up with four strategic foci: 1) China Studies spanned from the traditional humanities to the contemporary global development of China, including the recent Belt and Road Initiative; 2) Innovative Biomedicine captured our colleagues' world leading research in genetic, genomic and precision medicine; 3) Information and Automation Technology capitalized on our research strength in artificial intelligence and machine learning with potential applications for healthy and smart living; 4) Environment and Sustainability as an integrated research area addressed the diverse physical, ecological and human factors affecting the sustainability of our planet earth.

We presented our draft strategic plan at town hall meetings for consultation with our research colleagues. We anticipated noise from individual researchers, who tried to push their personal research agenda for inclusion in the strategic plan in the hope of getting additional resources. We illustrated the inclusivity of these strategic areas and welcomed participation from researchers who could demonstrate how their niche areas fit into our vision of addressing global challenges. This participatory approach promoted consensus and espousal from our research community. The four strategic areas adopted in 2016 prevailed in the subsequent Five-Year Strategic Plan 2021–2025. The next challenge was to translate our strategic research innovations into tangible benefits with significant impact to society.

Entrepreneurship Ecosystem

The image of academics used to be associated with the ivory tower, a figure of speech which began in the twentieth century to depict universities and science that were detached from the outside world. The work of academics sitting in an ivory tower was often perceived as impractical or irrelevant to the everyday life of ordinary people. We owed it to the society which supported the funding of our universities and research to pay back with our knowledge. I remember during the early stage of my academic career, some of my traditionally minded senior colleagues regarded my active community engagements as distractions from my academic pursuits. I disregarded their biased scrutiny. I believed that if I could deliver and excel in my academic performance, my societal involvements should not be counted against me. I conceded that some of my other socially engaged colleagues might have caused their seniors to frown by dispensing social commentaries without grounding in academic or research evidence. While they had their right to share their personal views or political opinions as intellectuals, those commentaries should be distinguished from evidence-based outputs bearing their academic affiliations. My convictions on translating knowledge and research evidence to serve society were vindicated with the advancement of knowledge transfer and entrepreneurship in the university research ecology in the twenty-first century.

In the global context of competitive and knowledge-based society, the integration of the components of education, research, and innovation in the knowledge triangle had become a preferred framework. In 2009, the Hong Kong University Grants Council (UGC) introduced a new stream of recurrent funding for universities for strengthening and broadening their capacity and endeavors in knowledge transfer, which was recognized as the third mission of the higher education institutions, apart from teaching and research. Following the initiatives in the United Kingdom and Australia, the UGC added the assessment of research impact to society in the 2019 research assessment exercises, beyond the quality of research publications. In preparation for this new requirement, universities began to ramp up their efforts to develop impact cases from our colleagues' research. Unfortunately, when universities lagged in setting the vision of higher education, external demand and funding often became the tail wagging the dog.

Entrepreneurship in universities began to flourish in American universities in the late twentieth century, when innovations by professors and students in top-tier research universities blossomed into phenomenal ventures. For example, the roles of Stanford University, the University of California at Berkeley, and the University of California at San Francisco in the evolution and success of the Silicon Valley as an entrepreneurial hub propelled the rise of entrepreneurship on college campuses. Asian universities were latecomers in the development of innovation and entrepreneurship programs. Innovation was typically associated with science and technology while entrepreneurship tended to be based in business programs.

China's Thirteenth Five-Year Plan in 2016 set out the focus on science, technology and innovation as the country's development goal. This spurred the Hong Kong SAR government to begin to strengthen its efforts to promote innovation and entrepreneurship in our universities. The Fourteenth Five-Year Plan in 2021 further strengthened the role of Hong Kong as an international innovation and technology center and a major platform of cooperation in the Greater Bay Area. Are universities in Hong Kong ready to take up the new strategic development goals?

An Infrastructure Fit for Purpose

As PVC/Vice-President for Research, I supervised two separate administrative offices at the university: The Research Administration Office (RAO), which primarily processed the research grants and awards administration, and the Knowledge Transfer Office (KTO), which helped colleagues with filing patents and administering the commercialization of their products. Coming from the non-STEM areas, I had little prior contact with the KTO, as our knowledge transfer activities at that time did not involve patents or commercialization. Knowledge transfer traditionally focused on the more applied STEM areas, especially Engineering and Medicine.

The existing offices of RAO and KTO were more administrative units headed by mid-level administrators who were basically gatekeepers of the bureaucratic procedures. Researchers had often complained about the internal roadblocks posed by the administrators on innovation. The two separate offices were not aligned to identify potential entrepreneurial opportunities arising from our colleagues' research. There was little communication between the staff of the two offices. How could this bureaucratic modus operandi facilitate the innovation and entrepreneurship culture at the university?

The opportunity arose when the heads of both offices left for personal reasons within a short gap after I took up office. I convinced the university administration to merge the two offices into a single unit, to be headed by a director and associate director who were senior and experienced researcher-practitioners. The merged Office of Research and Knowledge Transfer Services (ORKTS) was established in March 2014, the first such integrated office in the universities in Hong Kong. In introducing the new office, I highlighted the "S" in the acronym of ORKTS to promote a service culture for the office, which I reiterated repeatedly during my meetings with the office team members. I believed that administrative offices should be a service unit to help academic colleagues to achieve and excel in their pursuits. We should be equipped to bring solutions to help colleagues to solve their problems instead of acting as the central authority creating more obstacles with rules and bureaucratic procedures. Listening to the voices of our dedicated researchers, I took it upon myself to make life easier for them, given that I was in the position to do so.

In re-engineering the research infrastructure, I had a lot to learn along the way. I was fortunate to have the staunch support and guidance from Prof. Wai Yee Chan 陳偉儀, Founding Director of the School of Biomedical Science. An alumnus of CUHK and expert in molecular genetics, Wai Yee was recruited from the Georgetown University Medical Center and the National Institutes of Health to set up the School of Biomedical Science. He later became the PVC responsible for strategic development in 2018. I invited Wai Yee to serve with me on the Research Committee as Deputy Chairperson. Not only did he enlighten me on the midstream and downstream R&D (research and development) ecosystem with his experience in translational research and patents, but he also backed me up on the management of the new office. I could always count on his input and advice when I needed someone to bounce off my ideas. The greatest challenge, however, lay in identifying the right candidates to lead the new office as there were few researcher-practitioners with both R&D experience in the local academic community who also had the academic standing to command respect from our professorial colleagues. Through Wai Yee's knowledge and connections in the field, we finally recruited an excellent team headed by Prof. Walter K. K. Ho 何國強 to launch the vision of ORKTS after an initial setback.

Walter was a former Chair Professor of Biochemistry at CUHK and had been active in the field of biotechnology. Before retiring in 2010, he had been Director of the Hong Kong Institute of Biotechnology, which provided catalyst and essential infrastructure for the development of the biotechnology and Chinese medicine industries in Hong Kong. Wai Yee was his former student and convinced him out of his comfortable retirement to lead the nascent

ORKTS. As a seasoned academic leader and administrator, Walter connected well with the academic colleagues and motivated his team with professionalism and geniality. He recommended savvy solutions to manage the divergent demands of researchers, contractors, and patent licensees. With the confidence of having a capable leader at the helm, I could be more relaxed and let the team members fulfill their potential.

Building a new office was dependent on teamwork. Borrowing from research and practice in personnel psychology, I implemented a 360-degree appraisal of the performance of the Director and Associate Director, with their consent, involving feedback by peers, key stakeholders, and subordinates in addition to self-appraisal and appraisal by the supervising officer. This model of performance review had been used effectively in business management for a long time. At CUHK, this was a bold initiative for an administrative unit, which astonished our human resources office, but they could not find any reason to advise against it. The engagement of the unit managers in ORKTS in the appraisal process enhanced their sense of empowerment. The anonymous input helped to confirm my unilateral preliminary assessment and identify areas for improvement.

Staff training played an important function to stimulate our incumbent staff to develop new mindsets and new skill sets for the entrepreneurial ecosystem. Whereas academics had more opportunities to update their knowledge through conferences and research collaboration, administrators tended to stay put in their routine practices. We often got frustrated with administrators who told us why something could not be done otherwise because that was the way it had always been at the university. With the changing landscape in higher education, our supporting infrastructure needed to be fit for purpose. Picking up best practices from visiting our international partners during my overseas trips, I decided to provide the opportunities for my team to also learn from these role models. Above all, they were the ones working in the frontline. I deployed resources to organize a week-long training workshop on innovation and entrepreneurship management at an American university for the key staff at ORKTS. I also invited a representative from each faculty responsible for their impact and entrepreneurship to join. Apart from the substantive knowledge gained, the overseas training also helped the teambuilding at ORKTS, as well as forged a closer liaison between the academic and administrative colleagues.

Despite my lack of interest in business and personal finances, I soon became alerted to my official role in the capacity of PVC as chair of the committee overseeing dozens of dysfunctional subsidiaries and spin-off companies under CUHK at that time. Many of these companies were set up in the 1990s in a flurry of interest in commercialization promoted in the faculties of Engineering and Medicine. In the past, the university was not equipped to run commercial enterprises. After being set up, the companies were left to run on their own by the faculty members who were passionate about their pet projects but lacked the business know-how. Reviewing their annual accounts showed that some of them did not even have a balanced budget. They were run more like a research center than a commercial operation. I could not accept the laissez faire practice of going through the motion of receiving the annual reports from the university accounts office. A major review and a clean-up exercise were warranted.

Without any commercial expertise within the university's committee overseeing these companies, I invited a family friend who had been an executive at the Hong Kong Stock Exchange as well as the Securities and Futures Commission of Hong Kong to join the committee and advise us on the review. I was embarrassed to show him our messy portfolio, but he was always courteous and respectful in sharing his wisdom. I wondered how someone with his extensive experience and expertise would view the commercial ineptness of our university. Learning from his acuity in investment and company governance, we managed to pare down the portfolio of dysfunctional companies and strengthened the management of the remaining ones.

This exercise of cleaning up our companies prompted me to update and strengthen our policy on the incorporation, governance, and winding up of companies under the university's umbrella. This became handy when the government further invested in innovation and entrepreneurship in universities as a strategic development of Hong Kong's future role in the Greater Bay Area. A parallel revision of our policy on the establishment, governance, and dissolution of research units was conducted to manage the proliferation of research units.

In the process of strengthening the governance of our infrastructure, I also found that our existing policy on knowledge transfer and intellectual property was outdated and not suitable for purpose. We needed to create incentives for innovation and commercialization arising from basic research. The exercise of revising the intellectual property policy was more challenging, as it covered a wide domain of works including teaching materials, publications, database, software, and patents by faculty, staff and students. It involved balancing the interests of stakeholders with those of the university. Again, I invited faculty representatives to join our administrators in a task force to identify options to move the university forward with a policy that enabled collective ownership. We reviewed practices in world-leading universities and worked with external intellectual property consultant and legal professions. Following rounds of consultation with stakeholders, the process that began in 2015 was finally completed in 2020.

Mindset and Tools

Apart from building up the infrastructure, we needed to train our faculty and students in entrepreneurship. In 2013, President Joseph Sung came up with the idea of setting an incubation center on campus to promote student entrepreneurship. Unfamiliar with the concept, I quickly researched how this could be done. After reviewing the scope of activities and resources required, I concluded that in the CUHK context, we were not ready for an incubation center designed to support the creation of companies until the stabilization of their business models. The incubation program at the Hong Kong Science Park adjacent to our campus could have served that purpose. Instead, we should start with a modest pre-incubation center to stimulate creativity and entrepreneurship among students and support aspiring students to prepare and fine-tune their startups. I proposed to name it the PI-Centre, borrowing from the film *The Life of Pi*, depicting Pi's discovery of his purpose in life and his resilience in maintaining strong convictions even in life's most challenging moments. The importance of fostering resilience served as a reminder to student entrepreneurs that one in five startups would fail in the first year, and 90 percent of startups went bust over the long run. With the energetic drive of colleagues at ORKTS, the PI-Centre accelerated into being in 2014, offering up to one year of working space, facilities, training, mentoring, funding, and entrepreneurial consultancy service to selected student startup teams.

Entrepreneurship was not confined to students who already had the idea and aspiration of a startup. To cultivate the innovation and entrepreneurial mindset among university students, I proposed a Minor Programme in Entrepreneurship and Innovation (EPIN) in 2017, the first of its kind in Hong Kong. The pioneering curriculum design adopted an interdisciplinary approach, and the courses were open to all undergraduate students from different faculties, not just in business or technology. The EPIN Programme provided a platform for students to learn, practice and make things happen, through a simulated process of creating a new venture in which the students went through the different stages of "ideation," "realization," and "commercialization." It helped students develop the relevant mindset (e.g. creativity, perseverance, social responsibility and proper conduct in research and development) and skill sets (e.g. problem solving, project management and business planning).

Promoting innovation and entrepreneurship to faculty members revealed conventional biases. When I invited representatives from all the eight faculties to engage in a brainstorming session on how to cultivate and promote this ecology at the university, the representatives from the humanities and social sciences were aloof and skeptical. They looked down on entrepreneurship with disdain as a materialistic business activity that was incongruous with their virtuous and noble academic aura. I challenged them to think of social innovation and entrepreneurship, and how social enterprises had helped to advance services for the disadvantaged. By reconnecting entrepreneurship with social causes, the skeptical colleagues became convinced.

To promote faculty entrepreneurship, ORKTS consolidated its support functions through funding and training. In addition to administering the technology start-up scheme provided by the government, CUHK established a knowledge project transfer fund (KPF) to support professors from all faculties to initiate social innovation projects, exemplifying the translation of academic

The Shenzhen Research Institute InnoHub opened in 2018.

knowledge into social impact with direct engagement with local communities, often in partnership with external organizations.

Parallel to the scheme from the government to support technology start-ups, we initiated a Sustainable Knowledge Transfer Project Fund (S-KPF) in 2015, which provided incubation services for CUHK academics to launch evidence-based social enterprises. Besides seed funding, our Social Innovation Team supported our colleagues' social enterprises with business development consultancy, publicity and media engagement, and partnership liaison. While more attention had been focused on developing innovative technology into profitable business ventures, some professors had opted to apply their innovations to serve a social mission. As an example, professors in engineering and medicine collaborated to start a social enterprise using artificial intelligence technology to preserve and clone human voices to re-create voices for people with communication disabilities to regain the ability to speak. In contrast to the initial skepticism of the representatives from the humanities and social sciences, colleagues from these disciplines soon saw the benefit of translating their research into self-sustaining social enterprises instead of just short-term social service projects dependent on dwindling donations. A team led by a professor specializing in sign language started a social enterprise to provide sign bilingual (sign language and oral language) education and communication support services as well as sign interpretation services to deaf and hearing-impaired individuals, their parents, and normal-hearing children in schools and the community, promoting better communication and an inclusive environment. Another team headed by an educational psychology professor developed a robot for autism behavioral intervention based on their research that social robots were more effective than humans at teaching language to children with autistic spectrum disorder.

As interest in innovation and entrepreneurship grew in the university, the need for a physical hub beyond the small PI-Centre for students became apparent by 2017. I first suggested setting up an Entrepreneurship and Innovation hub (InnoHub) at the Shenzhen Research Institute (SZRI) at the end of 2017. SZRI was struggling to utilize its research space efficaciously by our faculty members after some of the research schemes in China could be applied directly from Hong Kong. On the other hand, the rapidly growing entrepreneurial and production ecosystem in Shenzhen could provide a wide range of support for CUHK students, staff, and alumni to transform and commercialize their research outputs. By May 2019, there were twenty-eight start-up teams settled in our InnoHub in Shenzhen. The expansion of the innovation ecosystem at SZRI revitalized its functions to achieve its mission of supporting scientific research, technology transfer activities and talent cultivation.

Responding to the requests of our faculty members, students and alumni, we explored the possibility of expanding an innovation hub at a centrally accessible location on campus within the constraints of space and resources available. I spotted an old residential building located next to the University MTR station. The lower floors of the building had already been turned into the office of a unit that was just moving outside campus. We applied for the vacant space to establish an InnoPort. The reputation of our innovation and entrepreneurship programs had earned us the confidence and support from the University. By 2020, the knowledge transfer team from ORKTS had enthusiastically designed and transformed the old offices into a modern and vibrant space for connecting people, bouncing ideas, gathering, co-working, and running events. By consolidating all the university's innovation and entrepreneurship activities under one roof, the Innoport served as the habitat for aspiring entrepreneurs to innovate and incubate their research knowledge and ideas into products that had social as well as economic impact. The knowledge transfer journey was no longer limited to a few selected ventures, but an accessible extension of one's research into the society.

As I reflected on the process of building the entrepreneurship ecosystem in the last decade, it dawned on me how it resonated with a theme in the

The PI-Centre coworking space in 2014.

The CUHK InnoPort came into operation in 2020.

Communique of the 2024 Third Plenary Session of the Twentieth Central Committee of the Communist Party of China, the contents of which were widely discussed at all levels of government in China and Hong Kong. One theme pertaining to the development of innovation and technology was highlighted in an academic seminar that I recently attended. The communique emphasized the importance of coordinated efforts to promote integrated reform of institutions and mechanisms pertaining to education, science and technology, and human resources, as well as to improve the new system for mobilizing resources nationwide to make key technological breakthroughs. Designating science and technology as one of the bases of Chinese modernization meant that the entire political and administrative apparatus needed to revolutionize itself first. This applies to the university's infrastructure as well.

As children, we often heard the saying by Confucius in the *Analects*: "Good tools are the prerequisites of a good job" (工欲善其事，必先利其器 *Gongyushanqishi, bixianliqiqi*). By tools, Confucius originally meant not only the hardware, but also the people and the methods. Here, the tools extended to the entire system. I hope my small efforts at CUHK have contributed to boosting the development of innovation and entrepreneurship for our next generation.

From Teaching to Cultivating Critical Thinking

I often met CUHK alumni who were not students in psychology, but who had either taken my course as an elective or had sat in my class in the early days. Other than the novelty of psychology as a subject, they told me that word had spread around that there was a new teacher who was a young female, whatever that meant. Before the introduction of teaching evaluations, how students chose their courses was often through word of mouth, not necessarily based on substantive course contents, but rather on obscure curiosities.

Teaching was often likened to acting. I lacked the dynamic flair of a performer who captured the attention of a large audience. My "counselling" voice could only reach an intimate group in a small classroom. Mindful that my voice could not withstand over an hour of non-stop monologue, I adopted a more interactive style of engaging students in role plays and discussion. Using local cases as examples and highlighting cultural differences from Western textbooks based on our own research stimulated students' interests. Values and ethics were also embedded in these discussions at the same time. Those were the key takeaways that the students remembered and treasured.

Students growing up in the Hong Kong education system had become too focused on getting good grades in examinations. Granted the public examination results would determine entrance into the preferred universities or major subjects, what students needed later in life was not "tips" in the public examination questions. Every time I saw the large promotional advertisements in the back of buses as I drove, I always frowned at the values portrayed in the so-called "tutor kings" who gained prophetic celebrity status in Hong Kong for their predictions on the questions in the upcoming public examinations. Yet, eager parents kept sending students to these tutoring schools after class. We tried to change this examination orientation in the university. Examinations only constituted a portion of the final grade. Instead, we added term papers to train independent research writing and group projects to cultivate teamwork. Increasingly, complex ecosystems in modern societies required new work cultures that centered on collaboration, peer-to-peer work, and collaborative leadership. Soft skills and values remained key learning objectives throughout the evolution of higher education.

I tried to engage the students to take an active role in class discussion, but Hong Kong students were more habituated to passive note-taking, regardless of what was being said. Once, I played the trick of talking gibberish for five minutes before asking what the students were getting in their notes. Even for those who detected something wrong, they did not dare raise any questions at the time. The students were so eager to take notes that they started to request teachers to distribute copies of their overhead transparencies in the old days, and now PowerPoint slides in class. I refused even though many teachers complied with the request. I always remembered my time in a graduate elective course at the University of Minnesota, when a classmate who was supposed to be a first-class honor CUHK graduate had to copy my notes every class because he could not keep up with the lecture. Note-taking was a basic study skill essential to learning. I'd rather have my students learn to listen and comprehend the gist of the lecture, and only jot down the key point. I volunteered to give a lecture to first year students in their orientation course, during which I raised four basic questions to them: "What do you want to know? Why do you want to know? How do you know? What do you want to do with what you know?" My hope was that when they graduated, they would gain more useful outcomes than a diploma as their job credential.

Critical thinking would be a more important learning objective in a knowledge society when so much information could be found just a click away online. There are so many online courses and teaching materials that could replace or supplement the contents of what we used to teach. As teachers, we had to learn to change our roles from transmitters of knowledge to facilitators of learning by guiding students how to learn. When the generative AI tool ChatGPT was first launched in 2021, some universities in Hong Kong decided to ban students from using it initially. It became apparent that the policy was unrealistic and would deprive students and researchers from benefitting from the learning opportunities offered by the AI tool. International universities had begun to learn how to capitalize on the advantages of generative and non-generative AI as efficient teaching and research aids by optimizing faculty and student time on tedious routine processes, as well as assisting in data analysis. A global consortium of higher education institutions also launched a study on the impact of the burgeoning AI technologies in the workforce and how education could respond by upskilling and reskilling academics and university leaders. Even more importantly, we should ponder how to educate our students on the critical analysis and ethics of applying AI technologies as human beings.

Noting how machine learning on digital media could feed us myriad messages to shape our interests and opinions, it became even more crucial that students learn how to appraise and validate the online information they received, broaden their perspectives from diverse sources, and cultivate judicious judgement through critical analysis. Unfortunately, many students had modelled rowdy politicians to become "critical" without the "thinking." The proliferation of media had enabled ordinary citizens to freely share their opinions while giving rise to unfettered spread of unconfirmed rumors, fake news, and other harmful acts such as hate speech and doxxing. It was unimaginable to find how an unverified hearsay spread by neighbors in a small city in Ohio, U.S.A. got circulated, ending up as a claim made during the 2024 American presidential candidates' television debate that Haitian migrants were eating pets. Although the false claim was decisively debunked by the city officials, it continued to take on momentum as a tool to promote intended outcomes. Politicians had become known for the tactic of repeating a lie often enough in their propaganda leading people to eventually come to believe it as a fact. As we became more aware of geopolitical conflicts in recent years, we only began to realize the extent of biased or false narratives and misinformation that we received in the media and social media, and how mob behavior could be incited through these platforms.

Facts, Misinformation, and Herd Mentality

In the past, we used to trust what we read in newspapers and what we saw on television news. We soon learned that presented facts could be subject to bias and distortions especially in a politicized climate. Media reports on the social movements in Hong Kong in 2014 Occupy Central Campaign and 2019 Anti-extradition Bill Movement brought to the fore the double standards in the narratives, especially by Western politicians and media when compared to those on the 2024 pro-Palestinian protests in American college campuses. Despite the violence and destruction rampant in the 2019 Hong Kong riots, the coverage glorified the students' "peaceful" pursuits for freedom and democracy and condemned police brutality. There was no coverage of the arson, rampage, and attacks on the police, MTR stations, innocent citizens who disagreed with their stand, as well as private businesses deemed to be supportive of the central government. Many of my American colleagues wrote to express their concern for my safety living under police brutality in Hong Kong. I had to correct them, saying that they only saw edited versions of the coverage, and the risks to ordinary citizens came rather from the violent protesters.

On the other hand, the 2024 pro-Palestinian protests on American campuses were more often portrayed in the conventional media as riots and terror threats, posing a harassment to other people on campus and blocking normal functions of the universities. There was little coverage of police brutality when police in riot gear were called in to clear the protesters' encampments.

An American politician had once praised the 2019 Hong Kong protest on July 1, HKSAR Establishment Day, during which the Legislative Council was ransacked, as "a beautiful sight to behold." The comment was later alleged to refer only the "peaceful" rally, demonstration, and march, totally ignoring the storming and ransacking of the Legislative Council after the march. Her quote came back to haunt her after the U.S. Capitol was attacked on January 6, 2021 by a mob of supporters of the then former President Donald Trump after his 2020 election defeat, when her own office was invaded and damaged. Over 1,500 people had been charged and convicted of criminal acts for this single attack on Capitol Hill, although they were subsequently pardoned by President Trump on the first day of his second term. I hope our students will be educated to broaden their historical and global perspectives and discern more objective and balanced views with critical thinking.

During the 2019 social unrest in Hong Kong, our students were inspired by the rhetoric of freedom and democracy as universal values of social justice. However, when pressed to explain the meaning of these values, few could articulate the underlying principles except to repeat the slogans as their aspirations for Hong Kong. I had always supported the development of social consciousness in our students. That was the background of some of our early days' extracurricular programs. However, I also emphasized the importance of social responsibility as an inherent corollary of individual rights. Despite idealistic goals, violence and infraction could not be justified as the legitimate means to an end.

The 2024 pro-Palestinian protests spreading across American campuses offered parallel lessons. Ivy League university presidents were forced to resign after they did not openly censure the protesters' behavior when grilled by politicians in Congress. Even U.S. President Biden came out to declare that violent protest, including vandalism, trespassing, breaking windows, shutting down campuses, threatening people, intimidating people, and instilling fear in people was not peaceful protest and against the law. While upholding the principle of free speech, he emphasized the principle of upholding the rule of law. No such condemnation was covered in Western media over the riots and campus occupation in Hong Kong in 2019.

Herd mentality and mob behavior has been studied for over a century in social science to show how people would conform to the social norms of the groups to which they belonged and followed the behavior of the majority at the expense of their personal judgement. Docile people would follow popular opinions and ideas even when they might not fully comprehend or support them. There is strong and growing evidence in social psychology research on why people believe misinformation and resist correcting those views. Why would so many people trust falsehoods? Research has found how people tend to seek out information that confirm their prior beliefs in what is called "confirmation bias" and come to a desired conclusion rather than an accurate one. Machine learning also selectively transmits similar messages to individuals' social media to fit into their identity or world view. When the same false information is repeated multiple times, especially with the amplification by circulation through the social media, it becomes lodged in memory. Even the new input of accurate information cannot easily unseat falsehoods. To inoculate against misinformation, we need critical and analytical thinking with a focus on lateral reading and scientific evidence to help us to recognize manipulation techniques, to identify untrustworthy content, and to avoid circulating materials without discernment. Given the dominance of and preoccupation with social media among the younger generation, cognitive training should take priority over sheer knowledge transmission in educating our students.

During their formative years, students are particularly vulnerable to peer influence. In the face of conformity pressure in social media, resilience to stand up for their independent views is an important part of students' personal development. I still remember how I stood my ground and resisted peer pressure to smoke cigarettes during my California high school days. I also recall crossing the picket line to go to my classes at UC Berkeley when many students called for cancellation of classes during the occupation of the People's Park and the anti-war protests. In the first place, I did not support the occupation of the People's Park, which was land belonging to UC Berkeley but was taken over as a public park by local activists and students who refused to leave when the university wanted to construct a soccer field on the site. Despite my respect for the students' objection to the Vietnam War, I regarded going to class my right to education, which was my primary purpose for being at the university in the United States. During the social movements in Hong Kong in 2014 and 2019, I urged my colleagues not to simply follow the requests of most of the local students, who wanted classes to be cancelled officially so they could join the protests, but also to support the minority of those who did not want to conform or preferred to stay in class. Without our balanced support, the minority of students might feel intimidated under social pressure. As responsible teachers, upholding our duty in education should be the priority. Teachers sympathetic to students who joined the protests could provide alternative means for them to catch up on the lectures they missed without depriving other students of their rightful expectation for education.

Social Responsibility, Diversity, and Inclusion

The need for diversity and inclusivity was critically underscored during the social unrest on campus in 2019. After the educational reforms in 2012 changing the previous three-year curriculum under the colonial university system to a more universal four-year curriculum, there was an expansion in internationalization with an increase in non-local students. In the preparation for internationalization, I had suggested in the University Senate that we needed to design comprehensive strategies to promote inclusivity and integration of the non-local students. Unfortunately, more attention was paid to hardware, such as ensuring provision of hostel spaces and enough courses taught in the English medium to accommodate non-local students who could not understand Cantonese. I was disappointed to observe how local students tended to ignore the presence of non-local students in class discussions and extracurricular activities, continuing to converse in Cantonese without regard as to whether the few outsiders could understand what was going on. These ethnocentric attitudes negated the university's educational vision of cultivating our students to be world citizens. If Hong Kong were to aspire to become an international education hub, as suggested in the 2024 Chief Executive's Policy Address, finding enough hostel places should not be the primary concern. Universities in

Hong Kong should strengthen their diversity and inclusion ethos to provide a more welcoming environment for non-local students.

During the height of the 2019 social unrest, the local students' nativistic attitude against mainland students was fanned by the wider sentiments of hostilities toward China. Anti-China messages were posted all over campus. A few courageous mainland students who posted their opposing views were bullied and attacked. Under the predominant anti-establishment political climate, even the university administration was under threat. While I had all along supported students' development of idealism and social consciousness, I argued that they should not forget the need for balance with grounding in social responsibility and constructive reforms. Violence and destruction had no place in education. Unfortunately, the senior staff responsible for student affairs pandered to students' demands and did not condemn the vandalism and disruptive actions during the unrest. Nor did they take a strong stand to uphold discipline when regulations and order were infringed. They thought leniency could help them connect with the students and keep the communication channels open. They were sympathetic to students' demand for "social justice." I disagreed with the students' violation of law and order in the name of the misconstrued ideal of "social justice."

Much has been written on the side of the protesters about the campus occupation in 2019. The voices of the unwilling participants had not been heard. I believed there was a need to provide a contrasting view on the side of the receiving end to give a fuller picture.

Back on our campus, uncivil graffiti with anti-government and xenophobic slogans were sprayed all over the campus buildings. No action was taken by the university administration to identify and discipline the perpetrators. In mid-October, radical students and unidentified protesters broke into the administration building to demand direct dialogue with the University President. Succumbing to the demands by the radical students to hold an open forum, which served more the purpose of a political show than genuine communication, the President's opinion was subsequently hijacked by the students' staged appeal and dramatized accusations of brutality and unsubstantiated allegation of sexual violence by the police, which turned out to be a lie.

The chaos culminated in a five-day CUHK campus occupation by the protesters starting on November 11, when the security office was taken over and school entrances were barricaded by bricks dug up from the sidewalks. To block traffic and people going to work in support of the call for a general strike, protesters threw furniture and objects from the campus Number Two Bridge crossing the MTR railway track and the major Tolo highway that served as the thoroughfare for the eastern part of the New Territories. Arrows and bows were stolen from the university sports center to use as weapons against police who attempted to clear the blockade on the bridge. Under the misconstrued notion of academic sanctity, the university did not allow the police to enter the campus. During the next four days, the university campus was sealed off by the protesters, when the two main entrances were also blockaded. Campus residents going out to work had to be interrogated when they passed through the check points guarded by the protesters. Classes had to be cancelled for the rest of the semester.

I was the Pro-Vice-Chancellor responsible for research and innovation at the time. Living off-campus, I could not drive back to my office with all the roads leading to the campus blocked. I tried to keep in touch with colleagues remaining on campus to ensure they were safe. In anticipation of increased violence, I had earlier arranged to reinforce the security of the campus facilities housing the Internet Exchange point which was set up in 1995 by then President Charles Kao to facilitate faster local Internet connection. Being the Hong Kong network's backbone, as much as 99 percent of Hong Kong's Internet interaction went through our exchange point. Fortunately, the core facilities remained intact during the occupation.

The occupation wreaked havoc on the rest of campus. Veteran trees once guarded by students from campus development were chopped, and bricks from the sidewalks were dug up by the occupiers to build roadblocks to fortify their occupation. From my living room window overlooking the north side of campus, I watched with horror black fumes shooting into the night sky as protesters practiced throwing petrol bombs in the sports field. During the day, campus buses commandeered by unlicensed drivers for joyrides wiggled down the hillside. The entire fleet of thirty some campus buses had been totaled after the occupation.

In the Science Building, colleagues noticed students guiding protesters to break into the laboratories. After appealing without avail to the President for help from the security office, which was overtaken by the protesters, or for permission to report to the police, a few dedicated faculty members remaining in their chemistry laboratories desperately tried on their own to protect the dangerous chemicals under their ward from falling into the wrong hands. They removed the door plates to mask the identity of the laboratories, locked the laboratory doors with their own bicycle chains and blocked the entrances with furniture. I admired their sense of duty and responsibility; at the same time, I had to remind them that their personal safety should come first. Their heroic efforts saved the dangerous chemicals, but that did not prevent the production of over 10,000 petrol bombs on campus, some of which were transferred to the occupied Polytechnic University when the protesters retreated from the CUHK campus after five days, while the remaining 7,000 were discovered abandoned around campus during the aftermath cleanup.

It was unclear to which extent the CUHK students were leading or supporting the occupation. Yet, the administration's attention was focused on the student union leaders and the protesters. The safety of students and staff not participating in the protest was sidelined. They were left to fend for themselves. Most local students living in the college hostels left campus to go home with the help of the college staff. The non-local mainland students felt particularly at risk. They refrained from speaking in Putonghua in public to avoid being identified as targets for attack. On the second day of the occupation, they started their exile on foot from a side gate in the remote part of campus, dragging their luggage across the flyover to the adjoining Hong Kong Science Park. The Students' Affairs Office and the senior management who remained on campus had been preoccupied with the protestors, neglecting the plight of the mainland students. With the railway track and the main roads blocked by the protesters, public transportation came to a standstill. The desperate mainland students were stranded at the Science Park after fleeing from campus. A colleague living in the vicinity took the initiative to rally her neighbors to help shuttle some of the students to the northern New Territories where they could make their way across the border to Shenzhen in mainland China. The others were rescued by the Marine Police, which sent a harbor patrol launch to pick up the stranded students from a pier near the Science Park and transported them to safety.

Meanwhile, a few of us contacted colleagues at the CUHK Shenzhen Research Institute to help take care of the students who crossed the border to the mainland like refugees. Many of the students came from different provinces and Shenzhen was not their home. When I visited the Shenzhen Research Institute after the social unrest to thank our colleagues there for their assistance, I was deeply touched by the accounts of their caring efforts. The small team of office staff took shifts to greet the students at the two Shenzhen train stations and shuttled them to the institute building. Meanwhile, they contacted the local district government, which quickly arranged free short-term lodging and meals for the students before they could either return to their hometown or felt safe enough to return to campus. I took a special trip to Shenzhen afterwards to meet and thank the district government officials for taking care of our students.

The violent episode underscored the dire need to emphasize that the right to freedom, including the right to free speech and free expression, must lie within the bounds of responsibility, integrity, civility and legality. Above all, exercising one's freedom should not infringe on that of others. Most of our faculty members, who cared more about carrying on their academic pursuits, found their research activities were brought to a standstill when they could not access their laboratories, and their graduate assistants fled campus. I could understand their frustrations and anxieties. Some of them had been rushing to finish their grant research and submit papers for publication; others were preparing their portfolio for substantiation. After taking count of loss and damages to the university's research facilities under my portfolio, I wrote to all faculty members to express my understanding of their concerns about disruptions to their research and requested the deans and department chairs to offer assistance for the affected colleagues to resume work. This was at least a small gesture of care and concern to many colleagues, who felt bewildered and neglected by the university and had to fend for themselves during the chaos. The notes of appreciation I received from some colleagues' replies showed the value of the human touch in times of crisis.

The centrality of human values of mutual respect, acceptance, and consideration—which were undermined during the social unrest—pointed to the necessity of formulating policies on diversity and inclusion at the university to reiterate our mission in moral education. Universities are grounded in core values and culture beyond the sheer transmission of knowledge. As institutions of higher education, a culture of openness, civility and inclusivity is required to nurture learning, communication, and the pursuit of truth. The motto of CUHK, "Through learning and temperance to virtue" (博文約禮 *bowen yueli*), which is based on the *Analects* of Confucius, underlined the emphasis on both intellectual and moral education. These foundational values were swept aside in the politicized environment. Demand for "universal," or more specifically Western, values of freedom and democracy overrode traditional values of temperance and dispensed with the rule of law.

In the aftermath of the social unrest, I urged CUHK to formulate a diversity and inclusion policy in the form of a contemporary version of code of conduct to operationalize the university's motto and core values. Spearheading this task, I engaged leaders from different academic and administrative units to articulate the core values for CUHK as openness, civility, and inclusivity, which were aligned with our motto and culture. By embracing openness, we expected all members of the university to endorse equal opportunities and respect the inherent and transcendent dignity of all human beings. The culture of civility would be embedded in the CUHK's shared beliefs, norms and practices, which prescribed empathy and respect for all and proscribed hatred and intolerance. The value of inclusivity would establish a safe and welcoming environment for members of the university community to develop and consider new ideas, foster learning from dissimilar others, and promote open and frank expression of one's opinion. A sense of belonging of all members of the CUHK community would be the result of respectful, caring and civil interactions. The right to academic freedom, including the right to free speech and free expression, was pledged in the policy with the proviso that the exercise and preservation of these rights must lie within the bounds of responsibility, integrity, civility and legality. The discourse on free speech in the United States following the pro-Palestinian protests on American campuses also highlighted the need to have competent information and verifiable knowledge before expressing any idea freely. Academic freedom was intended to allow people to have the resources to inform themselves and create competence.

Conscious that many policies would just gather dust on the bookshelf when there was the calm after the storm, we laid out the infrastructure and procedures for implementing the new policy CUHK with a three-pronged approach: affirmation of core values, promotion and support, and redress for infringement. A senior-level committee was set up to steer and review the policy, and to ensure its effective implementation, with a Diversity and Inclusion Office serving its executive arm. The policy was adopted in 2020, right before my retirement from full-time appointment at CUHK. The new infrastructure provided a centralized and permanent home to consolidate the various units on equal opportunities that I had previously initiated, including anti-sexual harassment promotion and redress, support for female academics, and support for persons with disabilities. Some of my female colleagues had been worried that without my championship, those initiatives would be disbanded after my retirement. It was gratifying to note how this response to the social unrest afforded the perpetuation of my equal opportunity legacies at the same time.

In Western countries, diversity, equity and inclusion (DEI) policies had focused on bringing more female or ethnic minority academics, leaders and professionals to the top of organizations. For example, in 2024, pursuing an active diversity policy in higher education in the Netherlands had been lauded for helping to achieve the target of having women lead half of the Netherlands' fourteen senior research universities for the first time. On the other hand, this focus had backlashed in the United States. Many universities with DEI programs in the conservative states faced backtracking opposition from ultra-right politicians, with funding cut from the programs or even having the DEI offices closed. Emerging from the American civil rights movement in the 1970s, these DEI policies originated from the intention to provide upward social mobility through affirmative action and other special measures to historically marginalized individuals who had previously been underrepresented, such as sexual and racial minorities. The focus on targeted staff hiring and student admission practices had led opponents of DEI practices to condemn them as reverse discrimination in the current swirls of political bifurcation. Many DEI offices in government and universities became banned and were terminated in the changing political tide. The risks of pro forma implementation of DEI policies trying to meet a target without a firm grounding in a culture of human dignity and respect for all would result in the core values underlying DEI policies becoming undermined. A lesson for CUHK.

Bittersweet Retirement

Over the four decades at CUHK where I have devoted almost my entire professional life, I flourished with the university from its budding stage to a world-class educational institution. I have personally grown through working with many talented colleagues on novel ventures that broadened my horizons. New challenges in the changing landscape gave me the opportunity to continue learning new frontiers. My academic career was much more fulfilling than just teaching and research. I was proud to have left my footprints across the campus along the way, establishing the discipline of gender studies regionally, propelling Chinese psychology to the world stage, transforming the research ecosystem to generate societal impact, and initiating policies to create a safe working environment for students and staff and foster stronger governance of the university, among other things. Advocating support for the previously invisible female colleagues not only boosted their confidence and fulfill their potential. Creating a sense of community that treasured excellence without forgetting about the human touch of caring for all rendered the university workplace a second home, where we spent so much of our time away from our own home.

My only regret was retiring from the university in 2020 near the end of the social unrest while the COVID-19 pandemic was ravaging across the world. I could not bid farewell in person to all those I cared about. Even more sadly, the curtain fell at the nadir of the university's reputation and staff morale after the social unrest, when I witnessed what our predecessors, alumni, and colleagues had faithfully assembled over the decades being eroded due to our dereliction in educating our students' sense of social responsibility and the misjudgment in crisis management by some members of the senior management, of which I was alas a disinclined member of the team. I hope the rebuilding process will not take decades.

CODA:
LIFE AND TIME

Post-retirement travels in
Cappadocia, Turkey, 2023.

9

Coming to the end of this book reminded me of one of my favorite piano music pieces, Beethoven's Piano Sonata No. 8 "Pathetique." At the end of the first movement, the recapitulation brought back the themes of the exposition in different keys before the dramatic coda, which included a brief reminder of the grave introductory theme followed by a swift cadence at the end. In the sonata-allegro form of a classical symphony or sonata, the typical coda section immediately follows the recapitulation section before concluding the movement, creating a sense of closure.

The Fluidity of Time

Writing this memoir has compressed almost three quarters of a century in my life journey into just a matter of months of sitting in front of my laptop for a couple of hours during my free days over the past two years. It seemed incredible how scenes from my past came flashing back in sped-up time. I was reminded of Albert Einstein's theory of relativity, which dispelled our belief that time was constant and universal. He demonstrated that both time (how long is one minute) and space (how long is one inch in length) were relative quantities, depending on the frame of reference and the state of motion. Einstein's scientific theory and famous equation revolutionized the field of physics and led to advances in the scientific understanding of our universe. For the layperson, the concept of relativity challenged traditional beliefs in the absolutes of truth and how wrong we had been in our understanding of the constancy of time and space in the ways we experienced our lives every day.

The scholarly treatise on time, *Eigenzeit Revisited*, by Helga Nowotny, former President of the European Research Council, offered an insightful social science-based analysis of the contemporary concept and experience of time. She illustrated how changes in society affected our sense of time. Modern technology that provided digital speed and connectivity of big data accelerated the speed and multiplicity of social interactions. I still remember thirty years ago when it took a week or more for an airmail letter—or what is now called snail mail—to reach a colleague and then another week or so of anticipation for a reply. Multimedia communication can be achieved now instantaneously with multiple participants. My husband used to take days and months of research on the evaluation of different consumer products going around multiple shops before deciding on a purchase. Such information can now be presented in minutes before you or even forced upon you on a small screen. According to Prof. Nowotny, this acceleration of time in modern society has reduced the distance between the present and the future. The compression of time has not necessarily brought a better life to people when expectations and demands increase correspondingly.

As a layperson in the topic of time, my experience of time was simply personal. Our notion of time varies based on our vantage point. During childhood, we often toil through the school year looking forward to the summer holidays. The school days seem too long and the summer holidays too short. When I was young, I rushed through college and graduate school and used to be the youngest among my classmates and my colleagues at work. At the end of my long career, I found myself among the oldest to retire. During the COVID-19 pandemic, three years were stolen from our lives in the blink of an eye, but counting the days and hours of quarantine in a hotel made it seem like the clock had stopped. On the other hand, counting could enhance our mindfulness. One way we taught relaxation was by counting one's breathing slowly. When I worked out at the gym, I counted one to fifteen reps for each set of my exercises, resting for a minute before the next set, staying mindful of the connection between my movements and my body. Ninety minutes soon passed without feeling pain or drudgery. For things that we wanted to do, time was never too long.

People often asked me how I had the time to do so many things. I told them we could always expand time to do what was important to us and constrict the time on what was less useful. It was up to us to manage our time. I was lucky that throughout my career, I could live close to my work, saving the time and stress of the daily commutes. When I first got married, my husband was surprised to find no television at my home. How much time could we save every day from not being glued to television, social media or video games? When I urged my colleagues to leave their offices to do exercise several times a week, they lamented they had no time as there was too much work to do. I tried to convince them that work could never be finished, but we could control our own schedule to fit in the exercise sessions, just like holding regular meetings. Before I retired, I could still fit in my gym sessions after work three to four times a week, or whenever I could by scheduling lunch instead of dinner appointments. Research has shown that exercise not only improves our health, mental health and cognitive function, but the time invested in exercise can be saved by the greater productivity and efficiency achieved at work. It is a matter of how we want to use our time in life. For me, my life has been time well spent.

In Between Nothingness

In the early 1960s when there was little urban light pollution, I could still watch twinkling stars at night from our garden in Number 8 Macdonnell Road. At that time, I wondered what was out there in the sky and beyond, and where the universe ended. Lacking the aptitude for astrophysics, my quest was more metaphysical. Looking down on earth again, I figured how miniscule human beings like us were. How different were we from the ants we watched swarming around traces of food on the ground? Over half a century later, the same questions about human existence in the context of the universe remain in my mind. Why would our supposedly more intelligent human race in this planet be engaging in repeated self-destructive and mutually assured destructive paths?

As a teenager, I often asked myself why I was born into this world. That was probably a question many people asked when they felt empty, apathetic or frustrated about life. These feelings could predispose young people to hopelessness and the risk of suicide. Sadly, suicide among young people has been on the rise. Modern conveniences and material possessions have not provided happiness or optimism in life. What is the meaning in life that gives people hope and gratification?

For me, this question on why I was born led to my quest for the meaning in life. I came to realize that before I was born (or rather, I was conceived), I was nothing; after my death, I would become nothing again. While I had no choice in deciding on my birth and probably my death, I had more choices in making the best of my life in between nothingness. It was also up to me to seek and create my meaning out of nothing in life.

Here I am referring only to the meaning in *my* life, not the meaning of LIFE in the collective sense. The meaning of living and existence of human beings or any life form with consciousness in this universe has been explored in philosophical, scientific, theological, and metaphysical discourse throughout history without a consensus on a definitive answer. It is beyond my capacity to go into the issue of a collective consciousness on the meaning of existence, even though the meaning of my life is derived from my connection with the collective.

Looking back, I had a rich and enjoyable life. Hedonic pleasures were only transient; what gave me enduring meaning in life was the connection with the people whose lives I had touched through my actions, including my former patients, students, colleagues, and the marginalized community, as well as with the people who had inspired me and guided me along the way.

Witnessing unfairness towards and subjugation of disempowered groups spurred my bold strides at different life junctures. Driven by the passion to right wrongs, the compassion to relieve the suffering of the disadvantaged, and the resolve to get the job done and improve the collective LIFE around me, I filled my life sphere with meaningful links to humankind. These linkages expanded my life beyond being an individual to being a part of a larger whole that shared the benevolence in humanity, offering a treasured sanctuary in a world often filled with tragedy, cruelty, and man-made destruction. I should not forget that eudaimonia is a luxury and privilege. Many people in different parts of the world throughout the centuries were less fortunate when they had to live in inhumane conditions struggling for survival. Staying alive and finding food to feed their starving families could have been their raison d'etre.

As we look at the night sky of our Milky Way galaxy in awe, thinking about the hundred billion stars that we now know exist but cannot yet fathom, as well as the hundreds of billion galaxies each with their hundreds of billions of stars beyond our own in the universe, we cannot help reminding ourselves of the transience and insignificance of our human existence. It is up to humans on this planet to collectively nurture our transient existence. What gave me meaning in life through contributing to human betterment stood in stark contrast to the anathema of human malice, perpetuated frequently by toxic political leaders who were ultimately supposed to take care of and bring a better life to their people. What should be the responsibilities of leadership? Given our world of shared destiny, what should be the role of world leaders?

Reflections on My Leadership Journey

I never considered myself a leader in the conventional sense. One of the support systems I built to foster leadership attributes in our junior female colleagues at CUHK was a mentorship program matching them with senior female colleagues. My mentees often asked me what being a leader entailed. My honest answer to them was not to think of themselves, but of the people they were going to serve. I shared with them that I lacked ambition and did not set out with an aim to become a leader. I just did what I thought was needed and what I could do one rung at a time, identifying and capturing opportunities that were opening my way. Driven by passion and compassion, I learned from the needs of stakeholders and considered what I could do to address their needs.

These learning experiences had probably strengthened my preparation to take up greater responsibilities along the way.

Much has been written on leadership styles, especially in Western business management literature. I would not venture to fit myself into one of the labels in the myriad of management typologies. In my own way, I simply followed my heart and my mind to do the best for society, reminding myself of the original aspiration of what needed to be done, be it helping the disadvantaged, serving the community, creating new mechanisms to sustain changes, or inspiring achievement of research excellence. During the process, I listened to the input of the stakeholders and engaged partners in the community to contribute to the common cause. They provided diverse perspectives to the issues at stake so that the measures we introduced would not leave gaps or create new problems. Putting ourselves into the shoes of the ones we were going to serve, we tried to design and adapt solutions to cover the multifaceted problems instead of following the bureaucratic one-size-fit-all rules and regulations. Acknowledging that no one person could know it all, I found strength through inclusive engagement and teamwork, exploring the best approach to get things done from the feedback, while acquiring new knowledge and skills from others along my way. In return, being able to continuously learn through these life experiences invigorated and enriched my life journey.

Some people associate leadership with power and status. I did not see my role in that context. Far from the "strong man" stereotype, I never had to raise my voice or bang my fist. I rejected the label of the "strong woman" or "superwoman," which was commonly used to describe successful women or women in power. My voice was too soft and my body size too petite to fit the "strong woman" image. In fact, successful men were not given the label of "strong men," which connotes a negative image of a dictator or political leader who controls by force.

For me, being in a leadership position meant that I just took up more responsibilities and accentuated the various functions that I could bring with my role: problem-solving, facilitating, motivating, empathizing, engaging, uniting, goal setting, and championing. Listening was just as important as or even more essential than speaking in the leadership role. From my vantage point, I had the advantage of having a farther and broader view in setting out the vision. I could be in a better location to bridge people with people and people with resources by connecting the dots. In a way, I was holding the keys that could open more doors for others. By breaking down the bureaucratic silos, I could create synergies and empower all players to achieve the collective goal. Being knowledgeable and prepared afforded me the boldness to venture into untrodden grounds. Ultimately, it was important for me to focus on whether and how I could have a positive influence on the people and the community I was serving. Perhaps it was this pragmatic and gentle perception of leadership that broke many of the barriers for me.

Mentoring the Next Generation

Going into retirement did not mean disengagement. We just move into different roles. In recent years, I have been asked to share my career insights to mentor younger colleagues at regional and international psychological conferences on how to become more internationalized. Reflecting on my own journey, I pondered how we could equip ourselves to reach out to the world beyond our ethnocentric locality. Borrowing from the philosophy of science, I advised that internationalization should be rooted in our *Weltanschauung* (world view), which constitutes a comprehensive conception of the world and the place of humanity within it. We could begin by understanding our immediate cultural contexts. With a firm grounding in our own culture, we might then pivot out to the surrounding region and the rest of the world. To avoid cultural imperialism—of which we had been victims—we need to open our minds to understand, appraise, and appreciate other cultures and perspectives. This provides the foundation for us to critically evaluate ethnocentrism and broaden our knowledge base.

While many Asian psychologists based in Western countries had begun to come forth to the front and achieved prominence, those based in their home countries tended to be shy and less assertive. They asked me what they could do to emerge from their isolation. I encouraged them to start with their mindset, leave their comfort zone, and break loose. As more junior colleagues had the opportunity to attend international conferences, I reminded them that participating in these conferences involved more than just attending sessions of renowned speakers, or presenting an individual paper, and then going off sightseeing afterwards. The value of these conferences lay in reconnecting with old contacts and building up new collaboration by joining the discussions inside and outside the sessions. As they built up their own research program, organizing symposia around a common theme and inviting international discussants to the symposia could help strengthen their research network. Although professional services might be time-consuming, serving as reviewers and editorial board members of international journals, and joining committees of international associations can open up new opportunities along the way. I envisaged that just as how the effect of butterflies flapping their wings in Brazil could change the air pressure that could eventually cause a tornado in the United States, vigorous research by non-Western psychologists could collectively make major impacts on psychological science. This would apply to other fields as well.

Whereas scientific disciplines were beginning to embrace the benefits of multiculturalism, cultural interactions at the world level did not seem to have brought multilateralism and more peaceful co-existence. In our increasingly interconnected world, the most pressing global challenges require global solutions through strengthening the spirit of multilateralism and international cooperation. Chinese leaders have coined the phrase "Human community with a shared destiny" (人類命運共同體 *renlei mingyun gongtongti*) as their foreign policy goals in the twenty-first century. Skeptics may consider this slogan more as propaganda than substance. If the proposer had not been from China, this concept might have been hailed as universal truth. Unfortunately, xenophobic mindsets of politicians in some other countries have stirred racial hatred and polarized their populace, escalating national and international conflicts. Dichotomized thinking is a type of cognitive distortion of viewing things as all-or-nothing and pitching the good against the evil that has been magnified in many polarized democratic systems. Personal interests, political agenda, and chauvinism have overtaken the original aspiration of democracies to serve their people and humanity. In the current geopolitical landscape of perpetuating unilateral hegemony not only in the political and military domains, but also in economic, technological, and cultural fields, Western powers often impose their values as if they should be universal and ubiquitous. They react to the rise of alternative voices from the Global South and non-Western countries as threats to be resisted and subdued. With Western control on the narratives in world media, China-bashing sadly continues to dominate the worldview. Lessons from the history of colonial subjugation in the past centuries has not yet been learned.

I am gratified that in my professional career, I have been able to overcome the dominance of Western psychology and helped to bring a Chinese voice to promote multiculturalism in the psychology discipline. The Chinese cultural perspective has highlighted the importance of interrelatedness with others, which is also shared in many other non-Western cultures, beyond the centrality of the individual self in Western psychology. This concept of interpersonal relatedness extends beyond psychology. I look forward to witnessing the Global South countries' success in bringing their cultural voices to serve humanity by promoting multilateral dialogue and cooperation in international affairs and diplomacy.

Gratitude

Research in positive psychology has shown that being grateful can lead to increased levels of emotional, psychosocial and physical wellbeing. Gratitude is much more than saying thank you. It is an emotional response arising from the recognition of good things in our lives and the appreciation of how this goodness comes into our lives. Expressing our gratitude helps us to connect to something larger than ourselves as individuals, be it other people, nature, or a higher power. Practicing gratitude focuses our attention to relishing good experiences instead of dwelling on negativity. It helps us to reduce stress, deal with adversity, and build strong relationships. It brings us optimism and greater happiness.

Life can be filled with vicissitudes of goodness and badness. In remembering my life journey, mostly positive episodes came to mind filling me with gratitude. I have been fortunate to have lived in an era of relative peace and abundance, witnessing the social progress in Hong Kong and the rise of my homeland from war-torn poverty and foreign oppression over the past two centuries. I am grateful for my upbringing in Number 8, which provided me the luxury of a carefree early childhood when I could devote myself to pursue my education as far as I could go, while watching the microcosm of human interactions that prepared me for navigating the larger society. As children, we took the privileges we had in life for granted without thanking the troop of domestic helpers in Number 8 who sacrificed their own families and their youth to take care of us throughout a large part of their lives. Similarly, in the modern version of home help, our population of foreign domestic helpers had left their own children in their homeland to take over our household chores, bring up our children, and care for the elderly so that women in Hong Kong could take up their own employment outside the home. I really appreciated the home help that afforded me the extra time for rest, exercise, and enjoyment after work without having to worry about household chores.

Even though my parents were not hands-on in bringing us up, they took good care of us in the way their generation knew best. Despite my short period of contact with my father before his early death, my memory of him is filled with admiration for his fair-mindedness and kindness in leading the clan. He ingrained in us the family values that stood the test of time. As a young widow, my mother had always been mindful of protecting us and ensuring that our physical needs were met. Even in her moderate stage of Alzheimer's disease, now in her nineties, the mumble-jumble utterance she kept repeating to me like a recorded message whenever I talked to her was: "Don't worry, I will always take care of you. You are my daughter." That was the essence of her memory associated with me that was retrievable from her deteriorating brain.

My family life would be incomplete without the staunch support and loving care of Japhet, my extraordinary husband. In many ways, we could not be more different: In terms of body size, he is tall for a Chinese man of his generation, and I am particularly diminutive. He has always been athletic and would engage in all kinds of ball games, whereas I am fragile and did not start any physical exercise until we got married. He is quick and sharp but inpatient, while I am more relaxed and composed. In his lectures, he would raise his booming voice when students did not quiet down and if that did not work, he would expel the unruly students from the classroom. My tactic was to lower my gentle voice even more into a whisper so that the noisy students would be shooed by others who wanted to hear what I had to say. Trained as a hard-nosed engineer, he focused on the product and mainly operated on the principles of science and logic. As a psychologist, I attended more to process and feelings, and often confused him with my dialectical thinking. Yet, we shared the common values of righteousness and altruism, as well as treasured each other's commitment to serve society and to defend the disadvantaged. Both of us preferred to stay home and enjoy classical music, which filled our leisure time. He always taught his students on the first day of class about the three essentials of life: physical health by leading a healthy lifestyle, keeping a balanced diet and taking regular exercise; mental health by holding a positive mindset, managing stress, and bouncing back from adversity with resilience; and living a meaningful life by knowing one's aspiration and taking steps to achieve it. To walk the talk, we managed to build up our bodily health, sustain our happiness, and find our meaning in life together, embodying the simple motto of New Life 330 (body, mind and spirit) that I adopted to promote holistic health in the community.

Japhet was multitalented at work and at home. He provided foresightful guidance and strategic formulations on my plans, which complemented my cautiousness in bold ventures. He showed me the inadequacy of being the worker ant who just kept on working hard and not working smart. Yet, he respected my preference for being low-key and modest in pursuing my own way. Whereas I was not someone who would blow my own trumpet, I was told that he often lauded my work with pride in front of others. In his view, a man who did not respect his wife should not deserve respect.

At home, he was Mr. Fixit, meticulously restoring all the household devices that I managed to dismantle or disrupt with my mechanical clumsiness. Without any training in home renovations, he quickly read up books borrowed

Exercising in the hotel gym during my travels.

Japhet playing soccer at the Chung Chi College Stadium in 1998.

from the architecture library to design all the installations in our new flat, which rivalled a professional job. He ensured that our surroundings were safe and well maintained. In a way, he has literally travelled with me on my life journey, not only by sharing my life mission, but also being my driver wherever we went, taking care of all the logistics of our trips, carrying my luggage and bags, sheltering me in crowded environment, shielding me from risks and so forth, so that I could have smooth sailing. Now and then, he would ask me what I want more in life. I know, somewhere in the back of his mind, he always wanted to provide me with a life befitting someone raised in the big mansion on MacDonnell Road. He had already sacrificed so much for me. To me, there was nothing more to be wanted than what I already had in my contented life.

My contentment did not mean stagnation in life. I have been able to continuously learn in life and from life. Lifelong learning beyond formal education has enabled me to flourish continuously, for which I am most grateful. My former patients educated me about life trauma, which propelled my social activism. The elderly audience in my first public mental health talk taught me to communicate at an appropriate level. Women I encountered across the world showed me the diversity and commonality of their experiences as women. Different cohorts of my students illuminated the direction for educating the next generation. My academic colleagues fascinated me with their intrinsic motivation to drive the frontiers of knowledge. There is still so much waiting for us to learn in life, which makes life worth living.

Throughout different stages of my life, I have been inspired by numerous community leaders, as well as the unsung heroes who paved the foundation and sparked my engagement to contribute to society. They showed me how selflessness could enrich one's life. I could not thank them enough for what they have bequeathed to our world. I am also grateful to my network of comrades and friends who shared my passion and compassion for making the world a better place for all. Treading our common paths together gave us the strength and mutual support in breaking the silence, tilling new ground, and bringing our voices to the fore. Watching and learning how the next generation might reach new heights in these endeavors will be perpetually gratifying in the remainder of our lives.

Japhet and Fanny playing music together at home in 2013.

In retrospect, my seventy-odd years of life have passed so quickly. I am forever grateful for having lived through these past decades the way I did. Beyond fulfilling the regular accomplishments of an academic and professional, I also had the opportunity to serve the community in so many ways that contributed small steps, albeit bold strides, to creating a better place for the people around us. Even with my soft voice, I found resonance to achieve our common cause. In a way, my life journey has opened new horizons for me and my community like a gentle stream of clear water that cracks through hard rock. These blissful memories are exhilarating, even though all the while, my life has remained peaceful, like water that is as smooth as a mirror. Was it the grounding in the Buddhist home atmosphere in my childhood that brought me tranquility? Or was it the imprint of my Chinese name 妙清 *Miaoqing*— depicting the Zen-like state of being wonderful, sublime, pure as well as clear— that formed my identity? Whatever it was, in my remaining life passage, I hope to witness more people using their voices to help human beings live more meaningful and peaceful lives as modern societies advance.

ACKNOWLEDGEMENTS

First and foremost, I thank my parents who have bestowed this life upon me. Along my life journey, I have learned and benefited from so many people who are too numerous to name here without repeating my admiration, appreciation, and gratitude that I have expressed in different parts of the book. Here, I will just focus on those individuals associated with the publication of this memoir, which calls for another facet of my gratefulness.

As I tried to recall my early family life, there were gaps about which I had to consult other senior members of my generation. My Sister Three, Deanna 妙屏, and Sister Ten, Marsha 妙芝, both living now in the Bay Area in California, shared their recollections of their childhood experiences with me. Deanna also showed me her immaculate old photo albums, giving me a glimpse of our home before my memory span. Marsha was fervent about my intention to write about our family life. She shared the articles that she had written about her own transformation from a diffident girlhood in Hong Kong into a self-assured Asian-American community leader in the San Francisco Bay Area. My cousin Albert 熾堂 updated me on Aunt Two, and forwarded a scanned copy of her well-preserved photos of the family when she passed away from COVID at age ninety-five. I reckon the *Rashomon* effect in our subjective memories of life in Number 8, which were colored by our own respective experiences. I have not confirmed the accuracy of my recollections with them. The truth is relative to our own perspectives.

Conscious of my inexperience in writing in a literary style, I asked my husband, Japhet, who is an avid and critical reader, to review my draft manuscript. This was the first time he had read any of my manuscripts. He often teased me about my prosaic presentation style, which does not excite the audience. He pointed out parts that needed illustration and spark. He reminded me of incidents that he had shared with me in the past forty years and was amused to learn about what he had previously not known about my early life. Above all, his unfailing emotional support accompanying me in the journey of writing meant most to me.

Other than my own family members, would other people care to read my memoir? Having worked with The Chinese University of Hong Kong Press (CUHK Press) for decades over many academic publications and official duties, I consulted Director Gan Qi and her colleague Minlei Ye about my idea of a memoir. Their enthusiasm and encouragement swept away my initial hesitancy. They recommended publishing it in both English and Chinese. My previous publications have been primarily academic in nature, formulated in standard research templates. I read up on memoirs written by contemporary scholars. Guidance and feedback from Minlei and Winifred Sin of CUHK Press on my draft chapters spurred the flow of my memories. As women of the younger generation, they felt enlightened by the historical contexts referenced in my life journey. They cradled the contents and design of the book with care and professionalism. They also shared with me other memoirs published by CUHK Press, among which was Prof. Helga Nowotny's *Future Needs Wisdom*.

Prof. Nowotny is a Professor Emerita of Science and Technology Studies at ETH Zurich, and former President of the European Research Council. Her intellectual memoir immediately resonated with me, given our mutual experiences as women scholars. Her talk at the book launch of her memoir at CUHK was inspirational. I felt we were kindred spirits in being intrepid in voicing our thoughts and carving out our own paths, albeit in different cultural contexts. As an accomplished scholar and a distinguished leader in research and innovation policy, she would have been my spiritual mentor had I met her earlier in life. I was greatly honored by her agreement to write the Foreword to my memoir, and was amazed by the speed with which she delivered a warm and generous review of my manuscript despite her hectic schedule. I cannot thank Helga enough.

Endorsements have become a standard expectation of book publishing. At the request of CUHK Press, I decided to approach the people who have shared significant aspects of my life journey. I was deeply touched by their responsiveness amidst their busy schedules or challenging times of their lives.

Prof. Diane Halpern, former President of the American Psychological Association, and my good friend and collaborator on several projects on the psychology of women, was the first person who came to my mind when I was asked to recommend endorsers to my book. I have always admired her erudite scholarship and fervent sense of righteousness. Before I approached her, the wildfire in Los Angeles in January 2025 had destroyed her neighborhood. For weeks, I was worried about her safety and was relieved to learn that her house was still standing although the community had become uninhabitable. I was hesitant to impose on her with my request during such taxing times. Her instant response was most touching: "Of course, I will do anything you ask me to do."

Prof. Joseph Sung appointed me as the first female Vice-President of CUHK in its fifty-year history when he was the Vice-Chancellor. He led the university with his heart and entrusted me with a free hand to execute his vision for innovating the university. After retiring from CUHK, he has embarked on a new venture to his career, launching the new medical school and serving as the Senior Vice-President at Nanyang Technological University in Singapore. I was flattered by his immediate acceptance with the remark that it was his honor and pleasure to write the endorsement. The honor was, in fact, mine.

Dr. Judith Mackay, my feminist friend and comrade in arms for almost fifty years in promoting women's development in Hong Kong, responded to my request with a succinct "absolutely yes." She reminded me that I once told her she used the phrase "absolutely" a lot when we served together on the Women's Commission in Hong Kong. "Absolutely" characterizes Judith's inspiring vigor, indefatigable spirit and firm commitment in taking on everything in her life. Judith shared with me her notes on the early history of the Hong Kong Council of Women and setting up Harmony House. Her lifelong anti-tobacco campaign and fight for women's rights presented an ardent role model for the younger generation.

I first met Mr. Woon Kwong Lam when he was the Shatin District Officer while I was serving on the Shatin District Board. He later invited me to join the Regional Council. Throughout his ministerial career in the Hong Kong government, W. K. demonstrated his intellectual acuity, integrity, and human sensitivity in serving the people of Hong Kong. Our life paths continued to cross after his retirement from his ministerial posts, including both of us having been the Chairperson of the Equal Opportunities Commission. After stepping down as Convenor of the Non-Official Member of The Executive Council, HKSAR, he agreed to serve as an honorary senior fellow to the Hong Kong Institute of Asia Pacific Studies and offered insightful advice to our academic colleagues at CUHK on public policy research. He has also become the connoisseur advisor of Japhet's and my travels in Asia.

Ms. Shelley Lee, another dedicated former senior government official, has been a motherly icon of the Hong Kong government. Her kindness and sincere concern for the underprivileged, the orphaned and the victims of catastrophes, which won her the acclaimed nickname of "Community Godmother," prevailed after her retirement. As a founding member and former Chairman of the Association of Female Senior Government Officers formed in 1979 to fight for equal remuneration terms for married women in the civil service, she has been a staunch supporter of initiatives to promote women's development. We first became acquainted when the late David Akers-Jones, then Secretary for the New Territories, enlisted us to brainstorm the establishment of support groups for women in the grassroots. Shelley has been my caring mentor in steering the course of my public service. She radiates with warmth and dynamism in every encounter.

Grounded in such abundance of munificence, the publication of this book has been most rewarding.

Lastly, my gratitude goes to you, the reader, for embarking on this journey with me. In this interconnected world, our lives form legs in the cosmic marathon relay. The legacies of past generations have paved the way for us and our next generations to take up the baton to make the world a better place for all.

Hong Kong, Spring 2025